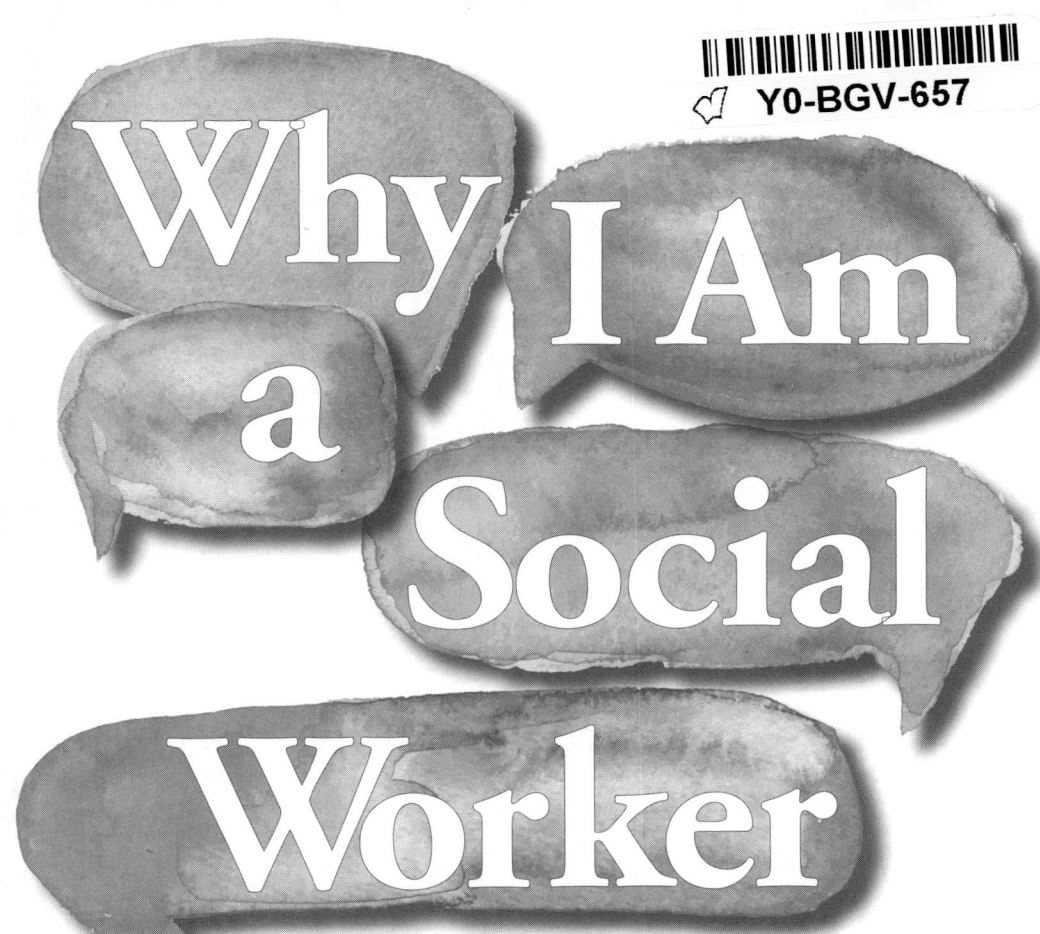

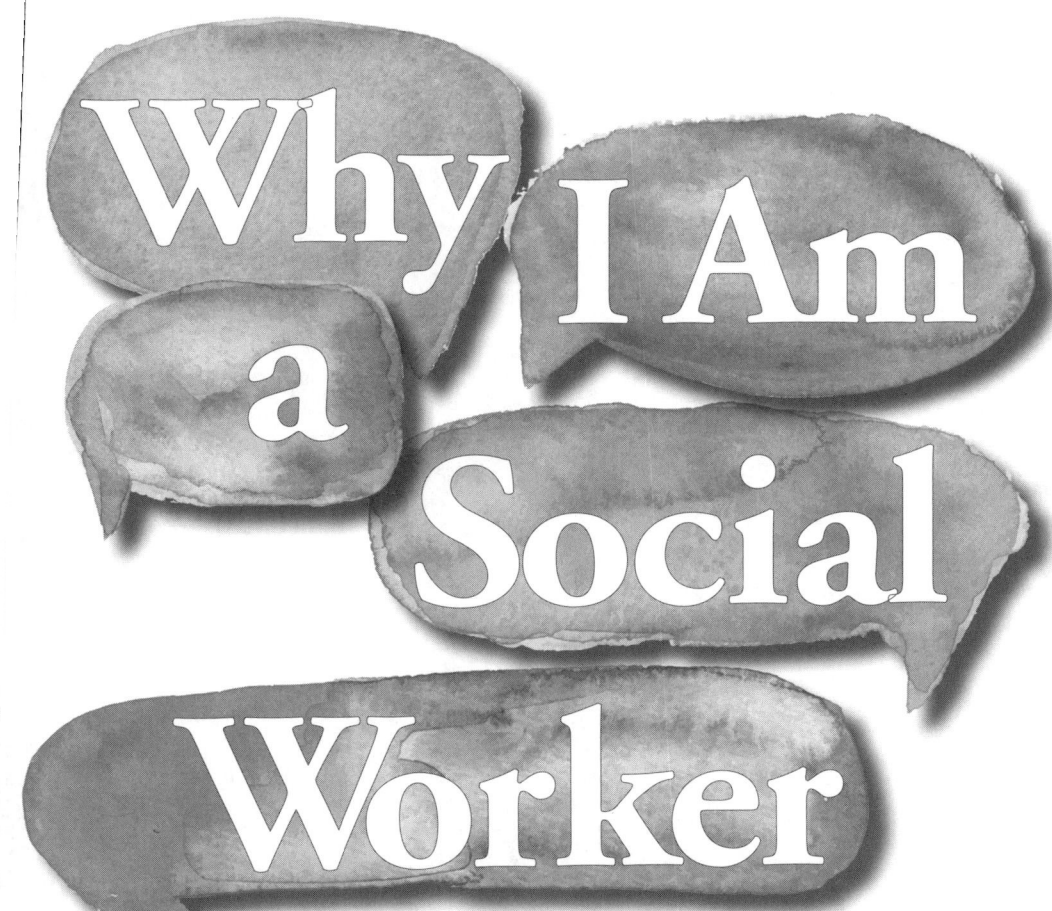

25 Christians Tell Their Life Stories

Diana S. Richmond Garland

All scripture quotations, unless otherwise noted, are from the New Revised Standard Version.

© copyright 2015
North American Association of Christians in Social Work
P.O. Box 121
Botsford, CT 06404-0121

ISBN 978-0-9897581-0-9

Dedication

I dedicate this book to the gracious social workers
who gave me their stories to share with you,
and to the memory of Alan Keith-Lucas and C. Anne Davis,
mentors now gone before us who helped me to hear
my calling to social work.

Contents

Introduction
    Social Work as Christian Calling   1

Children and Adolescents
1. **Patricia Cummings,** Regional Director,   19
   Presbyterian Family Care Services
       Charis Dietz, Co-author
2. **Allison Porter**, Child and Family Services Social Worker,   29
   Springfield Youth Center and John Hale County Hospital
       Lindsay Swain, Co-Author
3. **Joanie Armstrong**, Child Advocate and Adoptions Specialist   39
4. **Joseph Martinez**, School Social Worker   47

Adults
5. **Kate Martin**, Individual and Couples Therapist   55
   and Workshop Leader
       Erin Olson, Co-Author
6. **Myria Hester**, Therapist with Older Adults   63
   and Adults with Disabilities

Communities and Congregations
7. **Adam Bennett**, Executive Director, Serving the City Ministries   71
8. **Wes McIntosh**, Community Organizer,   83
   Metropolitan Area Interfaith Organization
       Leah Gatlin and Kelsey Wiggins, Co-Authors
9. **Christina Dobal**, Community Advocate   95
       Regina Chow Trammel, Co-Author
10. **Heather Quintana,** Missionary Social Worker and Pastor   101
        Lori M. Sousa, Co-Author
11. **Chanphen Yindee**, Operations Manager,   113
    Rak Lae Pra Pon Foundation
        Melissa Ishio, Co-Author

Physical Health, Illness, and Disability

12. **Martha Ellington**, President, Prism,   121
    An Adult Day Health Center   121
13. **Courtney Barrett,** Hospital Social Worker   133
14. **Kara Terry**, Nursing Home Care Manager   143
15. **Jon Black**, Hospice Social Worker   153
    Emily Bibb Mosher, Co-Author

Mental Health and Mental Illness

16. **Raelyn Greer**, Clinical Social Worker and   161
    Assistant Program Director, Department of Mental Health
    Bethany Parrott, Co-Author
17. **Sunshine Parker**, Therapist, New Beginnings Treatment Center   169
    Myria Bailey Whitcomb, Co-Author
18. **Diane Tarrington**, Senior Director of Social Services   177
    and Commissioned Minister, Volunteers of America
    Angela Dennison, Co-Author
19. **Kevin Arroyo**, Field Director, Center for Hunger Solutions   189
    Jeremy Everett, Co-Author

People Who Are Refugees and Immigrants

20. **Karen Richmond**, Refugee Resettlement Social Worker   197
    Amy Butler, Co-Author
21. **Aurora Flores**, Community Organizer, Immigrant Rights   205
    Emily Bibb Mosher, Co-Author

Criminal Justice

22. **Laura Crawford**, Clinical Forensic Specialist, The Refuge   215
23. **David Thomas**, Family Therapist, Juvenile Court   221
    David McClung, Co-Author

Workforce Development

24. **Joy Fitzgerald**, Director, Job Preparation Collaboration   231
    of the Women's Missionary Alliance
    Ally Matteson, Co-Author

Military

25. Ilene Borden, Military Social Worker, Air Force   239
    Nicholas A. Wright, Co-Author

Conclusion

26. Step by Step   247

Appendices

A. **Practice Settings**, Organizational Auspices   259
    and Levels of Practice

B. **Glossary**   261

C. **Interview Questions**   263

D. **References**   265

Introduction
Social Work as Christian Calling

If you were to ask people in line behind you at the grocery to name professions for a survey you are doing, they might look at you with uncertainty about your odd question. When they answered, they might list doctors, lawyers, nurses, teachers, pastors, and perhaps a few others—maybe architects and accountants. Unless there was a social worker in the line, or a family member of a social worker, social work might not be mentioned. People often have only a fuzzy idea of social work as a profession; they may assume that social work is primarily employment in public social service programs like child welfare and temporary financial assistance.

My grandchildren play pretending to be teachers or doctors or ballerinas; I have not seen them play "pretend I am a social worker," even though their parents have friends who are social workers and Grandma teaches social work. Few entering college students start out fixed on majoring in social work; they just know that they want to help people, and through a friend or mentor, they find their way into an introductory class or elective in social work. I often hear from my students, "I had never heard of social work as a profession." Social work is a little known and often misunderstood profession.

This book is one modest effort to change that misunderstanding, to describe the rich diversity and nature of this profession through the stories of the daily lives and professional journeys of 25 social workers chosen to represent many of the different people groups and human situations where social workers serve.

If this profession is not well understood, then how do people find their way into it? I teach a graduate Introduction to the Profession course in a Christian university. Many of the students in my class say that they feel "called" to help people—sometimes a specific population of people such as abused children or immigrants or people who live in poverty. That calling is an expression of their Christian faith. As they tried to learn how to become a helper of people, someone steered them to social work, "the helping profession" (Action Network for Social Work Education and Research, 2009, p. 6). I wanted a resource that would help my students as they reflect on their sense of calling, a book I could use to guide them in this process.

By telling the stories of Christian social workers describing their work and how their faith and calling informs that work, this book provides a way to explore the relationship of faith and practice on personal, emotional, and practical levels. This book is limited to exploring the breadth of ways Christians integrate their religious worldviews with their social work practice, given the diversity that exists within the religious perspectives we call "Christian." In the future, I hope to expand this exploration to include social workers of other religious faiths.

I wanted to write a book that is rigorous in its exploration of social work practice and will not varnish the difficulties and struggles, but also tells the story of the rich, rewarding work in all its diversity that social work can be. If you want to understand what social work is and how Christians see social work as a way to live their faith from the lived experiences of actual social workers, I wrote this book for you. If you are already a social worker, you will find here the stories of colleagues who are walking the journey of Christian faith through social work.

I believe the book will be useful for professors teaching social work, pastors advising students on pursuing their calling, and college career counselors. Very few of us have been prepared to help students explore their sense of calling, anchor their work-life in their faith as motivation for their service, and articulate the relationship of social work values and ethics with their religious beliefs, values, and practices. Social work is not alone; research in higher education indicates that most colleges and universities do little to help students explore spirituality and religiosity as it relates to the purpose of their lives and their career choices (Gallagher, 2007).

In sum, this book has three objectives:
1. To describe the path of Christians into social work, how their work is an expression of their faith, and how their faith motivates, sustains, and is challenged by their work.
2. To sample the breadth of social work as a profession, from public to private and from nonsectarian to religious congregational settings, and how faith finds a diversity of expressions.
3. To serve as a resource for exploring the ethical integration of faith with professional practice.

I could have accomplished these objectives didactically, by laying Christian values and beliefs alongside professional ethics and exploring commonalities and dissimilarities, or by providing research findings from a study of Christian social workers. I have chosen, instead, to use a narrative approach, allowing the relationship of faith and practice to emerge through the professional life stories of social workers who are Christian. How do these social workers describe the relationship of their faith and their work? What are their daily work-lives like, with their challenges, frustrations, joys and triumphs? What were their paths into social work and the particular kinds of social work they chose? What roles do their religious beliefs and spiritual practices have in sustaining them for the work, and how has their work, in turn, shaped their religious and spiritual lives? This book will provide you with a realistic view of the gritty realities of a profession that is at the forefront of serving those Jesus described as "the least of these" (Matthew 25).

This book is designed to complement the great work others have done to explore the integration of Christian faith with the profession of social work. I commend to you especially the writings of Alan Keith-Lucas (1985), David Sherwood (2010, 2012a, 2012b, 2012c), and Rick Chamiec-Case (2012, 2013). These scholars have described the landscape of social work practice from the perspective of a Christian worldview.

Lived experiences are always messy, with complexities and often with the necessity of taking action based on an incomplete understanding of the situation or the unseen implications of one's actions. You will honor these social workers whose stories I have told by taking their stories seriously enough to realize that, although they were doing the best that they could do in particular circumstances, your understanding of ethics and best practices may have taken you in a different direction, had you walked in their shoes. By definition, professions require ever evolving knowledge and skills, as well as professional judgment when the path forward does not unfold with great clarity or ease. The discussion questions at the end of each story suggest that you not take each story as an exemplar so much as a window into one social worker's lived experience of this profession.

Methodology

My first challenge was to identify the social workers whose stories I would include, and so I began with my own professional networks. I sought social workers who believe that their work is an expression of their Christian faith and who are employed in the diversity of settings and with the diversity of people where social work can be found. I used the telephone and sometimes teleconferencing for interviewing so that I could include social workers across the nation and even the world. We audiotaped and transcribed each interview. The quotations in each story are their actual words.

I conducted some of the interviews, but I also involved my graduate students at Baylor University, both masters and doctoral students, in conducting some of the first interviews. Sometimes those students (now alumni) wrote the first draft of the chapter. You will see their names as chapter co-authors. We used a semi-structured interview; you will find the questions that guided us in Appendix C. We allowed the social workers to tell their stories and simply used the questions as discussion starters, ensuring that the social worker had addressed all the questions at some time during the interview but not necessarily in any particular order.

I began the book in 2011 and did not complete it for four years. I found that as I wrote each chapter, new questions emerged. I was also curious about what additional reflections the social workers might have had after the phone call ended and they thought about the conversation. Few had opportunity before this experience to describe their work or how their faith relates to their professional practice. I know that my own experiences as an interviewee have often left me wishing after the fact that I could add my follow-up thoughts to the conversation. Therefore, I conducted second interviews to be able to tell "the rest of the story" as I wrote the book.

Before the second interview, I sent the manuscript written from the first interview to the social worker for any corrections and further reflection. At least 18 months, and more often three years had passed between the first interview and the follow-up interview, allowing opportunity for more development of the social worker's story. I wanted to be sure that I actually captured the multi-faceted motivations, frustrations, and ongoing reflection about the interaction of the life of faith and professional practice. I conducted all the second-round interviews myself. Finally, I sent the final manuscript of the entire book to all these social workers, giving a final opportunity for corrections and additions and so that they could see how their story fit with all the others.

To protect their privacy and the confidentiality of their clients and organizations, and to allow them to speak most candidly, the social workers have remained anonymous. I have changed all the names of people, organizations, and locations. If these social workers want to share their stories with others, these stories belong to them and they can certainly feel free to reveal their identity.

The Book's Framework

I could have organized the book in many ways, and I experimented with several. I first tried organizing by the context in which social workers served—public agencies, private non-sectarian settings, religiously affiliated organizations, congregations, and private practice. As I read the completed manuscript, however, I realized that, although the nature of the organizational context is a factor given much attention in discussions about the integration of Christian faith and professional practice, it actually did not seem to capture much of the diversity among these social workers. Theoretical discussions seem to assume that tax-dollar-supported and other non-religious organizations limit the integration of faith with professional practice, whereas such integration is overtly encouraged in religiously affiliated organizations. But as you will see in these stories, these social workers called to this profession by their Christian faith actually serve across the range of public and private organizations. Moreover, they focus less on their organizational context and more on the needs of their clients—whether the client is an individual, family, or community—when they consider the role that religion and spirituality need to play in their actual work. Therefore, you will find Appendix A provides a key to these social workers' organizational contexts, if that is of interest to you.

The organizational framework that emerged as useful focuses on the people groups and fields of practice in which social workers serve. Want-to-be social workers feel drawn to working with people such as vulnerable children and teens, adult couples, frail older adults, persons with mental illness, persons living in poverty, or immigrants and refugees. That framework is what I have chosen, but it is not as straightforward as it might seem. Social workers have a diversity of opportunities open to them and move from one field of practice to another. Few of the social workers I interviewed have lived their calling in one place doing one kind of social work over the courses of their careers. Rather, they lived their callings as journeys that carried them from one place to the next. Even over the four years when I was interviewing them, many of them changed employers, and sometimes they even changed fields of practice. Some who remained in the same organization moved over to another department or into administration. I came to see, as you will, that they may have begun thinking about their calling in response to the needs of a people group or particular challenging social problem. Over time, that thinking shifted from a static place to a sense that they are on an ever-unfolding path.

Given that complexity, the book suffers from an imperfect ordering at best. First, most current practice settings could actually fit in more than one section. Does the story of Courtney Barrett, for example, a social worker employed in a geriatric outpatient clinic of a state hospital, fit best in the adults section or in physical and mental illness? Between interviews, Courtney changed jobs and went to the VA hospital surgery unit, further complicating story placement in one section. And what about the fact that she is now in the process of launching a home health business designed to normalize life for older adults, providing services to help them stay in their homes rather than move to an assisted living or nursing facility? The book's organizational framework may inadvertently communicate a stasis that is not an accurate depiction of the journeys found in these stories. However imperfect, I hope this framework is useful in guiding your exploration of the experiences of Christian social workers. Think of it as a snapshot in time.

While I was working on this book in fits and starts over these four years, I was also working with my friend and co-author, Gaynor Yancey, to interview social workers employed in congregational settings, resulting in the publication of our book *Congregational Social Work* (Garland & Yancey, 2014). Therefore, I only touched lightly in this book on that field of social work practice. Because so little has been written about social workers on congregational staffs, I knew I could not do justice in this book to describing that setting adequately, so I refer you to that book for exploring the stories of social workers who have pursued their calling into congregational leadership. In this book, you will find a taste of this practice setting in the stories of Heather Quintana and Adam Bennett.

The Relationship of Christian Vocation and Work

The concept of work—including social work—as a Christian calling, or vocation, has emerged over the centuries of the Church's history. In the past century, the term "vocation" has taken on a much broader and secularized connotation, although Christian thought still sees that work is—or can be—a calling from God.

Christian leaders have not always considered work to be a religious calling, however. In the medieval world of the sixteenth century, the life of the mind and of contemplation was the highest order of human religious life. Work was necessary but had little spiritual significance. Religious vocation meant becoming a priest or monk or nun, devoting oneself to prayer and the study of the Bible. The church considered those who remained in the world of work and family life rather than the cloister to be less than the highest Christian calling (Hardy, 1990).

During the Renaissance, a new attitude of work emerged as God came seen not just as Creator but a cosmic crafter of the world. Human beings became like God by also being productive, not just by thinking (Hardy, 1990). The belief that one's work could be an expression of one's Christian faith is one of the very tenets of the Protestant Reformation. Martin Luther (1483-1546), himself a priest, asserted that it is through our stations in life—our jobs, our roles as family and community members—that God bids us to serve our neighbors. Through our work, we serve others. Work can be a "vocation," God's calling.

Christian vocation and calling included not only one's work life but also the ways we can serve others through all the relationships of life (Hardy, 1990; Kolb, 2009)—helping a neighbor, changing an infant's diaper, cooking dinner for one's family. Much later, as documented in Pope John Paul II's *Laborum Exercens*, the official Catholic theology of work became congruent with the Protestant position at every major point (Pope John Paul II, 1981).

Theological frameworks emerged for understanding work—employment—as Christian calling (e.g., Volf, 1991). Both Protestant and Catholic thought saw human work as a way we bear the image of God. Through our work, we participate in God's ongoing creation. Work is an opportunity to live the example of Christ in serving others and sometimes suffering for them (Hardy, 1990).

Over the centuries since the Reformation, European and American societies became more secularized, and so did thought about vocation and work. The scope of "vocation" diminished and came to connote simply the paid work a person does (Veith, 2011). Now people use terms like vocational training, vocational schools, and vocational counseling to talk about one's preparation for the work world (Schuurman, 2004). In fact, vocational training has come to connote the trades—car repair, welding, and plumbing—in contrast with the "professions" that require college and often advanced academic degrees. The secular meaning of "vocation" has strayed far from Martin Luther's theological understanding.

American Christian thought has translated that secularized understanding of calling back into the church, also missing the meaning that the Reformers gave to the world of work. In the church world in which I grew up, we used the language of being "called to full-time Christian service," referring to paid full-time employment in a congregation or another church organization. Full-time Christian service had come to mean being a pastor or another church staff member or a missionary. The term assumes that a work-life in or through the church is the highest form of Christian service, and that people who work in other settings can still do Christian service when they volunteer in the church's mission projects and programs, as part-time volunteers. Amy Sherman says that we have "shrink wrapped" the Kingdom of God, limiting it to work internal to the church rather than recognizing that all are called to partner with God in the redemption of the world (Sherman, 2011). Once again, the church perceived a life work outside of the church as somehow less "Christian," echoing medieval thought that elevated cloister over work in the world of community and family.

Putting this understanding of calling in a larger context historically and globally suggests just how limited and exclusionary it is. Most people do not have the freedom to choose to do inside-the-church work, no matter how committed or desirous of living the faith "full time." Freedom of choice about what kind of paid occupation we will take up is a luxury limited to only a very few people in the world. The circumstances and society into which we were born, the opportunities and limitations life deals us, and the expectations of others limit and sometimes block our choices, not just our own gifts and interests.

Biblical texts that address "calling" are limited neither to church work nor to choosing a path of paid employment. The concepts of calling and God's choosing us (election) are closely associated (e.g., Romans 8:30, 2 Peter 1:10, Isaiah 41:8-9). God is the chooser, the caller; we are responding to the Holy Other. In the biblical narratives of the Old Testament, God called not only kings and religious leaders, but also artists who "the Lord has called by name" built the tabernacle (Exodus 35: 30). Similarly, Jesus taught his disciples that that *he* chose *them*, not the reverse (John 15:16). God calls us to specific places and responsibilities: "Let each of you lead the life that the Lord as assigned, to which God called you" (1 Corinthians 7:17). God calls people to all kinds of work.

This book posits that, for Christians, all of life is to be lived following our bidding Christ; part of life is the work we do. Vocation is "the spirituality of everyday life" (Veith, 2011, p. 119). We cannot meet all of our own needs; we depend on others, and they depend on us. According to Hardy (1990), this need for one another is a sign that God intends us to live together in society, bound together by our common needs and mutual service.

Wherever people work, they can live the teachings of Jesus—doing unto others as they would want done for them. Those "others" whom Christians "do unto" are those who will purchase a product a Christian factory worker is assembling, or the citizens who will drive across the bridge a Christian engineer is designing, or the people who eat the produce a Christian farmer sends to market, or the ill patient a Christian doctor is treating, or the customers a Christian store clerk is assisting. Some work may not be especially meaningful in itself; most of us have found ourselves at one time or another doing work because we needed the income, not because the work itself was the expression of our gifts—waiting tables, stocking inventory, running a cash register. Still, we are part of the fiber of the community, with opportunity to contribute to the wellbeing of others. The focus of the Christian vocation is not self-satisfaction or enjoyment in the work per se, but rather, in relating to others as Jesus taught, including fellow employees as well as those who receive our work.

We are all part of a body, creating the communities and neighborhoods and providing one another with the goods and services we need to survive and flourish—or not. Ideally, our work is an expression of the special gifts and talents God has given us. As much as you may love playing music and singing, if you have no natural talent and willingness to practice, it is doubtful that your best work will be in professional music performance. If you are good at math and love organizing spreadsheets, you may do your best work as a financial manager. Paul was clear that no part of the body is more important or more vital than any other part; we are all "called" to do our part (1 Corinthians 12).

Researchers have found that those people who view their work as a calling are more satisfied and committed to their work, struggling less with depression and stress than those who do not (Dik & Duffy, 2009; Steger, Pickering, Shin, & Dik, 2010). Frederick Buechner has often been quoted: "the place God calls you to is the place where your deep gladness and the world's deep hunger meet"(Buechner, 1993, p. 95). That is, God usually calls us to the kind of work that we need to do and that the world most needs. He suggests that if we find joy in our work, we have met the first requirement. If our work is writing commercials for potato chips or making violent video games, we probably have missed what the world really needs from us. At the same time, if we are working at jobs that we find boring or depressing, we probably have missed what would bring us deep gladness—and we probably are not helping those we are serving very well either.

When the work fits our gifts and abilities, we can keep at the work because we are well suited to the task. Because we enjoy the work—most days—does not mean that our motivation is self-fulfillment, however. Rather, we feel meaning and purpose because we catch glimpses that God is using us for God's purposes. We are tools of God's ongoing creation. The gifts and abilities that God created in us and define who we are fit with the needs of others—and we experience that "fit" as confirmation that our feet are on the right path. According to 1 Peter, we are to use whatever gifts God has given us to serve our neighbors (1 Pet. 4:10). In so doing, we experience the joy of being God's coworkers (Palmer, 1991; Sherman, 2011).

Sometimes the very work that brings us the joy of purposeful lives is also deeply demanding and even depleting. There are times that we sacrifice a part of ourselves for the sake of the others we serve through our work. Every social worker has heard someone say, "I could never do what you do." That is true; some people do not have the gifts and abilities that social work requires. Those who do, however, may experience the joy of serving even in situations that lead to fatigue and perhaps tears.

Moreover, sometimes God calls people to tasks for which they are quite unqualified or that they do not want to do. Think of Moses with his speech impediment and objections to confronting Pharaoh; Jonah called to prophesize to a people he despised, fleeing from the task God put before him; Esther not wanting to risk her life by speaking for her people; and even Jesus asking God to take away the terrible task God put before him in the Garden of Gethsemane. The biblical narratives teach that when God does call people to something they are unable or unwilling to do, a display of God's power will follow.

Christian calling, then, is our work, but at the same time it is more than our work. Because God loves the world, our calling is always about our contribution to that world—in all the ways we live in a physical place and a human community. Calling is far more than the profession for which we prepare or the title we put in our e-mail signature or business card. Calling does not end when we retire from paid employment. We walk our calling all our lives, with all the ups and downs and twists and turns, never finished until we finish this life.

The History of Social Work as Christian Vocation

Some professional paths are intrinsically more directly in service of neighbors than others, and social work is one such profession. Many of those who shaped the beginnings of the social work profession in the late nineteenth century were religious leaders, applying the new social sciences of psychology and sociology to the mission outreach activity of the church. Specht and Courtney (1994) have suggested that even the name "social work" derived from the religious term "good works," a Christian concept (p. 21).

Many of the earliest schools of social work combined social work and religious education. At a time in which women were denied access to established church institutions like denominational seminaries and colleges, they founded these social work schools to prepare to serve as church workers and missionaries both in this country and in overseas missions (Garland & Yancey, 2014). For them, social work *was* a Christian mission, so it certainly *had* a Christian mission.

Early male leaders of the social work profession also grounded the very purpose of the profession in Christian teachings. In 1920, the president of the National

Conference of Social Work described the *calling* of social work as work for God's order "on earth as it is in heaven" (Lovejoy, 1920, p. 209). He grounded the profession in the words of Jesus announcing his calling to bind up the broken hearted, proclaim liberty to the captives, and open the prisons of those that are bound, saying "this is not a slight task to which we are called" (p. 209). Lovejoy equated social work with sacred ministry grounded in the life of Jesus. Two decades later, Edward Devine, a leader in the Charity Organization Society, wrote a historical reflection on the earliest years of the social work program and concluded that the power, purpose, and value of social work derive from Christian teaching (Devine, 1939). These two examples represent the heart of early social work.

During the early and middle decades of the twentieth century, however, new theoretical approaches of the social sciences that left no room for religion and spirituality came to dominate the helping professions, including psychology, social work, and psychiatry. These approaches saw religion and faith as unscientific and therefore a threat to professions that saw themselves as expressions of the social sciences. Social work, particularly social work education and academic scholarship, became increasingly secularized—and social work education has a strong influence on the profession as it prepares each generation of new leaders. In 1952, Bisno expressed the common sentiment of social work education that a Christian understanding of sin was in direct competition with social work's valuing of an individual's worth and dignity. He argued that Christianity, as he saw it expressed at least in Catholic social work, is "outside the main stream of social work thought" (p. 3).

Outside the mainstream described the reality of social work in religiously affiliated organizations and certainly in congregations. Professional social work and religious service agencies grew to ignore or even be openly hostile toward one another, even though professional social workers motivated by Christian faith continued to serve in public and private nonsectarian settings, quiet boundary crossers from the secularized profession to the religious agencies where they served. Professional leaders ignored the concept of religious calling, leading church historian Martin Marty to comment that social work had become "godless" (Marty, 1980, p. 463).

For a student to talk about Christian motivation for choosing social work as a profession could have meant rejection from social work school (Keith-Lucas, Kuhlmann, & Ressler, 1994). Even so, Christians quietly continued to enter the profession as a way of living their faith, often underplaying their religious motivations for choosing the profession because of the profession's suspicion of and hostility toward all things religious. Christian organizations and agencies continued to provide social services as expressions of the mission of the church, ignored by the social work profession (Garland & Yancey, 2014).

It took half a century before leaders in the social work profession rediscovered the church and the role of religious faith and spirituality in the lives of social workers and their clients. Positivism, the philosophy of science that limited truth to that which we can verify empirically—what we can observe—was challenged by new postmodern theories that questioned our ability to know the social world objectively. By our very observations and description of the world around us, we actually construct it, said the postmodernists. Our observations are always incomplete; we cannot assume that because we do not observe some reality that it does not exist (Hutchison, 1998; Jeavons, 1998; Meinert, 1998; Pardeck, Murphy, & Min Choi, 1994; Weick & Saleebey, 1998). There was room again for religion and spirituality—and God.

At the same time that scientific theoretical thought was changing, so was U.S. government policy. The federal government was dismantling its social welfare policies and programs and instead making grant funding available to private social services organizations. Those organizations included religiously affiliated agencies and even congregations through legislation such as the 1996 Personal Responsibility and Work Opportunities Reconciliation Act (PRWORA). The legislation launched the White House Office of Faith-based and Community Initiatives (Chaves, 1999; Farnsely, 2004; Farris, Nathan, & Wright, 2004). Social work academics and educators were also rediscovering the importance of religious faith and spirituality—and God—in the lives of clients, if not yet in the lives of social workers (e.g., Belcher & Cascio, 2001; Canda, 1999; Canda & Phaobtong, 1992; Cnaan, Boddie, & Danzig, 2005; Cornett, 1992; Derezotes, 1995; Netting, 2002; Sherwood, 1999; Walsh, 1995).

Social work education was also recognizing the role of religious institutions in the preparation of social work professionals. In 1985, the Council on Social Work Education (CSWE) first accredited a social work program that overtly prepared social workers for practice in church settings, the Carver School of Church Social Work located in The Southern Baptist Theological Seminary in Louisville, Kentucky. CSWE had been accrediting social work programs in denominationally affiliated universities for many years previously, since the beginning of accreditation, although many schools de-emphasized their religious affiliation in the processes of accreditation and even in their classroom teaching. Accrediting a program overtly focused on social work education for the church had never happened before. By the beginning of the twenty-first century, CSWE had accredited almost 200 undergraduate and graduate social work programs that were identified as "religiously affiliated" (Council on Social Work Education, 2012), and many were becoming more overt in their integration of religion and faith into their programs.

During this same period at the end of the twentieth century, leaders in social work began revisiting the concept of vocational calling, although they couched that calling in secular terms. They were concerned that the profession was losing its commitment to social justice, public welfare, and to serving persons in situations of poverty, or otherwise disadvantaged and oppressed. In the late decades of the twentieth century, increasing numbers of social workers were less interested in care for populations historically of concern to the profession, and more interested in providing clinical services in private practice settings with paying clients. Leaders feared that social work was losing its calling (e.g. Reamer, 1987; Specht & Courtney, 1994). Because of this concern, Canda and others found an audience in the profession when they described how many social workers come to the profession seeking to live into a religious calling on their lives (Canda, 1989, 1995, 1999).

In the decades when religious motivation was highly suspect in the mainstream of the profession, the North American Association of Christians in Social Work (NACSW), founded in 1954, had provided a haven for Christians who sought to integrate their faith with their professional practice (Keith-Lucas et al., 1994). In 1974, NACSW began publishing the journal, *Social Work & Christianity*, that provided an opportunity for publications that addressed the relationship of social work and Christian vocation. NACSW published two important books on the topic of Christian calling and social work as a profession that continue to be relevant today (Keith-Lucas, 1972, 1985).

Understanding Social Work as Christian Vocation Today

Rick Chamiec-Case has provided a conceptual framework for how Christian social workers think about the integration of Christian faith and social work practice (Chamiec-Case, 2009). He describes the *latent integration* model, in which Christian faith permeates whatever the Christian does and so influences professional practice whether or not the social worker is intentional about it. In other words, the social worker simply integrates faith into practice because one's self is the primary tool in social work practice, and if that self is Christian, then practice is an expression of Christianity. Latent integration does not necessarily require intentionality or reflection.

Chamiec-Case's second model of integration is the *calling* model, in which a social worker has experienced God calling them to social work. As you read these social worker's stories, most but not all of them identify social work as their "calling," even though they may have only identified that calling upon reflection after entering the profession. The Chamiec-Case model of calling implies a beckoning into—first comes calling and then comes the choice of social work as a path of living that calling. But according to many of these 25 social workers, they have been operating from a latent integration model, only to reflect back along their life journey to experience afterwards what they perceive to be God's calling all along the way. Calling for them is not a beckoning so much as a reflection backward to see God at work in their lives.

Chamiec-Case also describes a *sustaining/coping* model of faith and practice integration (Chamiec-Case, 2009). The conviction that God calls Christians to care for persons who are vulnerable, poor, or in distress gives them energy and strength for work that is often stressful and even discouraging. For these Christians, they are social workers not because that they believe their efforts will result in a changed world broadly or even perhaps the worlds of the clients they serve. More fundamentally, they believe that God calls them to show their devotion to God through service to people and advocacy for justice—even when their efforts seem fruitless.

There is much more depth and breadth to Chamiec-Case's research on calling than I can develop here; I commend to you his original work as a parallel reading with this book.

In an exploration of the integration of faith with social work practice, some of my colleagues at Baylor University interviewed our students, practitioners, and faculty colleagues. They described this integration as "the road trip of a lifetime" (Scales, Harris, Myers, & Singletary, 2012, p. 130). They discovered that students found their way into social work in a variety of ways. For some, parents modeled service during their childhoods. Some walked through doors and opportunities that presented themselves. Some found themselves drawn to serving a people group or addressing a human problem, and social work was the way to best go at that task. For some, their goal was church ministry, but they were seeking the skills and knowledge that social work would provide them for that ministry. Some seemed unclear, still looking for a compass. Confirmation often only came long after school, when they had opportunities to work in the profession and realize that it fit (Scales et al., 2012; Singletary, Harris, Myers, & Scales, 2006).

The Stories of Calling

How do you understand calling? Does our call come from outside ourselves—is something or Someone calling us into a particular work or task? Or does it come from within, in a process of discerning what looks like a life that fits our gifts and what we enjoy? In fact, most of us have a multitude of motivations for what we do, some of which we may only be dimly aware, if aware at all.

Bible stories present a variety or examples of God calling people to a task or a lifework. Often there seemed to be an actual audible voice. God spoke to Abram who left home and kindred to answer. God spoke to Moses from the burning bush. An angel spoke to Mary. A great flash of light and thundering voice knocked the angry Pharisee Saul down and blinded him. These biblical callings suggest calling may be a onetime voice heralded by bright lights and burning bushes or heavenly visitors.

Other stories suggest that God speaks to us in our dreams or in dreamlike states. In a dream, Joseph received a warning to take Mary and Jesus and flee to Egypt. The boy Samuel heard a voice in the night, mistaking it at first for his mentor Eli; it took Eli's guidance before Samuel understood what his own ears were hearing.

Still others heard no voice directly but chose a direction because they trusted another to have a word from God. Esther acted based on the urging of her Uncle Mordecai. Sarai went with Abram to a new country because Abram told her God had called them.

Many of these biblical narratives imply that calling comes at a defining moment in time as a great task to which God calls. But for many of us, calling seems more a process over a lifetime of listening to the stirrings in our souls in response to scripture and the world around us, of listening in the silence of prayer or the sharing in corporate worship, of dreams waking and sleeping, of the voices of people we trust telling us how they see our gifts and possibilities. Bankson has said that calling begins with a feeling of connection to something or someone (Bankson, 1999). We walk by the ocean, hear a choir sing gloriously to God, catch a new meaning in an old Bible story, experience anger at an injustice on the streets of our town or in the evening news—and we may feel a longing that we sense comes from beyond ourselves.

Sometimes those intuitions only come as we look back on the events of our lives and see that we were not just wandering aimlessly—our steps brought us to where we are because it seems that is where we were supposed to be.

Stories of calling have been my way of understanding social work as a Christian vocation. Anne Davis (b.1937-d.2006) was a pioneer, the first dean of the Carver School of Church Social Work at the Baptist seminary in Louisville, Kentucky, and my friend. I began my teaching career under her leadership in 1979, and she shaped much of my thought about the integration of Christian faith and social work practice. Anne loved a good story—she embedded her understanding of truth in stories—the stories of ordinary people, of growing up in a poor rural area of Virginia, and, of course, biblical stories. Because she so shaped my own sense of calling, I share her story of calling with you.

Anne's story is common for women in congregations in the middle of the last century in Caucasian Baptist life; my own experiences of being a Christian girl growing up during that era parallel hers. She was very active in her congregation's life, and, feeling led by the Holy Spirit as a teenager, she committed herself to "full time Christian service" or what others called "vocational ministry."

Anne did not have a clear picture of what type of ministry she would do, but her congregation invited her to preach, although she knew that was a rare experience for women in Southern Baptist life during the 1960s. "At that point, all I knew a woman could do was be a missionary to China," she recalled. She did not particularly want to do that, "But I would have, if nothing else had opened up," she said in an interview, laughing (Laine Scales, personal communication).

Anne had to wait until her college years to discover other types of ministry that would shape her calling and career. In college, she heard about the Carver School of Missions and Social Work in Louisville, Kentucky, one of those training schools that had been founded by women in the beginning years of the social work profession (Garland & Yancey, 2014). There she found herself prepared as a social worker, supported by scholarships from the Woman's Missionary Union of Southern Baptists.

During her early years of professional practice, she served under the auspices of a congregation and then a denominational missions agency, the Southern Baptist Home Mission Board. Supported by donations through congregations of Christians giving to mission offerings, she worked in community development and social services in poor communities in Kentucky. She would later organize and lead the first and only accredited graduate social work program in a seminary, with the goal of providing new generations of social workers for the missions and ministry of the church (Scales, 2008). Yet she could never have imagined that outcome as a teenager preaching in her rural congregation, wondering if God was calling her to be a missionary to China.

This brief snippet from Anne's story illustrates what I found in the stories you will read in this book. Calling is a journey that begins with little vision about where it will lead but enough faith to trust the One who is calling onward. There are twists and turns that make the next section of the path ahead impossible to see. Discussing the concept of calling is much different than living it.

Before we interviewed them, the social workers whose stories I have told may or may not have given systematic thought to the concept of Christian vocation, to what motivates them, or to how their work and their faith intersect. To ask them about their "calling" meant their going back to think about the path they have walked and what led them along the way. For some, the sense of God beckoning them into this path was very real. Some heard what they describe as the voice of God, perhaps in their thoughts or dreams if not as an audible voice from the heavens. Others have trusted intuitions that come in their experiences of holy quiet, expressive worship or searching scriptures and inspired readings. Others seemed to stumble along, only becoming aware of a sense of purpose—or calling—by looking backward. They did what they did because a path opened before them and they simply took it.

Is it less a calling if we are only dimly aware, or not at all aware, that God is leading us? Does God intervene in our lives by actually directing us, or are we simply called to be faithful to the teachings of Jesus wherever our paths wander? As you read their pondering of their journeys, I hope you will reflect on your own vocational path thus far.

Moore has commented that stories have meaning in themselves; they do not need someone else to point out their meaning. We may analyze stories to amplify their hidden wisdom, but the analysis should never replace the richness of the stories, which always carry "a surplus of meaning" (Moore, 2008, p. 219). Hearing the stories of others almost always points us back with new insight for understanding our own life paths. In the most ordinary events of our lives, we see glimpses of the sacred weaving of God in our lives (Garland, 2003b).

I have shared these social workers' stories as they told them. You will undoubtedly find yourself disagreeing with some of the decisions they made in their professional work; perhaps you would have tackled a situation differently. I certainly do not agree with them in every respect, both how they think about the integration of faith and practice, or with the actions they took in the stories of practice they told me. There are as many Christian worldviews as there are Christians; you will not agree with some of their beliefs and practices based on their faith, nor do I. They are not my stories to change or critique. I hope I have told them well enough that you can hear how their beliefs and faith practices have shaped and been shaped by their work as social workers—and their understanding of what difference it has made in their social work that they are Christians. My hope is that their stories will give you new ways of thinking about your own path as a social worker.

> Trust in the Lord, and do good . . . Commit your way to the Lord; trust in Him, and he will act. . . . Be still before the Lord, and wait patiently for Him (Psalm 37: 3-7)

Gratitude

I did not write this book alone. It began as a dream with my colleague, Vicki Kabat. Together, we sketched out the prospectus and wrote the first draft of the first chapters. I would never have launched this project without her encouragement. She was patient when I allowed other projects to put this one on a long hold that became years. She retired before I could pick up the work again, encouraging me to finish the book without her.

You will see a number of chapter authors who were my students in my MSW and PhD classes who took on conducting an interview and writing the first draft of a chapter as a class project. I am grateful to all of them. Jan Collins, Audrey Henderson, and Gloria Holloway each worked with me successively over the years as my graduate assistants and transcribed most of the interview recordings. Rick Chamiec-Case, NACSW's Executive Director, has been a close friend and occasional research partner for more than three decades; Rick patiently encouraged me to write this book, even when I repeatedly asked for extensions. I am grateful to my colleagues Jim Ellor and Dennis Myers in the Baylor School of Social Work for contributing suggestions and editing early renditions. I am also grateful to my Baylor colleagues Gaynor Yancey and Laine Scales, who read the final manuscript in its entirety and made encouraging and helpful suggestions. For almost two decades, Baylor employed Jeanie Fitzpatrick as my assistant, and we have enjoyed a close friendship far beyond the workplace. Subsequently, NACSW employed Jeanie as copy editor for this book, and her hand has much improved its readability. The book is better for the contributions of all these colleagues; any shortcomings are my responsibility. Beyond all others, I am grateful to a New Testament scholar who is also my husband. For 45 years, I have learned from and drawn upon David's deep insights into scripture. I have cherished our partnership in calling as well as our companionship and love all along our own journey together.

I am especially grateful to these 25 social workers who entrusted their stories to me. They took hours out of very busy lives because they wanted to share their stories with you. They did so knowing that their stories were not just stories of courage and dedicated service to others but also stories of their own mistakes and struggles, and of the dark nights when they wondered if somehow they had lost the path of calling on which they thought God had planted their feet. In all of the "ordinariness" of their daily lives and work, may you see the thread of the sacred, woven throughout their days—and yours.

Questions to Ponder

1. What vocations did you try on through pretend play as a child? What were the influences that led to the appeal of that pretend work, and how do you see those related to what you are doing now, if they are?

2. How do you think your family would define the profession of social work? Your friends?

3. Before you read this chapter, how would you have defined the terms "calling" and "vocation"?

4. Consider the term "full-time Christian calling." Does it apply only to those employed by congregations and religious organizations, or do you see it more broadly?

5. Which of Chamiec-Case's models of integration of faith and the social work profession (latent integration, calling, or sustaining/coping), or combination of these models, fit you best?

6. How do you see God directing—or not—our paths? Are we free to choose any number of paths, or is there just one that is unique and "best" for us?

7. If you believe that God leads us, is a vocation less a calling if we are only dimly aware, or not at all aware, of that leading?

8. How have you experienced calling and vocation in your own life? What aspects of your life have a sense of calling touched?

Children and Adolescents

Patricia Cummings
Regional Director, Presbyterian Family Care Services
Charis Dietz, Co-author

Patricia Cummings grew up knowing that her parents had adopted her. Even before she understood the concept of adoption, her parents read her a children's book that explained that adoption means that they had chosen her; that she was special. She always felt loved and secure. Because of that life experience, she thought she would grow up to work as an adoptions social worker.

Her parents were active members and leaders in their congregation. As a teenager, Patricia says she felt called to ministry. Her denomination did not allow women to serve as pastors, however, and she did not know of any other route into ministry that was open to her. She completed her associate's degree and left college for marriage at the age of 19. In the years that followed, she and her husband struggled with infertility. Month after month of not being pregnant was painful; she deeply wanted to be a mother. She finally came to the place of saying, "Okay, Lord, you and I both know there are a lot of children that need someone to love them and care for them." She and her husband adopted their son. And the experience of deep disappointment and then the joy of becoming an adoptive mother herself after living with the reality of her own adoption fed her sense of calling to care for children who are vulnerable to the loss of family.

In those early years, Patricia worked in the office of a middle school in their small town, where she also functioned as the school nurse, even though she does not have a nursing degree. But there was no school nurse and so when teachers sent sick children to the office, Patricia did what needed to be done. She reflects back,

> I saw so many kids that really weren't sick, but they were sick at heart. If they were physically sick, I would call their family to pick them up. If there were problems, I tried to help them—but I really did not know how to help. I just cared.

That experience of caring without being able to help sent her back to school to obtain the tools she perceived she needed for helping children and, even more, the families of children. She completed a BA in psychology at a Baptist college within commuting distance of her home. After graduation, she worked for four years in the state child protective services agency. The agency provided the *training* she needed for working with situations of abuse and neglect, but she wanted more *education*. That is, she knew how to do the tasks assigned her, to conduct an assessment, to make decisions about the safety of children, and to follow procedures. She wanted to use her experience to create ways to help families *before* child protective services became involved—to think creatively and with a wider vision.

Patricia started her MSW degree at the state university, but once again, family responsibilities presented what seemed like a barrier to her education. Both of her parents were ill and she had the responsibility for their care, so she dropped out of her graduate degree program. After time at home providing care for her parents, she once again was looking for a job. This time, she found employment with Presbyterian Family Services. Her employment came with the promise of the agency's support—and the condition that she finish her MSW. Her son was now grown, so she jumped at the opportunity. Presbyterian Family Services sent her to a religiously affiliated university that was close enough that she could commute, because they wanted her to have a degree that integrated religious faith with professional social work. Working full time at Presbyterian, it took her three years of commuting to campus to complete her degree part-time. She graduated in 2003, at the age of 47. It may have taken her awhile, but she had found her route into social work.

Presbyterian Children's Homes & Services

Patricia began the Family Child and Family program for Presbyterian while she was an MSW student; she still supervises the program almost two decades after that first employment conversation, where she was offered a job and the support she needed to complete her MSW. Her staff works to provide families the services they need to help children flourish, whatever that may mean. Although they receive some of their referrals from the state child protective services agency where Patricia began her career, they only serve voluntary clients—the state agency or a court cannot require a family to receive their services.

Presbyterian has tried to remove all barriers that would keep families from benefiting from their counseling services. As a denominational agency, it is able to offer services without charge, supported by the Presbyterian Church. The social workers provide services in client homes because they believe they can be more effective by providing services in the family's own context. Therefore, transportation is never a barrier.

I asked Patricia to tell me about the kind of work that the agency does, and she told me about a family with whom she worked almost a decade ago and who still drops by to say hello and let her know how they are doing. Patricia received a referral from the high school about Beth and Carrie Porter, sisters ages sixteen and seventeen. Beth and Carrie were living alone with their younger brothers, who were in elementary school.

When Patricia visited, she learned that their dad had left them in a house for which he paid the rent, but he had provided nothing else. There was no furniture in the house, no electricity or heat. When their mother had died nine years previously, their father became responsible for their care. He was an alcoholic and went through a number of partners and marriages, and the children received little supervision or even provision for basic needs. Now not only had he left the girls with their own two brothers to care for, but also with four other children, the children of his current girlfriend. He had plugged an extension cord with one light bulb on the end of it into the house next door so that they had that single light at night. Before the extension cord, the girls had been holding a flashlight for each other to do their homework in the long dark evenings. The girls took jobs at the Dairy Queen in order to buy groceries. They alternated evening schedules so that one of them could be home to take care of the six younger children.

One night, the house next door burned down and Beth and Carrie lost their single light; that was a breaking point for Beth. The next day, Beth began to cry at school. When a teacher probed, Beth found herself telling about their situation despite all her father's warnings not to share the family's troubles. Patricia remembers:

> She was afraid because her dad had always told them, "If you ever tell anyone, what is happening, CPS will come and split you all up, and you'll never see each other again." So they had this huge fear all their lives of losing one another. So when I received calls from the school, I went to the home. As I assessed the situation, I realized that Beth, almost eighteen, really had the capacity to parent her brothers. We arranged to move the girlfriend's children out of the home.
>
> I asked Beth what was her greatest need, and she said she was trying to figure out how to get to the elementary school to get her little brother's report card, because you had to have a teacher conference to get a report card. She rode the bus to school, and she was trying to figure out how to get to the elementary school to have that teacher conference.

Patricia helped Beth move into a rent-subsidized apartment and arranged for furniture supplied by a congregation. She helped Beth with the legal processes of obtaining custody of her siblings. She arranged to transfer her mother's Social Security benefits from the dad to Beth so that they had some income. Patricia stayed in close touch with the girls as they completed high school. She helped Carrie to apply for and receive a full scholarship to the state university.

They were good students; they went to school every day. Carrie went to college, and Beth found employment and parented her little brothers. I worked with them for three years, developing their life skills such as Carrie's learning how to write a resume and apply for jobs, and how to budget. I was the adult with whom Carrie and Beth could discuss parenting the boys and making life decisions they both faced. I provided them with counseling. Carrie had been sexually abused during those early years by a relative who had been temporarily living in the home, and although the perpetrator was prosecuted, she never received any counseling.

Carrie and Beth were very active in their church, but because people there knew their father, they had been hesitant to reach out for help. Patricia became the adult in their lives on whom they could lean for those years, until they believed they could do it on their own.

> No one wants a social worker in their life forever, and when they reached the point that they felt like they could do life on their own, we mutually agreed that we would close their case. I was here if they ever needed me. So from time to time, they always have called me or come back by just to see me.
>
> A few years ago, a church asked me if I had a family to refer to them for a program called Open Table, where people in the congregation agree to walk alongside a family living in poverty and help them with life decisions, providing support. I talked to Carrie and Beth, and they both wanted to participate. They still lived in poverty; they had food and electricity, but they wanted more for themselves.

Patricia participated with the church group, at Carrie and Beth's request, now in the role of a volunteer mentor, not their social worker.

The family of siblings has done well. Carrie graduated from college and has a very good job. Beth completed a vocational nursing program and is employed as a nurse. Their incomes have lifted the family out of poverty. The older brother received an athletic scholarship and is on track to graduate from college. The younger brother is a junior in high school, playing football and staying on the academic honor roll. Patricia added to the story:

> They faced challenges, though, and that is what the Open Table church group helped them through. Carrie has Lupus, and she became very ill during her junior year and quit college; she had no insurance. Beth did not pass the final nursing test. So the church group helped them with resources and encouragement

to return to school until they both graduated and obtained stable employment, had reliable cars to drive, and knew how to budget their money. Most of their family members had not graduated from high school, and they were the first to go to college. They have done so well.

Patricia said that she has learned that change does not come through programs; it comes through relationships.

> I really see that change comes about through that relationship, the professional relationship and empowering the families; the program just provides a context for a relationship to form. Through the relationship, the family learns to trust us, to trust enough to learn from our education and expertise that we can share.

Working with Families

In some ways, Carrie and Beth's family was exceptional, since Beth was close enough to eighteen that Patricia could work with them toward their being responsible for their family without having to place them with adult relatives or in foster care. Few children can live on their own, obviously; they have to have parental figures in their lives. Patricia began her social work practice wanting to work with children. Soon she began to realize that she could help children by counseling with them for a few weeks or months, but if she worked with their parents, she could create change in the family systems that would help children far more than anything she could do in individual counseling with the children themselves. Her focus shifted to parents, guiding them in supporting the healthy development of their children. That is what she did with Patricia and Beth, and so prevented foster care placement for their brothers. The goal of the agency is to keep families together whenever possible.

Patricia is proud of how flexible the agency is, with its capacity for addressing most of the needs of families, even when their needs are outside the agency's usual services. To illustrate, she told me how, not long before we talked, Randy Poage walked into the office; it is not unusual for people to show up without an appointment. Another agency had sent Randy to Patricia because he was going through a divorce and needed a social study done for a court custody hearing. Patricia had done lots of custody work in the past, but she no longer offered this service. But someone had given Randy her name and said she could help him. She wanted to say that she was sorry, that she did not do social studies for the court anymore. But she also knew that she did not know his situation.

> I did not know how fragile he might be; I have seen people just crumble if I tell them I can't help them. So I invited him into my

office, all the while thinking to myself, "I know I'm not going to do that social study; I should tell him now and save his time."

Fidgeting nervously in the seat, he asked her if she wanted him to tell her his story. Clients often have to tell their story over and over in order to receive the services they need. She wanted to spare him that, knowing already that she would not be able to help. She asked Randy if anyone had given him a list of professionals who now were doing custody work. Instead, he launched into telling her the story anyway—and she listened. His heart was breaking at losing his wife and children. He worked at a minimum wage job, struggling to pay child support; he really did not have the resources to pay an agency for the social study he needed so desperately if he were to keep visiting rights with his children.

After listening to his heartbreak and his longing for a relationship with his children, Patricia decided to contact a colleague at another agency, asking if a social worker there would at least talk with him.

> I told her I would try to help find a way to pay for her services through another agency. Instead, she offered to do the social study pro bono, saying "If you tell me he needs it done, I will do it; don't worry about the money." I was so surprised; social studies take a lot of time and usually cost a lot of money.

So she made an appointment, hung up the phone, and handed Randy the slip of paper with the social worker's name, address and the appointment date and time. When she stood and shook his hand, Randy said, "Thank you; you are the only person who would help me." Then he thought, lifted his eyes and looked her squarely in the face, and said, "No wait; you didn't just help me. You are the only person that *listened* to me." For him, as much as he needed the help, he needed also to have someone care enough to hear his story. Patricia thought about how she had not wanted to take the time or put him through the emotion of telling his story, and realized she had been sensitive enough to realize that he needed and wanted the connection with another person who cared enough to listen. Because of her work, Randy's children would have their father back in their lives.

From Families to Community Practice

In the early years, Patricia worked directly with client families. She still works with a few families herself, even though it is a fulltime responsibility to supervise the social workers on the agency's staff across the region for which she is now responsible. She likes staying grounded in work with families so that she can readily understand what her staff experiences. There are also times that there is a good reason for the regional social worker not to work with a specific family—perhaps they are related in some way or are friends—and so Patricia takes those clients herself.

She also loves providing training for staff and experiences deep satisfaction in helping them work through challenges, growing and flourishing as professionals under her supervision.

In addition to providing counseling services in homes, Presbyterian's social workers also advocate for their families in the community. Patricia helped to develop a child advocacy center in her town and served as director of the board for four years. The center is still thriving; she is pleased that it is a strong organization; "they no longer need me."

In the months just before our last conversation, the agency promoted Patricia to Regional Director, one of four in the state. She now travels much of the workweek and often is gone three or four nights each week when she is opening a new program in another city or dealing with a challenge. Even when programs are running smoothly, she is away a night or two a week.

The agency is expanding their community-based programs and is able to do so because they have closed two residential programs. The teenagers being referred now to residential programs have significant mental health issues, and the agency is not equipped to provide those services. Instead, Presbyterian has decided to close their child residential programs and instead expand what they do best, which is to work with families in the community and with foster care. As part of that expansion, Patricia described a new residential program she oversees that she just opened:

> In one house, there will be seven single moms and their children. The other home is for six girls transitioning out of foster care at age eighteen and who have no families to support them as they move into adulthood. They can stay with us for up to eighteen months, with the goal of achieving self-sufficiency. They must be working or going to school or part time of both of those.

Rural Social Work

One of the most significant challenges Patricia faces is living in a rural community. She inevitably runs into clients at the grocery store or in church. Because of the close working relationship she develops with families and the mutual affection that develops through the work together, she is careful to explain that she cannot be their friend, and she will not even speak to them if she runs into them in the community unless they speak to her first. But she says, "they don't remember that—or they don't want to remember that." One evening, for example, she took a client's baby to the hospital and there encountered three former clients—the nurse who cared for the baby, another patient in the emergency room, and then the x-ray technologist. All three wanted to catch her up on their lives, but the context was not appropriate, and when Patricia did not encourage their sharing with her, at least one former client's face fell in disappointment.

On the other hand, there are great advantages in rural social work. Patricia knows the agencies and knows the other professionals in town, and they know and trust her—like the congregation that provided Beth and Carrie with furniture and, later, with the Open Table program, and the colleague who provided pro bono services to Randy. That is a real asset for Patricia's clients—she can obtain resources that otherwise might not be available to them.

The Reward

It gives Patricia joy when she sees clients regain hope that their lives can be better, even when others have given up on them. It is rewarding to see clients make progress and change their lives as a consequence of the agency's involvement. The rewards are also in seeing communities changed because of the work of the agency.

Just before our initial conversation, Patricia and another social work colleague had organized a community-wide school supply drive for the fourth year. In previous years, every congregation and every agency had doled out a few school supplies to children who could not afford them—Patricia had identified sixteen different places that gathered donations and then provided school supplies for families requesting them. Families had to be savvy in knowing where to go; not all families received what their children needed. Patricia asked, "Could we serve more children more effectively if we all worked together?"

Not everyone was enthusiastic—some were not sure they wanted to give up their own service project. In the end, though, Patricia was excited to see that all the congregations and agencies joined in to raise the funds for 2,400 backpacks with needed supplies in them, by grade level. Every child who needed supplies received an age-appropriate stocked backpack. And the community took pride in their strong collaboration. Many people participated, and they had different ideas about how they should tackle the project. There were conflicts. But, Patricia says with a broad grin, "We did it together; and we are already talking about what we learned and how we can improve for next year."

The Role of Faith

When Patricia and her staff conduct an initial assessment with families inquiring about services, they ask about their faith, what role it plays in their lives if it does, and whether or not they are part of a congregation. Some clients want to talk about spiritual issues, trying to find the meaning in the suffering they are experiencing. Others do not. Some have come from very different perspectives, and Patricia has learned to say, "Teach me about your faith."

Ms. Schmidt came to Patricia for help when she learned that a family member had sexually abused her daughter. Coming to Presbyterian was a big risk for Ms. Schmidt; she belonged to a non-Christian faith tradition, and her community expected her to keep the family's troubles within the community. Patricia needed to understand the teachings and values of the community in order to help Ms. Schmidt decide how to help her daughter and relate to her community. Since her faith community was part of the crisis, Patricia asked Ms. Schmidt to teach her about her community and their faith beliefs and practices as they relate to the crisis in Ms. Schmidt's family.

Patricia always makes the focus on the client's faith, not her own. When the session ended, Ms. Schmidt surprised Patricia by asking, "Would you pray for me?" Since the woman assumed Patricia has a Christian perspective since she was sitting in a Presbyterian agency, Patricia asked for clarification—did Ms. Schmidt want her to pray for her in the coming days, or was she asking for prayer together now? Ms. Schmidt responded, "I want you to pray for me this week because this next week is going to be really hard." Patricia responded,

> I said, "I would be honored to pray for you, if that is what you want." Ms. Schmidt smiled, and said to me, "I'm pretty sure that we're praying to the same God."

Presbyterian's mission statement says that it provides Christ-centered services to children and their families. Patricia is a Christian but not a Presbyterian, and her staff members come from a variety of Christian traditions. They may not agree on some of what Patricia calls the nuances of doctrine, but they do agree that Jesus focused on people's strengths. She referenced the story of Jesus talking with the woman at the well (John 4). When the woman told Jesus that she had been married five times, he responded by saying that she was telling the truth. Patricia notes that Jesus pointed out the woman's strength—her truthfulness. Jesus encouraged people, Patricia says, and so that is what she and her staff try to do—identify people's strengths, honor their experiences, and encourage them in their own paths.

> Even if I never bring up the Lord or faith or anything, if I'm building on their strengths, and that is what social workers do, then that's also what Jesus did. It is really about what they want and need, and not my trying to make them think as I think.

After our last interview, Patricia reflected more on the meaning of her faith in her work. She sent me the following message in an email:

> In the midst of crisis, clients often have so few that believe in them. Maybe they have broken relationships or lost hope that things can ever be different than they are. I believe that people can have a better future regardless of where they have been, the crisis they find themselves in, or the consequences of their

decisions. There is no condemnation in Christ; He loves us and gives us opportunity every day to change and live a more full and meaningful life. During times of deep hurt and hopelessness, God has always been faithful to "carry" me when I felt helpless to walk the difficult path. In the same way, I pray to be so "present" with a client or staff member that they see there is no condemnation but rather hope and encouragement, and that my hope for their future can carry them until they can recover their own personal hope.

Now, in addition to her responsibilities at Presbyterian, Patricia has returned to her graduate program as a part-time teacher. For more than seven years, she has been teaching a course on professional practice with children and families. As varied as her responsibilities are, they all relate to caring for children—through her own work with children and families and their communities, in her supervision of the work of other professionals, and now in the teaching of future professionals. When she felt the tug of a calling on her life to ministry more than forty years ago, she had no way of imagining the path on which that calling has led her.

Questions to Ponder

1. Trace what you consider to be the most significant of Patricia's life experiences leading to her current work as a social worker in a Presbyterian agency. What does her life illustrate about vocation and calling?

2. As you read the story of Carrie and Beth's family, what appear to be the elements in this story that led to a successful outcome? How do you see this as a story of the integration of faith and professional practice?

3. Describe Patricia's shift in focus from children to parents to communities. What drove that shift in her focus?

4. Why did Patricia not want to hear Randy's story? And why did she listen anyway? What difference did it make? What does this story illustrate for you about professional social work and Christian faith principles?

5. What principles did Patricia use in shaping how she engaged in conversations about religion and faith with Ms. Schmidt? What do you see to be the outcome?

6. What do you think about Patricia's statement that Jesus used a strengths perspective in engaging people as a centering principle for her staff?

7. How does Patricia relate her faith to her practice with clients?

Allison Porter
Child and Family Services Social Worker, Springfield Youth Center and John Hale County Hospital

Lindsay Swain, Co-Author

After completing her MSW, Allison began her career as a social worker in a middle school before taking the position of Treatment Team Coordinator at Springfield Youth Center (SYC). Although she has since moved on to a hospital position, Allison believes that the three years she spent at SYC first defined her path as a Christian living her faith through social work.

Springfield Youth Center (SYC) is a psychiatric residential facility for children who have landed in trouble at school or in the community, often involving arrest for illegal behavior—robbery, assault, and/or drug possession. Many of the eighty SYC clients have diagnoses of behavioral and emotional disorders. Once they leave SYC, they have to face the criminal charges that led to their arrest. Their progress at SYC is an important factor in the court's decision about what happens next. If they successfully complete the program, often the court will simply drop the charges against them. If they are not successful at SYC, then they usually face at least being on probation for a period of time, or, for more serious offenses, being in a locked juvenile detention facility. Clearly, the work they do, or fail to do, with the staff of SYC significantly affects their futures.

When Allison arrived at SYC each morning, a group of teenage boys greeted her; they were hanging out in the living room of the SYC boys' residence before they headed to school. Talking with them for a few moments, often sharing a laugh, was the beginning of Allison's morning routine. She enjoyed these informal exchanges with her students, and it provided the opportunity for her to help them be comfortable with her.

SYC calls the clients "students," emphasizing that SYC is an educational facility and normalizing the services SYC provides, since all children are students. SYC provides individual, group, and family therapy for the eighty students that stay for an average of six to nine months. SYC has both girls and boys who range in age from thirteen to seventeen. While in care at the SYC, students attend school on campus, participate in therapy, and live in housing units defined by gender and treatment level. Allison's office was in one of the boys' units.

Allison served as the Treatment Team Coordinator for the students living in her unit, leading the direct care staff, a nurse manager, the campus psychiatrist, and the student's family to structure the appropriate treatment for each individual student. She met regularly with the teachers and other staff members that interacted with her students, gathering information and offering feedback about how everyone's work fit into student treatment goals. The entire staff worked with the students and each other to help change the behaviors that landed the students in enough trouble to end up at SYC.

I Want to Be a Social Worker When I Grow Up

Allison believes that God had been preparing her for a career as a social worker all of her life. As a child, others easily confided in Allison and she cared deeply about people. When she was in first grade, her friend Susan shared with Allison that she was being physically hurt at home. Allison told her parents, and they contacted the school and Child Protective Services. The agency evidently decided that there was no imminent danger and so left Susan in her home while they investigated the allegation of abuse. However, Susan's family became even more violent after learning that Susan had told others that they had hurt her. Susan turned angrily on Allison; "You weren't a friend; a real friend wouldn't tell."

In Allison's first-grade mind, Susan was right; a friend should not tell secrets. After all, her telling had not seemed to help but just made life worse for Susan. Allison deeply regretted reporting Susan's abuse. So in the second grade, when her best friend, Rebecca, shared a similar secret, Allison told no one. Two years later, Allison's father, who worked at the local newspaper, learned that Rebecca had been found dead inside a clothes dryer. When Allison's parents told her about her best friend's death, she told them that she had known that Rebecca was being hurt at home and did not tell. Although Rebecca's death was ruled accidental, once again Allison believed it was her fault that she had not helped her friend. She decided that when she grew up, she would help children in need in a way that she was unable to help Allison and Rebecca.

Allison's first encounter with a social worker was during a middle school mission trip. She and her church youth group worked with a large urban mission organization, City Reach. During the week of service, the youth group stayed at a local apartment complex, where Allison met the City Reach social worker. Throughout the week, the social worker provided Allison with opportunities to learn about social work. When Allison returned home, she was confident she would someday be a social worker. Allison went on to enroll in a university with a social work school, majored in social work, and stayed to complete her MSW.

Springfield Youth Center

The opportunity to live her determination to help children came in her first job as a middle school social worker and again when she took the position at SYC. Allison learned that many of her students at SYC, rough and threatening though they might appear, and violent as they may have been, were reacting to their own childhood experiences of violence and other forms of abuse. Some had grown up in families so stressed by poverty and other challenges that they ignored their children's emotional needs in the simple attempt to survive. Allison tried to form a close relationship with each one, which was the most rewarding as well as challenging aspect of her work. She knew that her relationship with them, particularly the older teenagers, may provide a last chance to make the changes needed before they became adults and faced adult consequences for their misbehavior, regardless of the circumstances that had shaped them. Ready or not, they had to be released the day before their eighteenth birthday, and after that, trouble would mean the adult criminal justice system—jail or prison—where the emphasis would be much less on redemption and much more on punishment.

Allison believed that if she could just reach one student and help him to change, then it would be a sign that she was doing the work to which God had called her. Allison recalled a particularly rough day, when a highly unusual snowfall left the facility short staffed; it snows very rarely in their region of the country. The students were restless and short tempered because the weather trapped them indoors. A couple of fights broke out and staff had to physically restrain several students. Given the deteriorating group mood, Allison and her colleagues decided to take the students outside in the snow. Even though some of her students were seventeen years old, they had never played in snow. Allison and the staff showed the students how to roll snowballs, and her students worked together to make a snowman. Even though the students had been on the verge of fights all morning, now they laughed and played together. Seventeen-year-old George later said in a group counseling session, "You know, I realize that I don't have to be fighting my way through life. I am missing out on doing fun things like this." It was the beginning of significant change for George. Allison took pictures and had the students write stories about their snowman; she posted the pictures and the stories to remind them all of the day.

Part of Allison's work with the boys was learning the role of religion and faith in their lives, whatever that may have been, and helping them connect to the strength they could find there for the challenges they face. As for her own faith, she believed that she was living it by seeing the value of each student, praying for him, and helping him to find his own power to make life choices. Her Christian belief in people's freedom to choose well or badly was the foundation for telling her students:

You have been given the ability to make choices, and with that ability, there is the knowledge that you may not make the right choice, but that is your choice.

Allison's role as a social worker at SYC was broader than the clinical services she provided to the boys on her unit. One warm spring day, the students were celebrating the end of the year with an annual field day and barbeque bash. Allison played outside with her students, went down the water slide with them, and relished watching them participate in normal childhood activities. But the day ended abruptly and tragically. In the midst of all the fun, a beloved staff member, Mr. Mike, suffered a fatal heart attack. Mr. Mike had served at SYC for two decades and was an anchor of support for students and staff alike.

In the days that followed, while the other therapists struggled with their own grief, Allison reached out to students in other units. She helped them express their grief in appropriate ways by making a big scrapbook, with each teenager preparing a page, often a story illustrated with their drawing of a memory of Mr. Mike and the impact he made in their lives. They gave the scrapbook to Mr. Mike's wife. Allison recognized that the teens needed a way to express their feelings other than talking as a group. Allison and the chaplain also helped the teens organize and conduct a memorial service on the campus. Mr. Mike's whole family attended. Allison recognized that not only was preparing the scrapbook and conducting a memorial service ways for them to process their own grief, but also caring for Mr. Mike's family in such tangible ways was the kind of contribution to the lives of others that was the program's aim for teenagers who had often been destructive in the community rather than contributors.

Special Connections

Remembering how her childhood friends confided in her with an innocent trust, Allison felt the weight of the trust her students put in her to help them shift the course of their lives. She knew that there would be few other such chances for many of them. Years later, she remembers her students—and she believes they remember her.

One of Allison's most challenging students was Jason. His diagnosis included mild Asperger's Syndrome, a pervasive developmental disorder that involved delays in the development of many basic skills, including the ability to socialize with others, to communicate effectively with others, and to use imagination. Children with Asperger's Syndrome have difficulty making friends and even starting and participating in a conversation. Because of these developmental challenges, Jason was isolated from the other boys, often handling situations and his own emotions with aggression. Jason connected with Allison, however. She worked with him to identify and understand his emotions, including his anger, before he acted. Even when he was flailing in anger and a staff member was restraining him, all Allison had to do was say his name and he would calm down.

Although change was slow and Jason continued to be aggressive and difficult, she knew that he was trying. During group counseling sections, he became more open and receptive to the other students. He even told the other boys on the unit that they were his first friends. After his discharge from SYC, Jason continued to call Allison on a weekly basis to update her on his life, to tell her how he was using his coping and calming strategies. Even though it was not an expectation of SYC that therapists continue to work with discharged students, Allison encouraged Jason to maintain the connection with her. He needed the lifeline of someone who understood and cared.

Another student Allison thinks about often is John. John arrived at the SYC and announced to her that he was not interested in making any life changes: "You're not going to talk to me about drugs; I'm still going to do drugs when I leave here." But after seven months of meeting with Allison regularly, and her underscoring that nobody could make him change if he chose not to, he confessed that he was ready to discuss his drug problem. With Allison's support, he began to work toward freeing himself of drug use. He chose not to go home for holidays to avoid the drugs that were so readily available in his neighborhood.

John decided to go to another placement after his time at SYC ended so that he could continue to work on staying drug-free. The admissions director at the new facility called Allison to say, "I don't know what you did with that kid, but there is a connection that kid has with you; he talks about what you taught him in therapy." John's mother told Allison that she had given her son back to her. Allison reflected on the changes John had made:

> I didn't even realize I was, but somehow I got through.

Recently, Allison attended a marching band competition with a close friend who is a teacher. As she walked through the stadium, Allison thought she heard her name. As she turned around, she recognized one of her children from the middle school where she had served as a social worker before taking the position at SYC. The student ran up to her, excited to share his life updates. He thanked Allison for her involvement in his life, and shared that he was about to graduate from high school, something he said he would not have been able to do without her help in middle school. It was a precious moment for Allison, one that she has turned over and over in her mind, seeing it as a reminder that God called her to this work.

Of course, not all of Allison's experiences with clients have turned out happily. Paul came to SYC angry and stayed angry; he was aggressive and violent and had multiple legal charges pending against him. The men in his mother's life had abused him sexually and violently. No one protected him, and so he believed no one cared about him. Allison remembers trying every strategy she knew to connect with him, or to help him connect with other students. When the time for a family session came, he began throwing objects and had to be placed in a restraint chair and given medication to calm him. She still shivers, remembering the withering look of hatred and the words he threw at her, wishing her dead, as the staff carried him away, still restrained in the chair.

> That happened on a Friday, and I struggled all weekend, knowing I would see him on Monday. I worked out a plan: on Monday, I told him. "Friday is over; this is Monday. We need to move forward." But he did not connect—not with me, not with anyone. The violence continued; the destruction of property continued. He was even trying to make his own drugs; the kids had learned an old prison trick of putting toothpaste on orange peels and giving it time to mold and rot—and then eating it, if you can imagine. It causes a brief experience of high. He was doing that and teaching the other students. I finally had to call his probation officer and they removed him in handcuffs. I never saw him again.

In the course of her work with the young men on her unit, Allison began to study the failures her students experienced to determine how to make the program more effective. Many of them were in her locked unit when they first arrived because of their history of violence. As they progressed through the program, they could move to open units in the facility where the doors were unlocked and they did not have to live, go to school, and eat their meals behind locked doors and have recreation in a locked yard. In those open units, they received increased privileges to attend the campus school, use the campus recreation facilities, and have freedom to interact with other clients on the campus. The transition to an open unit was supposed to be a reward to motivate positive change. Yet the students would fail—getting into a fight or otherwise breaking the rules—and so be returned to the locked unit.

Allison came to realize that the transition to a new unit was not just a reward but also a stumbling block, because the move also brought a transition to a new staff members and even a new therapist, so that any attachments they had formed with staff, social worker, and fellow students were severed. Given the boys' histories of insecure attachments and life disruptions, they needed the continuity of the same adults in their lives.

Allison consulted with others on the treatment team and led a presentation to the agency's management advocating that they convert the locked unit to an unlocked facility, so that clients could receive greater privileges to reward their progress without the disruption of a move to another unit and staff. Allison worked with the students, saying, "This is our chance to make this place better for you." The maintenance staff removed the locked doors indoors and the fence and locked gates outdoors. With the boys' help and their suggestions for its design, the classroom became a game room, and they began going to school with the rest of the campus. The unit could still be "locked down" if there was violence or a threat of a runaway, but over the first nine months of its conversion to an open status, there was no need. As a consequence of this success, today there are no locked units at SYC. Allison reflects back on this victory:

> It was incredible to see. The boys reflected on the change they had helped to create, saying, "We showed them that we did not deserve to be locked up." They had helped to plan the transition; they reveled in their ability to create positive change for themselves and also for those that would come to SYC after they were gone.

Hospital Social Work

Allison knew she was living her calling and she loved her students and her colleagues. Still, she was still living in the same town in which she had grown up. She felt God's direction to seek a new direction in a new place. She felt drawn to medical social work.

> I realized that a lot of the trauma that happened in my students' lives had involved the trauma of a death or serious illness of a family member.

Allison applied for a hospital social work position in a city a hundred miles from home and then she experienced her own trauma. She became very ill, and her doctors thought she had pancreatic cancer. She knew that she could not change jobs in the midst of a major health crisis, so she withdrew from the interview process. The supervisor said, "Let us know once you are beyond this health crisis if you are still interested." Six weeks later, Allison began to feel better, and her doctors were amazed that her pancreas seemed to have healed and biopsies were normal. On the same afternoon, after she left her doctor's office with the good news, John Hale Hospital called and asked if she would be interested in a position as a case manager. Allison took the position and ventured out to live in a new place doing a new kind of work.

Allison began her work in the hospital working with all kinds of patients—those who had experienced a physical trauma as well as those who had attempted suicide with resulting medical trauma. Allison provided short term counseling while she assessed a patient's need for placement in a psychiatric facility for continued treatment. She thinks she understands now the urging she felt to move to a professional position and a city all new to her:

> It has made me a better social worker by broadening my horizons and experiences. When I went to graduate school, I thought I would work only with children and adolescents. Now I am working with children and adolescents who have grown up—and they still need a therapist and a social worker who is going to fight for them. I have learned that I can work with teenagers, but I can also work with anyone.

Allison also works with families in the neonatal intensive care unit (NICU) when babies are born too early or with serious medical issues. She provides care for women in federal prison who deliver their babies at John Hale Hospital. They have to relinquish their babies into someone else's care when they leave the hospital to return to prison.

> It is really sad for a mom who has bonded with her baby throughout her pregnancy and then has to hand the baby to a family member or a foster parent two days after birth, recognizing she will not be able to be a part of her baby's daily life. I walk with these mothers through that while they are here.

Allison has also worked with children in the hospital because they have been victims of violence; Allison has testified in court about whether or not the court should return a child to the family—revisiting her own life experiences that drew her into social work. This time, as a social worker, she can help.

> I truly believe that every fiber of my being is a social worker. It's what God created me for. God made me with certain attributes and gave me experiences in my life to shape me and to create me to be what God wanted me to be. God not only gave me the skill set, but He gave me the ability to recognize those God-given gifts in my clients, and to call on their own faith as they face the struggles in their lives. I say, "What is it that has helped you get through day to day thus far?" By my actions and my acceptance and my caring and my support, I can show what Christ is like.

One of the biggest changes in Allison's faith life has been coming to a place where she communicates acceptance, not judgment. She realizes that she can never know all of what they have experienced, but she can provide love and recognition that each one is also a child of God as she is.

John Hale is a county hospital dealing with traumas flown in from across the region. They also have women who come from outside the United States to birth their babies in a hospital equipped for dealing with high risk deliveries; the patients pay for services prior to receiving a travel visa. Ms. Zimba came from Kenya at the end of her pregnancy because she is an older first-time mother, in her late forties, and was pregnant with triplets. She was hospitalized for a few weeks prior to the delivery of her babies to ensure their safety.

Allison worked with Ms. Zimba and learned that she had experienced severe trauma earlier in life—rape, torture and the loss of pregnancies as a result. She wanted desperately to have a child, but she was shocked when she learned she was pregnant with triplets. She arranged to come sight unseen to the United States to have her babies in safety, even though there would be no family support. All three babies were born alive but premature and were placed in the NICU.

Allison worked with Ms. Zimba every day after she was released from the hospital, arranging transportation to the hospital for her to spend time with the babies still in the NICU, and then working with her to manage the long trip home with three newborns. With Ms. Zimba's agreement, Allison called a meeting of everyone in the small community that had formed around Ms. Zimba, helping them to help her as she took each baby home to her temporary living quarters. Allison made arrangements to fly two family members from Kenya to help her on the long return. Before she left to fly back to Kenya, Ms. Zimba came with the babies to take a picture with "the White social worker who helped us."

Allison has a copy of that picture. It reminds her that social work is a journey that can provide a world of different experiences: "Who knows where it will take me next?"

Questions to Ponder

1. Summarize the path Allison traveled from childhood onward to become a social worker. How do you see life experiences influencing the path she has taken?

2. What are the advantages and disadvantages of calling SYC clients "students?"

3. Was taking the group of SYC teenage residents out to play in the snow professional practice? If so, what made it social work and not just a fun diversion on a tense day?

4. When the beloved staff member died, how did Allison help students express and work through their grief? In what ways do you see faith, her own as well as her clients, as being integrated into her work to help the students to respond to this event in ways that would help with their therapeutic goals?

5. How do you think about client outcomes—successes and failures—such as those Allison describes with her clients from the perspective of Christian calling to this profession? For example, are good client outcomes a sign that Allison has chosen the right path?

6. Although Allison was a direct practitioner at SYC, she also successfully advocated for a significant change in the organization that led to the removal of locked units. Analyze, based on what you have read, the elements that led to her success.

7. Allison has had a wide array of clients with a variety of life experiences—teenage boys arrested for violent or otherwise illegal behavior, suicidal patients, imprisoned women relinquishing their children to foster care shortly after birth, and international women birthing children far from home. Of all her experiences, which are most appealing to you? What about working with those clients seems to be a good fit for you?

8. A residential treatment facility for adolescents and a county hospital working with all kinds of patients are very different settings for practice. What do you see, from what you read in this story, to be the similarities that enable Allison to go from one to the other?

Joanie Armstrong
Child Advocate and Adoptions Specialist

Joanie enrolled in a small liberal arts college as a journalism major since she enjoyed writing; she had never even heard of the profession of social work. She quickly realized that the journalism classes did not fit her; she was shy and interviewing people for stories was torturous. One of her roommates was majoring in human services. The roommate talked about wanting to help women and children who were involved in the sex trade or prostitution. Joanie resonated with her roommate's desire to do something that would "make a difference in the world."

Joanie changed her major to human services at the end of her junior year. Human services was a small program in her college, and most of the classes were taught by the same professor—a social worker with an MSW and a lot of experience in the profession. The professor became a mentor for Joanie, and on her advice, Joanie decided to go directly into an MSW degree program after finishing her undergraduate degree. She chose a graduate program in a Christian university more than a thousand miles from home:

> I knew I would need help in figuring out how to work in my faith with my practice of social work. My background and worldview were conservative. I was concerned that if you are a social worker, you have to be a liberal and accept everyone just as they are. I wanted to be in a Christian environment where I could sort out my identity and worldview as both a social worker and as a Christian.

In graduate school she learned that accepting people where they are, as they are, is not just a social work concept, and not just a liberal concept, but a concept that fits with Christian teachings of the unconditional love of God and the creation of every person in God's image.

Joanie received a scholarship to support her preparation in graduate school for gerontological social work. She loved working with older adults, and so when she graduated in 2007, she returned home and applied for several gerontological social work positions, but "nothing was really coming together." She was on the waiting list for hire in the state agency of Adult Protective Services, when a friend of her husband recommended that she apply instead for a similar position in the state department of human services, only working in *Child* Protective Services.

> It wasn't my plan to work with children or in child welfare, but that's where I ended up.

"I Could Never Do That Kind of Work"

If there is a popular media stereotype of social work, it is child protective services—a cool, matter-of-fact woman with business portfolio in hand, knocking on an apartment door in a poor neighborhood steeled to remove children from a home where they are being neglected or abused (e.g., Bridge, 2008; Kline, 2013). There are elements of truth in the stereotypes; social workers in child protective services *are* the front line responders, along with police, who bear responsibility for protecting children who are being harmed by the adults that are supposed to nurture and care for them. During the years Joanie worked for Child Protective Services, friends and acquaintances often said to Joanie, "I could never do what you do; it must be so hard." Her job was indeed sometimes incredibly difficult, but Joanie felt that God had given her the personality and skills to be able to do the work. Because of those gifts, Joanie does not think it was as stressful for her as it might be for others. That is how she explains her sense of calling to the work of protecting children; it was rewarding and right that she do what she could do for children that others could not do. The shy college student who left journalism because interviewing was uncomfortable found her place in advocating for and protecting neglected and abused children.

For the next five years, until her second child was born, Joanie worked in the adoption program of Child Protective Services, or what the agency calls "the back end" of the child welfare system. The agency had already removed the children in Joanie's caseload from their birth families' homes because of abuse or neglect and placed them in foster homes. It was Joanie's task to work with the children and their birth families to reach a decision about whether or not she should recommend that the court return children home or terminate parental rights so that children could be adopted. If the court terminated parental rights, then Joanie helped everyone prepare for adoption - the birth family, the adoptive family, and the child.

Joanie arrived at the office each day at 7:00 in the morning; she worked ten hours a day, four days a week, a schedule she chose because she needed the three days away for her own family. The agency recognized that providing schedule flexibility is one way to help support the resilience and coping of social workers who are doing such demanding work in the community.

Joanie was responsible for the cases of the twenty to thirty children in foster care. The agency expected her to work with each child for four months, during which she was to assess the bond between child and biological parents during supervised visits and the harm that might come from severing that relationship.

Joanie's early morning hours were often spent writing—and she remembers being drawn to journalism because she loves to write. Now she wrote reports for the family court that would ultimately decide whether a child would or would not go home to the birth family. Joanie's written assessment was the foundation on which the judge made that decision; Joanie had to decide what was best for the child, documenting her reasons. After the court decision, Joanie continued to work with children who were then in foster care waiting for adoption. She wrote status review reports for the court, updating the judge on the progress of the case, how close she was to finalizing the adoption, and how the child was faring.

Later in the day, after a stint of report writing, Joanie left her office to visit the children and families on her caseload, trying to see each of them at least once a month. Whatever else she did on each visit, Joanie's primary responsibility was to make sure that children were safe.

Joanie described her work with Toby, age nine months. An angry and frustrated parent had shaken him when he was two months old, trying to make him stop crying and causing permanent brain injury that could have resulted in death. Toby survived, however, and he was thriving in foster care. During her visits with Toby and his foster parents, Joanie checked on how he was developing. Because the shaking had injured his brain, Toby was lagging in reaching developmental milestones; Joanie made sure he was receiving physical therapy. Toby's improvement over a matter of months was remarkable. In September, at age six months, he had just begun to roll over, could hold up his head for only short moments, and could not yet sit up. By December, though, he was crawling and pulling up on the furniture to a standing position. He still had difficulty sitting without toppling over, but he was catching up in other respects with babies his age.

Toby's foster family was a couple in their early thirties, Jeff and Angie, who had already adopted two children from the foster care system, both medically fragile. They adopted Anna as an infant; she had been born with a heart abnormality, and doctors said she would likely not survive six months. If she did survive, she would never walk and would always need supportive care. But that was eight years before Toby joined their family, and Anna was thriving. Just months before Joanie placed Toby with Jeff and Angie, she had brought them Hannah as a foster child. Hannah had suffered unspeakably, severely burned over 90% of her body. When the court ruled to sever the rights of Hannah's parents, Jeff and Angie adopted her.

Joanie trusted Jeff and Angie. Still, she had to be diligent to check for any signs of neglect or abuse. Raising any child is physically and emotionally demanding, but medically fragile children place increased strain on a family—and this family already had three medically fragile children. When Joanie visited, she found Toby had bruises—a bump on his forehead, a rug burn on his knees, an irritation on his leg near his diaper. It was Joanie's job to decide what might be a sign of maltreatment, and what was not. Toby was still unsteady and so falls from pulling up on furniture were going to happen. He would fuss with long pants on and was happier scooting around the floor in just his diaper—and so the scraped knees. The foster parents had changed brands of diapers, and Toby had developed an allergy. Joanie had to ask for details so that she could assure herself and the court that the minor injuries were all accidental, the normal bumps and scrapes of mobile infants.

Although Joanie never experienced one of her foster parents abusing a child, not all foster families are like Jeff and Angie. Abuse in foster care had happened to other children the agency served, so Joanie was always watchful. Although Joanie never experienced that social work nightmare, there were times when she worried that children in her care were not being treated fairly or kindly. She had to weigh the outcomes for a child when foster parents were willing to adopt a child in their care, but for the wrong reasons, such as wanting their biological children to have a friend and playmate. There have been times when Joanie became aware that, although foster parents were not harming a child physically, they were emotionally abusive. She said,

> Emotional abuse is hard to prove. Our laws only protect kids from physical abuse. I learned that if a child had been in a foster home for a long time, it was difficult to take any action, even when I was really concerned, unless there were physical signs of abuse.

Jake, age nine, had been in a foster home for several years, and the family was planning to adopt him. And yet the foster mother wavered, letting Jake know that she was not sure she wanted him in the family permanently, even using the threat that she could call the agency and have him removed if he misbehaved. Haunting a foster child with the threat of homelessness, underscoring his insecurity, is a form of emotional abuse. The foster mother could also be warm and loving, however, and the easiest path for Joanie would be to let the adoption go through. Instead, she worked with the foster mother to explore all the options open to her, including helping Jake prepare for adoption by a family where he would fit better. Together, they worked with Jake to prepare him for a move rather than what sometimes happens, which is the removal of a child in the heat of a foster parent's anger at misbehavior, leaving a child with the guilty feeling that they have caused yet another life disruption.

Weighty Decisions

Joanie lived with knowing that the decisions she made would have a profound impact on children's lives. She remembers the children and the weight of those decisions. Joanie had just returned from maternity leave after the birth of Dillon, her son, when we first talked. She said that everything had changed with Dillon's birth, not only in her personal life but also in her work.

> I think I saw my kid in all the children I worked with. My work felt more personal; I had now experienced how challenging parenting can be, and still, I found it even harder to empathize with parents who abuse or neglect their children.

Martin was an infant on her caseload, hospitalized with a brain injury that occurred when his angry mother had shaken him as Jason had been shaken. From the hospital, the agency had placed him in a foster home, even though his maternal grandparents asked for custody. The social worker first working with Martin denied the grandparents' request because he had been living in their home when he was injured, although it was Martin's mother, their daughter, and not the grandparents who had shaken Martin. The foster home had been a good home for Martin; the foster parents were "the perfect family." The love and care Martin was receiving was the answer to a social worker's prayer; and they wanted to adopt him.

Joanie was not sure what to recommend. She visited the maternal grandparents and found them also to be loving and gracious—and they really longed to have Martin. She felt deep empathy for these grandparents grieving over the grandson they had lost to foster care. Joanie thought the social worker who had denied them custody had acted unfairly. Now she had to decide.

> Either way, someone was going to be hurt, either the grandparents who loved and grieved for him or the foster family that had really grown to love him and was planning to adopt him. It was one of the times that my work drove me to tears.

Joanie called a meeting of her colleagues to help her sort through what to do. She reminded herself and her colleagues that their primary responsibility was assessing the safety risks of the options before them, not allowing other issues to sidetrack them. Together they mapped the strengths and resources as well as the concerns of the options before them. Joanie had to face that as much as she hurt for the grandparents, they had not protected Martin from their daughter's violence, a woman who had a long history of drug use and domestic violence. They did not seem to understand the risk of allowing their daughter to care for Martin unsupervised. In the end, Joanie decided to recommend leaving Martin with the foster parents and to sever parental rights so that they could adopt Martin.

Joanie steeled herself for telling the grandparents her decision; "That's the thing I hate the most about my job—having to deliver the bad news." Like the social worker in the myth, she would be knocking on an apartment door, steeled for the task before her, but she certainly did not feel "cool" or matter-of-fact—she did what she needed to do with tears and empathy for the family.

Joy

Despite those difficult decisions and the grief that seeped into her life from her work in child protective services, she also found joy, a deep satisfaction that she was doing work that mattered. She especially loved working with older children, being a supportive person who listened to them, who sought to understand the story of their lives and to give them a voice in the decisions adults were making that would determine their futures. She also loved the people she worked with—her supervisor and the other protective services professionals—all of them advocating for children.

She would joke with her husband that once a year she allowed herself to have a "major breakdown," to feel like she was not doing anyone any good, that the work was in vain, that the problems children faced were too big for her to make any real difference. But those feelings would wash over her only once a year or so, and in the face of the burnout of so many social workers in the hard work of child protective services, she thought that was not unreasonable. Most of the time, she was aware of her sense that God had put her in her work, that every interaction she had with a child, a birth parent, or a foster or adoptive parent did make a difference, in that moment of time—and that is enough for her.

Joanie reflected that she believes her job is doing what the Bible talks about—caring for the orphans and the widows. "I feel like I'm doing God's work and maybe being Jesus to these children and their families." Because she works in a public agency, Joanie says she is careful about bringing up matters of faith. But it does come up. She gave an example of her work with Chris, an eight year old who had been in multiple foster homes since his third birthday. Because of physical abuse as an infant, Chris had some developmental delays and behavioral problems.

> He was just an eight-year-old little boy whose parents had abandoned him. Foster home after foster home had kicked him out because of his behavioral problems. I spent a lot of time working individually with Chris, trying to prepare him for the next move to a new foster home. I was trying to help him to see that even though he had a lot of people in his life who had given up on him, he had a lot of people who loved him. He said to her, "And I know God loves me, too." So I responded, "That's right, God does really love you."

She says she wants to tell all children that God loves them, especially children like Chris, with so much loss and insecurity defining their lives. She is careful not to say those words too quickly, however, when they have no reason to believe her. Children need to experience love and security with adults before they believe that there is an unseen God that loves and cares for them.

Next Step in the Journey

When her second child was born, Joanie took a maternity leave and then she and her husband decided that she would resign her fulltime job so that she could be with her children. She has continued her work with foster care and adoptions, though, and so she became certified as an Adoption Service Provider, which means she serves as the social worker in independent adoptions on a part-time basis.

> It turned out that God had set up all the opportunities for me to become an adoption service provider. I had the five years of experience at an adoption agency that is required. I had finished my licensure requirements while I was pregnant with my daughter.

The law in her state requires birth parents to meet with an adoption service provider before they can relinquish their rights to the child. Joanie's responsibility is to make sure that they understand their rights and that they are not being coerced to relinquish their parental role. She also determines what other services they may need because of the loss of their child. She loves working with birth mothers, helping them to know that their feelings are normal, and communicating that they are courageous and selfless to make the decision to relinquish their children because they are not in a life situation to parent.

Joanie said that before she began this work, she had a simplistic picture that adoption was a happy process. She has learned that it is painful for everyone. There is the obvious grief of the birth parent relinquishing a child. Adoptive parents are often coping with the grief, too, over not being able to have a biological child. They also face the worry and stress of the adoption process, and the differences involved in raising an adoptive child rather than a biological child. "The skills of parenting an adoptive child are not innate; they have to be learned," Joanie says. It is Joanie's job to help them learn those skills, and to become comfortable with their children knowing that they are adopted and even being in contact with the birth parent.

> Children love many people. They love their birth parent and their adoptive parent. I help them face their fears and learn how to navigate those relationships.

As much as Joanie felt cut out for child protective services work, she has that same sense of her new role as an adoption services provider. She cares for birth mothers who need her support in what she believes is one of the hardest and most courageous decisions they will face in life. She loves the educational work with adoptive parents who are so open to learning how to grow a strong adoptive family.

Joanie has taken on yet another social work role that she relishes. She is now teaching an undergraduate social work class in social policy in the university where she earned her undergraduate degree. In that small school, she is now the social worker with practice experience who finds herself inspiring students to pursue a master's degree in social work.

Questions to Ponder

1. Joanie chose a Christian college for her social work program, concerned about her ability to fit her Christian world view with the profession of social work that she perceived was "liberal" and would require her to accept people "just as they are." How do her concerns mirror or contrast with your perception of how various Christian perspectives view social work's ethics and values?

2. Making a decision about Martin's future drove Joanie to tears. What process did she use for moving from tears to determining what she would do?

3. What is there about child protective services work, as Joanie described it, that you think could lead to emotional exhaustion and burnout? What did Joanie bring to the work that allowed her to thrive and work creatively in this stressful work?

4. Joanie said that she is careful not to say too quickly to children who had experienced so much loss in their lives that God loved them. What reasons might you consider before you would teach children that God loved them despite the hard times they had experienced?

5. Joanie said that "God set up all the opportunities" for her to now be an adoption service provider. There have been a series of detours—the disappointment in journalism as a major, the inability to find a job in gerontological social work after graduation. How does her career path thus far fit your understanding of Christian vocation?

Joseph Martinez
School Social Worker

4

In December of his senior year in high school, Joseph's mother left his father to protect herself from what was becoming a dangerous relationship. Although neither of Joseph's parents had hit one another with more than a slap or yet inflicted any actual injury, their arguments had become physical. Joseph's father was attempting to control the increasingly conflict-ridden marriage by making Joseph's mother more dependent on him, taking control of all the finances and isolating the family socially from family, friends, and church. It appeared that the relationship was cycling closer to real violence. Sensing the increasing danger, Joseph's mother left.

Joseph went with her to live for a month in a shelter for victims of family violence. There were other young boys living with their mothers, but Joseph, at age 18, was the oldest male living in the facility. Joseph remembers that although some of the shelter staff were kind and supportive of him, his eighteen-year-old self felt the atmosphere of the shelter was clouded with a generalized distrust of men—and he was one. Moreover, Joseph's parents wanted help in putting their family back together, but the staff's support was conditional—they were only supportive of ending violent relationships, not restoring them.

As Joseph reflects back now, knowing what he knows about domestic violence, he does not want to minimize the violence between his parents, but he says that violence does not always mean that a relationship has to end. He believes that some people can change if they are motivated and given the help they need. Joseph's parents wanted a better life with one another. Somehow, they worked through the crisis. Joseph's father worked hard in counseling, and later that year, Joseph's parents reunited and are still together. To Joseph's knowledge, there has been no physical violence since that awful time when he was high school. That shelter experience left Joseph with the belief that "There has to be a better way to care for people." He did not imagine, however, that he would have any role in helping struggling families—he had no desire to work with children or with situations of domestic violence.

Named a National Hispanic Scholar based on his outstanding school performance, Joseph received a full academic scholarship. His father paid his living expenses for the first two years of college, and then Joseph supported himself with part-time work and loans. He declared business as his major but some friends suggested that social work would be a better fit; he switched majors and then stayed on to complete his MSW.

After graduate school, the Family Court offered employment to Joseph as a guardian for children caught up in their divorcing parents' court battles over custody. Joseph assessed each child's situation, including hearing from the child directly, and brought his recommendations to the court about what was best for the child. With young children, that meant using the skills of play therapy to understand the world through the children's experiences. With older children, it meant establishing the kind of trust that children needed to talk privately with Joseph about their experiences inside the parental war zone. Joseph then made his recommendations publicly as an advocate for the children in open court so that they did not have to speak in front of their warring parents.

Joseph remembers one such case that decided his next career shift. The trial had been long and heated. Something in the process triggered old feelings for Joseph that he was in danger, and he found himself frightened, although he knew rationally there was no physical danger at all. He vividly remembered the feelings of being in the midst of parental battles and the insecurity of being homeless. He knew all too well how his young client felt, or at least, his emotions told him he did.

> I almost fainted on the witness stand. I knew my case backwards and forwards. I was responding to everything very professionally as the attorneys were cross-examining me. They were doing their job, and they were not terribly aggressive. Still, I feel myself feeling a little light headed, so I was trying to figure out what was happening. I had not locked my knees. I did have breakfast. I realized I was just very, very nervous. I had to push through it and I did.

Afterward, Joseph did some careful inventory of his situation. The job was putting him in the role of mediator between warring parents—a position that was all too personally familiar. He knew he was in danger of projecting his own experiences as a child onto the children he served. He talked about his feelings with one of his colleagues, and his colleague helped him to realize that he could take his calling to be an advocate for children into another arena.

Joseph soon resigned his position with the court to become a special education social worker in a large urban school district; he had been in that position five months when we first spoke. All the children whom Joseph serves have a disability that has affected their ability to learn in school—autism, speech impediment, audiological impairment, and/or developmental delays. For example, a child with a disorder on the autism spectrum may have difficulty engaging with peers and staying focused on classroom work. Joseph works with teachers to structure learning environments that help children overcome the challenges to their learning, and with parents to help children learn at home the skills they need to succeed in a school environment. He also provides one-on-one counseling to children with mental illness or behavioral disorders.

Joseph organizes lots of meetings all over the school district that include both the school staff and a child's family, crafting with them an individualized learning plan for each student. Most of his time is spent in those schools in the district that do not have their own school counselor or social worker, which means he spends significant amounts of time driving between schools. Once a month and sometimes more often, Joseph meets with the Community Resource Collaborative, a collection of professionals from child protective services, local school districts, and mental health service providers—whoever is working with a child who needs more than what one agency can provide.

Joseph was the first social worker in this position. Over the months, his supervisor saw the impact a social worker could have, and so she found funds for a second social worker. Now Joseph finds himself leading the social workers in the district.

No Two Days are the Same

No two days are alike for Joseph. When I asked him to describe to me a "typical" day, he opened his calendar to a day in the previous week as a prompt as he let a day's story unfold. Joseph began that day in the school that serves as his home base. He starts each day there, checking e-mail, returning phone calls, and planning the rest of the day.

By mid-morning he was driving across the district to pick up some school supplies and uniforms for Darren, a teenager with mental illness who is homeless and staying with friends—couch camping. Darren's single mother struggles with mental illness, and so Darren turns to friends when he needs to escape. When Joseph arrived at the school where Darren was supposed to be enrolled, however, Joseph learned that Darren had moved to another friend's home—in another school. So Joseph drove to the new school to walk the school through the process of enrolling a student with no parent and no home. But Darren was not there, and after attempting to find him, Joseph ran out of time and clues for where he might locate Darren. He left several voice mails with families that had cared for Darren, hoping to track him down.

Turning from the frustration of the hours unsuccessfully trying to find Darren, Joseph raced to a team meeting with a school's special education department chair and a psychologist who had evaluated another child. Joseph had also met with the child and his parents, and together, the team developed an initial educational plan. Once that meeting ended, Joseph returned to his search for Darren, including running by one of Darren's friend's homes, and some favorite community hangout places—and still no Darren.

Back at one of the schools, Joseph met with a physical therapist. She told him that one of the students needed a walker and some other medical equipment that will allow him to have more freedom of movement. Joseph told her where to refer the family for financial help for the equipment they needed and made a note to himself to follow up the next day to be sure they were able to get what the student needed.

The day ended with Joseph learning that his application for a workshop scholarship for Alonzo, a teenager with developmental disabilities living in a homeless shelter, had been approved. The workshop helps teenagers with special needs and their families to make the transition to adulthood. The scholarship was the fruit of another day's search for his clients—that one successful. Joseph knew the family and when he learned about the workshop, he had gone looking for Alonzo's mother and found her. Joseph had been concerned because Alonzo's family had not given much energy to the transition to adulthood that Alonzo was about to enter. They had been too busy just trying to survive from one day to the next to think about what would happen when Alonzo, whose disabilities would hinder his ability to work or live independently, was no longer legally a minor eligible for the services Joseph and others were now providing through the school system. For Joseph, it is rewarding to know that he had helped Alonzo's mother lift her eyes from trudging through her days to planning for Alonzo's future—and her own.

Not all of Joseph's clients are living on the edge of survival, not sure where they will be sleeping the next night. Some of the families with whom he counsels have the resources to be able to put their children with disabilities in private educational institutions. But they have chosen not to; they want to help the public school system work for all children, including their own. Joseph helps them to navigate and sometime push the network of social services to be sure that all systems are giving the best care possible to the children in their community.

Gap Filler

Joseph calls himself a "gap filler"—"I'm the person that somebody calls when they have no idea how to address a situation with a child." When a student has needs beyond the normal patterns of care that social services provide, someone calls Joseph. When everyone feels stuck, it is Joseph that figures out a path forward.

Some people in the system where he works think that doing a good job means returning phone calls and e-mails promptly and keeping office hours. They seem to be just going through the motions but giving little attention to the actual impact they are having on the lives of children. It is a big system, and it is easy to feel lost in it, to become a cog in the machinery of monitoring children's lives rather than questioning, pushing, and advocating for changes that will help children not just survive but thrive. Joseph is working for change. He works hard on the assessments he writes that go to school principals and other administrators in the school district. He realizes that his ability to really help his clients often hinges on how well he writes—a report to a principal, an application for a scholarship.

When Joseph had been working for the school system for a year, he began to see that the position needed restructuring. His time was spread too thinly across too many geographically distant schools to be able to do his best work. He worried that students who do not make trouble are ignored; these are students who could be much more successful than they are now if they received the services they need. Joseph began working on recommendations for how to improve the system, to make it more efficient and effective in identifying and serving children.

He and a new social worker in the system are collaborating to create a new dimension to their work. In addition to working directly with children, they have set aside a day each month to provide training for teachers to help them understand what the children in their classes are going through when Child Protective Services is engaged in their lives, and what they experience in being moved into foster care because of their home situation. They are also working directly with Child Protective Services not to close cases too quickly, so that children who need them have all the resources of that large social service system available to them, even as they are transitioning back to parental homes or other living arrangements.

Thy Kingdom Come

Joseph's entire career thus far has been working in the machinery of social services for vulnerable children, and the bureaucracy and inattention to the quality of the services they provide can be maddening for him. Yet, through it all, he continues to be committed to the work of helping children who need an advocate; it is how he is living his faith.

"It can be really discouraging work," Joseph said. Sometimes Joseph feels like the only one trying to keep a child burdened by significant challenges from falling into a life wandering the streets or seeking the protection of a gang because, for whatever reasons, the child's family is simply not able to be that safe place. Joseph has to fight feelings of despair when his efforts fail. He remembers what a field supervisor said to him, "A Master of Social Work is not a master of results, but a master of the process." Joseph said:

> There is no excuse for not staying abreast of research and new theory and techniques in practice, but I have to remember, too, that I am not in control of outcomes. I do not control what my

clients do or the decisions their families make. My wife and I volunteer in the Stephen Ministry of our church. The ministry teaches that it is not true and not even biblical to say that God does not give us more than we can handle. Time after time in the Bible, God gives folks jobs bigger than they can manage. That is when we need to turn to Jesus. My wife and I pray over dinner each night together. One prayer we make often is that, if we feel like we used all the tools in our box that day and we were still unsuccessful in what we were trying to do, then we hand that to God and ask God to help what we could not do, and continue to strengthen us for the next task.

Joseph remembers a favorite professor when he was an undergraduate student almost twenty years ago. The professor told the class, "I am not a Christian social worker; I am a social worker and a Christian." Joseph agrees that social work is a profession that does not look different because the professional is—or is not—a Christian. Yet his faith is his motivation.

There are a lot of parallels between what Christians are called to do and what the social work profession expects of us.

Joseph remembers other fellow students who considered social work but chose another path, expecting that the social work profession would not allow them to be evangelistic about their faith. Joseph does not share their concern. Joseph sees resonance between social work's commitment to self-determination and the freedom the Creator offers people in choosing their own path, whether that path includes them living faith as Joseph understands it or not.

For six years after graduate school, Joseph stayed away from church; he had attended a Methodist church with his mother growing up. His congregation had what he considers a simplistic view of how God blesses and punishes people based on their behavior. In his work, however, he was watching parents traumatize their children as they warred with one another. He could not believe that God always prevents bad things from happening to good people, as his church seemed to teach, "because of what I was seeing in my practice, I was really struggling with making the head and heart meet." Now he reflects back and wonders if a community of faith could have helped him with that struggle. Instead, he left the church.

Years later, Joseph and his wife, Aria, began attending a church that "fits" for Joseph. They have found home in an Episcopal church, where they serve as acolytes each Sunday.

It is a long way from anything I could have imagined. We put on the white vestments, carry a cross and a candle, and walk all the way up the chancel. It was a nerve-wracking experience for us for several months, but now it is a very meaningful way we worship together and with our congregation. I am an altar server, which involves washing the priest's hands before communion. It is so different from how I grew up, and such a powerful blessing that I have no words to describe.

Joseph's pastor teaches that there are five basic concepts of Christian faith—creation, the fall, redemption, sanctification, and transformation. In creation, we are the beloved children of God; in the fall we're all sinners and fools; and in redemption we meet Jesus. Through sanctification we receive the power of the Holy Spirit, and through transformation we are given something to do with that power. That teaching about the path of faith resonates with Joseph's understanding that we are called to do, not just to believe. Social work is his "doing" his faith—his own transformation.

Joseph prays the Lord's Prayer—"Your kingdom come; Your will be done on earth as it is in heaven." Joseph says:

When I talk to people about what I do for a living, that is the language I use—I try to live my life as a prayer for God's kingdom to be present through me.

For Joseph, the kingdom of God means justice, and justice means that the kids can go to sleep and not be preyed upon in their own homes. He said:

Justice means that everyone—adults and children—have a safe place to sleep, enough to eat, and can walk down the street without fear. Justice means recognizing that those who commit crimes will someday be released from prison and they need to be reintegrated into the community and given a place they can contribute rather than harm. Christian faith ought to have a lot to say—and to do—to make God's justice a reality.

Joseph muses that social work really fits him, but he does not really feel that God "called" him to the profession. It just resonates with him and how he understands the world. He remembers a couple of young clients, two brothers ages six and nine, whom he counseled. Both boys had been sexually abused by their father and Child Protective Services placed them to live with their maternal grandmother. They were struggling, not just with the trauma that comes from being abused, but also with the upheaval from their home, the loss of relationship with the father they loved even though the relationship was abusive, changing schools, and moving from a middle class neighborhood to the poverty of the grandmother.

The changes were too much for the boys to handle. They were having trouble sleeping. They were wetting the bed, crying in school, and fighting other people and one another. Joseph realized even though the father had violated the sacred trust between parent and child, they were grieving his absence. They loved him—and he was now gone from their lives. They were also mourning the loss of their school, their friends, the swing set in the backyard, and all life markers that ease any child through the challenges of life. Joseph counseled with the boys for months, and life improved. The school staff was patient and understanding, and with Joseph's mentoring, they made new friends. They adjusted to life with their grandmother.

When it was nearly time for Joseph to end his work with them, he went to their school for one of his final sessions, and they came running across the playground to greet and hug him. Seeing the children running toward him, a teacher who was walking with him leaned over and whispered in his ear, "You're about to get pay day." Those broad smiles and hugs were enough for Joseph. Social work fits him, and in his own way, he is living the prayer, "your kingdom come."

Questions to Ponder

1. Joseph's first job after school was as a court advocate for children. He left that position when he realized that he was reliving his own past experiences in ways that might interfere with the work. How do we know when our personal experiences are an asset to our work? And when do they actually interfere with our work?

2. How did Joseph realize and deal with the interference of his personal experiences?

3. Some of the clients Joseph serves are living on the edge of homelessness and survival; their tenuous situations means Joseph spends a lot of time simply trying to locate them as they move from one temporary home to another. How does driving around a city tracking people down fit in professional social work—or does it?

4. List the skills that Joseph's work requires. Which of these skills seem unique to school social work, and which seem to be common in the other case studies of social work practice you have read thus far?

5. Joseph's job was to assess and provide services to children. In addition, however, he was assessing and making recommendations for systemic changes. If you were Joseph, how would you address the balance between attention to individual clients and attention to the service systems?

6. How do you see the nature of Joseph's work, the journey of his life, and his role as acolyte in his congregation fitting together?

7. Joseph says that his faith does not shape his professional practice, but it motivates him. What does he mean by this distinction? Does his experience resonate with your own, or not?

8. How has Joseph's work influenced his faith?

Adults

Kate Martin
Individual and Couples Therapist and Workshop Leader
Erin Olson, Co-Author

It was ten o'clock on a crisp, sunny autumn morning. The air was cool enough for a light jacket, but winter was still a few weeks away. Kate Martin enjoyed her bike ride from the college where she was teaching a class back to her home, which is about two miles from campus. During her ride, she reflected on her morning class; the senior social work students were sharing their experiences with clients in their various field placements. Kate had felt herself catching the energy of this new group of social workers as well as their passion for working with people facing life challenges. They reminded her of why she chose social work as her profession.

The bike ride gave Kate not only the time to think about her morning, but also to prepare herself for the individuals and couples she would see in her private therapy practice the rest of her workday. Arriving at home, she grabbed her lunch and hopped in her family's car to drive to her office. She had glanced at her planner earlier this morning; she would be seeing clients all afternoon and into the evening.

The Path to Becoming a Therapist

Kate's parents were both social workers. They lived and taught that God expects Christians to care for others and be agents of change in their communities. Her parents had taken different paths in social work—her dad worked with people with developmental disabilities and her mother had been a clinical social worker. The variety of career options in social work appealed to Kate, along with the direct connection she saw between social work and her call as a Christian. Kate's high school friends told her she was a good listener and someone whom they trusted with their problems or concerns. Her decision to pursue social work in college seemed like an obvious one.

After graduation with her BSW, Kate worked for a year in a neighborhood organization because of her interest in community organizing. She quickly realized that while she felt drawn to community organizing, this kind of social work often requires years of rapport and network building. Kate entered graduate school with an interest in pursuing clinical social work instead, deciding she would engage in community work as a volunteer rather than professionally. Her master's level internship in a local hospital led to her employment there after graduating with her MSW, and she stayed on for five years. She decided to open her own clinical practice, and four years ago, she joined ten other therapists in the building where she currently has an office.

Kate feels confident she made the right decision. She says,

> When a couple starts to experience healing and health in their relationship, I go home flying high knowing I'm right where I'm supposed to be.

A Long Day in the Office

After teaching her class, biking home, eating lunch, and driving to the office, Kate greeted her colleagues, grabbed a cup of coffee, and sat down at her desk to review her client files—an important part of her routine that gives her time to think about her upcoming clients. Her first appointment of the day was a young couple she has seen weekly for the past three weeks.

The couple, Becky and Matt, had been married four years; they had been trying unsuccessfully to have a baby for the past two of those years. They had sought medical help and now were going through treatment for infertility. The medical interventions in their sexual relationship designed to address their infertility, along with the disappointment and frustration they felt as the months went by with no pregnancy, had begun to erode their relationship. Because of conflict and distance between them, Becky had become depressed. Kate was helping them to communicate their feelings to one another in ways they could each feel supported rather than turning their frustration onto one another. The next step for Kate would be addressing Becky's depression. Over the weeks, Kate had seen improvement in their communication and support for one another.

Still, the basic challenge of wanting a baby, of the cycles of hope followed by deep disappointment, continued. Becky is a Christian and she questioned why God, whom she believes has all control and power, had not allowed her to have children. In her own mind and heart, Kate asked the same question, wondering about the meaning of God's plan for our lives. As a parent herself, she prayed that Becky would also be able to have that experience. At the same time, she has learned that prayer does not always bring the answer we want; her job is to walk with Becky and Matt through the uncertainty, the questions that seem to have no good answers, and the decisions they are now contemplating. Should they try to adopt? Keep trying for a pregnancy? Or find their way forward into life without their own children?

After her hour with Becky and Matt, Kate's next appointment was with Brian and Sheila. Six months ago, Brian had told Sheila that he had been having an affair for the past year, and they made an appointment with Kate a week later. Kate has been working with them ever since. Sheila had been unable to forgive Brian and the couple was now seriously contemplating divorce. It helped that Brian had finally agreed to end his other relationship, but it had taken him some time, further eroding their relationship. Sheila still could not allow herself to trust him.

After the session with Brian and Sheila, Kate paused to jot notes about the two sessions she had completed. She keeps progress notes on each session to help her remember what she and her clients have accomplished. Writing things down about the session also helps her process the events that occurred and she is able to begin thinking about where she might direct their next session. Although paperwork is one of her least favorite parts of the job, it is essential. Kate finished the last of her coffee and headed to the reception area to get her third client of the day.

Maryann was waiting for her; this session would be the first time Maryann's husband, Phil, would not be coming. After six months of counseling with Kate, Phil and Maryann had recently filed for divorce. They had been married for ten years, but they had drifted apart over the past four years. Phil had decided three weeks previously that he did not want to try working on their marriage anymore and Maryann had agreed to sign the divorce papers once he filed them. Kate hoped to help Maryann begin to envision her life after Phil as a woman who was divorced. Kate says:

> I find hope in my work with couples and individuals when they are able to mend hurts and repair brokenness. Couples do not always mend their relationships; but even in the ending of relationships, there can be hope. People can come to a fuller understanding of who they are in relationships while also gaining some individual integrity.

Kate saw two individual clients later in the afternoon—one struggling with postpartum depression and another with significant anxiety due to a stressful job. Between sessions, she took a quick leave from the office to pick up her children from school and take them home, giving her time to check in with them about their day. It was her husband's day to cook dinner because it was her night to do evening hours at her practice. She had extended her practice into the evening hours to fit her clients' work schedules.

After supper, Kate saw two more clients. Kate has scheduled clients three long days like this each week. She uses Tuesday and Thursday to work at home on paperwork, school work, and family responsibilities.

A Focus on Couples

Although Kate sees individuals in her practice, her specialty is couples work. Kate has worked with a variety of couples, regardless of their marital status or sexual orientation. Kate's perspective is that her beliefs and values do not have to agree with her clients for her to be able to provide them with professional care. She says:

> People do not have to be Christians to grow a stronger couple relationship. For that reason, I do not call my practice 'Christian counseling.' If my clients ask me, I will share that I am a Christian, but I will tell them that I work within their framework. I am not out to change their worldview; my goal is to strengthen their relationship.

As a consequence, Kate has worked with married couples, divorcing couples, cohabiting (unmarried) couples, couples in marriages open to sexual liaisons with others outside the marriage, heterosexual couples, and gay and lesbian couples. About her openness to working with couples in a diversity of lifestyles, she says:

> There are certain lifestyles that what we know from the research on attachment do not work very well for building trust and a secure attachment between partners. I will share that research if appropriate; usually that would be a conversation with couples who have a marriage open to other sexual liaisons. I do not address right and wrong but rather, how openness to other sexual relationships undermines the secure couple attachment.

Kate has worked with marital couples separated from one another and trying to reconcile as well as couples where infidelity has occurred and they are trying to figure out what to do next. Couples also come to see her about relationship struggles—fighting, sexual problems, and emotional intimacy issues. Kate also provides premarital counseling for engaged couples, often at the request of a pastor whom they have asked to perform their wedding.

Kate provides contractual services for congregations in the area; the congregation pays for the counseling of members their leaders refer to Kate. Sometimes pastors ask Kate her position on issues like sexual orientation or divorce. Kate explains:

> Pastors want to know how I respond to those issues in my practice, and some of them do not like what I tell them, but a pastor's role is different from a therapeutic role. I have to speak clearly to them about my role in working with couples with diverse orientations and worldviews.

Kate has also found a significant amount of satisfaction in her work around community education, partnering with churches and other community organizations that are interested in "promoting relationship help and marital health." She gives couples the tools they need to develop and maintain healthy relationships. She also is able to screen for when they may need more help than she can provide in an educational group. She loves being back in community work, which was her first interest as a college student. Community marriage education has fulfilled that earlier interest in practice at the community level.

Not all of her work leaves her "flying high." Kate is a social worker at heart, but private practice has also required her to learn and use good business practices. She is responsible for calling insurance companies and writing reports needed by courts, physicians, and other professionals involved in the lives of her clients. In order to balance what she enjoys in her work with what drains her, Kate has attempted to maximize what is "life-giving" for her—like the marriage education courses in the community—and she tries to put boundaries around what drains her—the business side of her practice.

Faith and Social Work

The interaction between Kate's Christian faith and her career as a social worker in private practice has always seemed clear to her. She says:

> Social workers enter people's brokenness and, in relationship with our clients, we can work toward healing and repair. I see that as a clear way of living out God's call to be agents of change and redemption. It is not that I bring my clients redemption, but I help them find own their way into greater health and love. In that sense, I believe I am helping equip people to have more security and support in the relationships that they have, which creates more functional people, self-aware people. I do see that as a way of nurturing discipleship. When people are healthy in their families and in their marriages, they are more equipped to serve and to come alongside others.

Kate said she can be that agent of redemption with clients whether they are Christians or not. Doing God's work in her relationship with clients does not necessarily mean praying with them or even talking about her beliefs or theirs. Kate wants to emulate Jesus in her relationships with clients and in doing so tries to be available, engaged, caring, empathetic, helpful, and present, as well as gentle or direct depending on what the situation demands. While some of her clients are people of other faiths, that aspect of their lives is important for Kate to know, but not usually the focus of the work Kate is doing with them.

Kate experiences her work with couples—and individuals as well—as a privilege. Kate says that she only considers praying with a client if the client asks her to do so. She says what is even deeper than verbalized prayer is the "sacred space" of her work with clients. Clients have told her that their time with her feels like a sanctuary for them because they finally have permission to express what is really going on in their hearts and minds. They experience healing.

> They experience something here with me and with each other that I believe is set apart and sacred because of how I frame our work and who I am. The reality is that I think that they could learn some of that elsewhere too, with a therapist of a different faith tradition. Still, it is how I view my purpose in the work.

Beliefs involve not only religion and faith, but, for many people, take expression in their politics as well. Kate described a woman who had called a few weeks before our last conversation, interested in setting up an appointment for therapy. First, however, she wanted to know Kate's political orientation; she asked, "Are you a conservative or a liberal?" The woman would not make an appointment until she knew the answer. Kate chose not to answer that question over the phone, but stated that she would be willing to talk more with the woman in a face-to-face conversation. The woman ultimately decided not to schedule an appointment and moved on to pursuing a different therapist who would answer her question.

Through this experience, Kate realized that it would have been easy, out of anxiety or out of a desire to want to help this woman, to answer the question and fulfill this potential client's perceived need to know about her political beliefs. If the same situation had occurred a few years before, Kate believes she may have felt the need to persuade the woman to schedule an appointment or may have wanted to prove to the woman that she was "okay." Kate came to recognize, however, that she is not called to offer services at all costs; "we can't be all things to all people." Kate thinks it is tempting as a Christian therapist to feel that God will give you the strength to work with any and every client.

Self-Care and "Super-Therapy"

On Wednesdays, Kate has supervision with Sarah, one of her colleagues. Kate recognizes that teaching, providing therapy, raising three young children, and nurturing her own marriage is a heavy load. She has known colleagues who became bitter and exhausted with the work, so she is intentional about taking care of herself to avoid burnout. She has found supervision on a weekly basis very helpful.

Kate has paid Sarah not only to provide clinical supervision, but also personal therapy. They named this hour in her week "super-therapy" and together they work through reviewing Kate's cases as well as her "own stuff," so that personal issues do not interfere when she is working with a client. In previous places of employment, Kate did not receive consistent supervision and she found herself very fatigued and emotionally drained by her work. "Super-therapy" leaves Kate with renewed energy to work and her life beyond work.

Kate has also found that networking with other people in the helping professions has helped her to take care of herself. She regularly meets for lunch or coffee with two other women who are in the helping professions and together they talk about and help each other understand "what it means to be me in this profession." Running and biking provide Kate with her own personal space to get away from the stresses of work and therapeutic relationships. She also recognizes the importance of play in her life and is intentional in spending time in play while she is home with her children and husband.

Moving Forward

At the beginning of her career, Kate had hoped eventually to be in private practice doing psychotherapy and she has achieved that goal. Now she finds her work expanding back into the community practice to which she was originally drawn. She particularly enjoys working with congregations to provide needed community education around relationship and marital health. She is concerned that pastors and other church staff members are overwhelmed with the needs of marriages and families in their congregations.

In the two years after the first interview, Kate had decided to say no to the university part-time teaching so that she could focus on developing the partnerships with churches and with community organizations to do more community education. She has added educational programs on parenting to her repertoire of programs on couples' education and is doing more workshops in congregations and in community organizations. She provides one-hour presentations as well as four-hour workshops and weekend retreats—and she loves the work. She has developed a network of congregations where she serves as a consultant as well as providing regular family education programs.

Over the past three years, she completed a certification by a research institute and uses their materials, based in extensive social scientific research, as the foundation for much of her work. Just the Saturday before our last conversation, she had provided a four-hour workshop, "Growing a Vibrant Marriage," for a group of ten couples in one of the congregations with whom she consults. She is now considering developing a "Part Two" workshop for the many couples who have participated in the first workshop, perhaps addressing more deeply a topic like conflict management. Although the research is not based on Christian beliefs and values, when she is providing workshops in congregations, Kate leads discussion of how the content aligns with "what we as Christians know to be true and healthy about relationships."

Kate has found this work nourishes her. She says about her work as a therapist:

> It can be lonely work, lively but lonely, because I am developing these relationships with people that I do not acknowledge outside the counseling room. It is heavy relational work. Teaching draws on different skills and is energizing in a different kind of way, so that balance is so important to me.

Whether she is working as therapist with a couple in crisis in her office or leading a workshop in a church fellowship hall, Kate sees this as her way, as she says, of "answering God's call to bring redemption."

Questions to Ponder

1. Kate's days are long, yet it is a schedule she chose that includes bike rides to work, long days three days a week and two days to work at home—and an afternoon break to take her children home from school. What about the way she has structured her work does and does not appeal to you?

2. Kate calls herself a "therapist" rather than a "clinical social worker." What are the pros and cons of the choice she has made?

3. Kate sees herself living her Christian faith, providing "sacred space" for working through the challenges her clients face, serving as "an agent of God's redemption." What difference does it make whether that work takes place in her private practice office or in a congregation's fellowship hall during a marriage education course—or does it?

4. Kate talks about "flying high" on days when she sees change happening in her clients and their relationships. It is on these days that she knows she's "right where she needs to be." What experiences have you had in your life where you've seen this? How do you know when you're where you need to be?

5. Kate describes the woman who decided not to make an appointment since Kate would not give her political orientation over the phone. How would you have handled this situation?

6. Kate sees her current work partnering with churches and community organizations to provide marriage and relationship education as a continuation of her community organizing work. How does it fit what you know about community organizing—or not?

7. Kate is intentional about the things she does to take care of herself such as her "super-therapy," running, and making time with friends and family. How do you take care of yourself

Myria Hester
Therapist with Older Adults and Adults with Disabilities

Myria had always wanted to be a teacher, so she pursued an education degree in college. Her degree requirements included observations in a classroom. During the semester she spent observing in an elementary classroom, she noticed that the same children kept coming to the teacher for help; they needed a jacket when the weather turned cold, or school supplies, or even something to eat. They were always the same children. Myria wondered how the school followed up to find out what was happening in these children's homes that led to their coming to school without ample clothing, hungry, without school supplies. She asked questions and she learned that working with family systems was the domain of school social work. Intrigued, Myria switched majors and completed her undergraduate degree in social work.

Myria wanted to go on to graduate school, but she had no idea how she was going to afford it. She applied, and then she learned about a scholarship program that would prepare her for working with older adults. She jumped at the chance. She loved working with older adults in her field placement, which involved her rotating through a variety of agencies working with adults, from community-based services to nursing homes and hospice. "I wanted to do it all," she said.

Upon graduation, though, she could not locate a position in social work with older adults. Instead, her first position after completing her MSW was with Child Protective Services. She needed a job; she was a single mom and had bills to pay, so she took it. "And I learned to love that, too," she says.

In fact, she found herself working not so much with the children themselves but with families—and with many older adults. Most of the children on her caseload were in "kinship care"; the foster families were actually the children's extended family—aunts and uncles, siblings and grandparents. These relatives were providing care for children whose parents were in prison or for some other reason not able to care for their children. Most kinship foster parents were older adults, grandparents raising their grandchildren—the very group Myria had hoped to serve. She saw their joys but also the demands and difficulties these older adults faced in trying to raise young children, including economic hardship, stress, and sometimes depression.

Myria's family lived in another state, and she wanted to be closer to family, so she left Child Protective Services and relocated. There the Area Agency on Aging (AAA), a comprehensive public service agency serving older adults and their families, had created a new program to address mental illness and, specifically, obsessive-compulsive disorders. AAA offered Myria a position to develop the new program and serve in it as a therapist and hoarding specialist.

When an agency assessment found that an older adult was at physical risk because of hoarding, the agency assigned their care to Myria. The older adult or a family member in the household collected and had not discarded items so that they so filled the living space with "stuff" that it was difficult to move through the home safely or keep it clean. Hoarding is a compulsive behavior and a symptom of significant anxiety and emotional distress.

The program consisted of a cleaning crew cleaning the home, and then Myria working with her clients to deal with the feelings of loss and grief or other anxiety issues that had led to expression in hoarding behaviors. Myria used cognitive behavioral therapy (CBT) in her work; she usually saw older adult clients for ten to fifteen sessions that took place in their home. Her work was a learning process for Myria as well as for her clients; in particular, she was developing new ways of addressing anxiety and depression in clients who have dementia or other cognitive impairments.

Myria loved her work at AAA. In each session, she learned more about her clients' hopes and fears. "Adults in their 80s and 90s have hopes and dreams, too," she says, but society tends to think hoping and dreaming are for younger people and so no one takes the time to listen to seniors. Older adults are often more openly spiritual as they come into the ending phases of life and "want to get things right." Myria has learned patience; younger people tend to reach the points they want to make faster, she says, but older adults reach their points through stories that may meander. Sometimes Myria has to think through the significance of the stories she hears for the struggles that are now confronting her clients. She appreciates learning about their lives, from their rich histories to their current roles as ushers or choir members in their churches or caregivers for their grandchildren and great grandchildren.

A Typical Day at the Area Agency on Aging (AAA)

Like social workers in many settings, Myria's day at AAA started at her office computer, checking e-mail and responding to referrals. She phoned all the referrals she received to determine if the client fit her programmatic responsibilities. After those initial phone calls, all of her work took place in the community and homes of her clients. She began her work with clients in an assessment process in their homes.

If Myria deemed that a home was biologically hazardous, she scheduled a bio-hazard team to spend a day cleaning. On those days, Myria spent the entire day with her clients, helping them to understand and come to terms with the shame of having others go through their possessions and disposing of what they have treasured. Myria said it was always an exhausting day for everyone, including herself; "it is an eight hour therapy session." She then returned once a week or so, depending on the clients' needs, working to restore hope and self-esteem. Myria found it especially exciting when clients invited others to visit them or plan a party; before treatment, they had been too ashamed or fearful to let others see the insides of their homes.

Myria described this process with one of the first clients with whom she worked at AAA. Ms. Trevon was deeply ashamed of the "mess" of her home. When Myria asked her to rate her home on a scale of one to nine, with one being no clutter and nine being completely cluttered, Ms. Trevon rated her home a nine. She said she could not believe that she allowed her life to become such a mess. Myria noted that she saw the "mess" in her home as a symbol for the mess of her life. But she was motivated to make change.

Ms. Trevon had not asked for help herself; the referral came to Myria from Adult Protective Services (APS). Ms. Trevon had become ill and was hospitalized. Her illness prompted an APS assessment and APS ruled that Ms. Trevon's situation was unsafe; they would not allow her to return to the home in its current state. Ms. Trevon had two small dogs that she voluntarily gave away when the home was assessed as unsafe even for dogs. Ms. Trevon moved into the home of a friend after being released from the hospital. Myria began her work.

Myria's assessment found that Ms. Trevon was grieving over losing her dogs, her home, and her "place" in the neighborhood. She felt guilty and ashamed that she had brought these losses on herself. She felt anxious and overwhelmed, with her life controlled now by strangers—social workers from APS and AAA. Myria began her work with a question:

> I asked her, "If the world were perfect, what would your home look like? How would you like your home to be?" We talked about how they might reach that point. Ms. Trevon agreed to the cleaning.

Myria scheduled the cleaning team, but before they began their work, she described the cleaning process in detail to Ms. Trevon. Myria led her in thinking through how she would feel when her neighbors saw the team working in her home and a dumpster in her yard—and how she would cope with those feelings. The shame she felt was overwhelming—and Myria promised to be with her throughout the process.

The cleaning took three full days. The cleaners first took out the garbage and boxed up belongings. Ms. Trevon and Myria worked together at a table in the back yard while the cleaners worked inside the house. Myria helped Ms. Trevon decide what to keep, what to trash, and what to put in a donation pile. When it seemed that an item should be discarded or donated, but Ms. Trevon wanted to keep it, they discussed what it meant to her—empty bottles, an old sweatshirt she never wore, papers long outdated.

When the process ended, Ms. Trevon moved home. She planned a pasta party; she invited her friends—and Myria. After the party, Myria visited with her for one last session, and they agreed that their work together was complete.

In addition to working with individual clients like Ms. Trevon, Myria also developed a ten-week self-help support group for clients struggling with hoarding, to help them learn better coping skills and to support one another in the life changes they were making. Ms. Trevon made new friends in the group; she stood by her new friends as they faced and coped with the changes they were all striving to make in their lives.

Turning Seventy

Although Myria specialized in working with hoarding behavior, she also worked with other clients of AAA as needed. Myria remembers Ms. Murphy who was very healthy, only taking a single medication for high blood pressure. But Ms. Murphy could not drive and had limited mobility due to degenerative arthritis. So when her physician diagnosed her with depression and she declined the medication he offered her, he suggested that she call AAA; she did and was assigned to Myria.

Ms. Murphy was approaching her seventieth birthday, and she had very negative images about aging. She believed the marker of her impending birthday meant she would then officially be "old." She would stop dying her hair, stop buying new clothes—just stop. Every thought she had about turning seventy was negative.

After working with Myria for a few sessions, Ms. Murphy realized that life would not suddenly end at seventy—it would stretch before her just as it always had, with an ending somewhere just as an ending had always been there. She realized that her age did not have to stop her from what she wanted to do—she had choices. Yes, she had limitations, but she had been coping with those limitations and she could go on coping with those limitations. Myria was delighted the day she visited Ms. Murphy to find that she had once again dyed her hair and planned a trip with friends. Life was better, and she had avoided the stigma of taking medication for depression, which was a significant victory for Ms. Murphy.

Next Step

After three years at AAA, a change in management brought a shift in funding, and the hoarding program ended. Consequently, Myria changed employers a year before our last interview, taking a position working with older adults and adults with disabilities at Jewish Social Services. She still uses her expertise in treating hoarding behavior, but her responsibilities are also broader. She says that, in many ways, she is working with the same population group. She does have younger clients now as well; many of her clients are ages 30-50 and have multiple sclerosis.

She still meets with her clients in their homes, not in her office. She finds she can use environmental cues that help her understand her clients' situations more quickly, and she can help clients who would not be able to come to her office because of their mobility challenges and lack of transportation. She sees four or five clients on an average day; most are dealing with depression or anxiety. Some of her clients' homes are actually nursing homes, because their disability does not allow them to live independently.

She had just seen a client when I talked with her, Ms. Borden, a woman in her eighties whose son had died four years ago. He was the youngest of Ms. Borden's three children, in his fifties at the time of his death from cancer, married with grown children of his own. He had been the child to whom Ms. Borden was closest; he helped her with life decisions and the many daily concerns of life. Myria said about Ms. Borden's grief at losing her son:

> She really beats herself up because she thinks that she should be over the grief. Her son died in July, and then his birthday is in October. Christmas is supposed to be a time of celebrations, but instead she grieves for him then, too. I see her those times of the year.

Myria uses cognitive behavioral therapy with Ms. Borden, addressing the guilt she has that if she had just been more involved with her son's life, perhaps she could have changed the sequence of events that led to the cancer. The approach is helpful in helping Ms. Borden separate the rational from the irrational thoughts she has. Myria has also encouraged Ms. Borden to share pictures of her son, talking about the stories each picture generates. As they talk about those life stories, Myria encourages Ms. Borden to reflect on the great life events she had with her son, that she had been very much a part of his life, and that they had had a good relationship. Slowly, she is coming to accept that it was not her neglect that led to his developing cancer.

Myria's supervisor has encouraged Myria to terminate services with Ms. Borden rather than carrying her from year to year, but Myria has been reluctant to do so. Although Ms. Borden does not keep regular appointments between Christmas and the anniversary date of her son's death in July, it seems to comfort Ms. Borden to know that if she needs a booster session with Myria, she can come back.

As she finished telling me about Ms. Borden, she said, "Oh, let me tell you one more story." She then told me about Mr. Morton. He has dementia and lives in a group home, and Myria was not at all sure that he was appropriate for her services when she first visited him. Mr. Morton's case manager had asked for in-home mental health services, believing that Mr. Morton was depressed. "I thought it was just going to be a friendly visit; he was not very verbal, answering questions with just a word or two." Myria decided to try Reminiscence Therapy, helping him to remember past times when he felt strong and happy. She asked Mr. Morton what his favorite music era was, and he said anything between 1960 and 1969.

> I brought my phone and played a little American Band Stand, and then we watched some clips of television shows on YouTube - three or four minutes of shows like Andy Griffith, Father Knows Best, Gun Smoke, and Perry Mason. He loves Appalachian music, so I played bluegrass, and sometimes Gospel music.

Mr. Morgan began to talk more. He told Myria about his father's death from black lung disease; he had been a coal miner. He talked about his siblings, about his mother's death, about his own work as a laborer in the mines. He taught her about his religion, which is Jehovah's Witness.

> When we started, he was not talking. Now we talk about football, about his hopes and dreams of going home to West Virginia. Oh, and he is wearing pants now. I forgot to mention that. For the first three or four sessions, he did not wear pants or shoes. The group home staff would just put a blanket over him. I remember the day I came in, and saw he was wearing shoes and pants. I said, "You have pants on, Mr. Morgan." And he said, "Well, I reckon I should be presentable."

Myria laughed. "I don't always hear 'thank you,' but that was better than a thank you. We laughed together—it felt good for him and also for me."

Myria did not want to stop the interview; it is clear she loves her work and loves her clients. She said:

> Let me tell you about Ms. Trist. She is thirty-one years old and is mother of a fifteen year old and a five year old. She has multiple sclerosis (MS), which has now made her blind. Last year, she lost custody of the five year old because she said she wanted to be a normal mother and be able to take her daughter to the park. She did, and she fell and passed out, and a neighbor called for an ambulance. Her passing out in the community had happened before.

Because there had been other incidences of her passing out with her daughter, Child Protective Services became involved and placed her daughter in foster care. Myria went on to explain that not only has the MS caused blindness, but Ms. Trist also has serious tremors, difficulty walking, and has to use a walker.

> She says she feels like an alien and she thinks she looks like one. She has lost a lot of weight, and she is depressed, and angry, and anxious about the future. She is angry at God, and she feels guilt for being angry at God. She is so honest, so open about her struggles, that I enjoy working with her. I am going to see her and her daughter right after this interview. I am trying to help her do what she needs to do to regain her daughter's custody.

Myria has been on quite a journey in these years since graduation—from her original interest in teaching children that then morphed into working with the family systems of children and then her care for older adults. Myria mused that in all of her work, she has dealt with family systems and the safety of vulnerable family members who need advocates, whether young children or older adults with mental and physical illness or disability.

Myria thinks that being a Christian has somehow made her flexible and open to new experiences, open to God leading her wherever she is needed. Now that she is working in a Jewish agency, she muses that that her Christian faith still integrates seamlessly with her practice; that really has not changed. Her faith—and her professional practice—lead her to treat her clients with empathy and unconditional respect and acceptance. Those principles for practice would apply in any social work context. Although the agency is Jewish, most of her clients are not. A few are Jewish, and a few are Muslim, and many are Christian, and some have no religious affiliation. Myria says:

> I need to be competent to talk about God and faith if that conversation can be helpful to my clients. I never ask unless they broach the topic or give me cues that they want to bring faith into our work together. But when a client is suffering from depression or loneliness, seeking to find peace, it is appropriate for me to ask if religion and faith have a role in their lives.

Hope

Myria says she feels called to do this work—and that keeps her going. Every job she has had since seeing the needs of children in poverty as an education student in college—all of it led "to this path and doing this work." She says she cannot imagine doing anything else.

Sometimes her work is thankless, and sometimes she sees no change in the clients she is working so hard to help. But she says:

> Just like we cannot see Jesus but know He is with us, then sometimes I may not see the change but I have to trust that change will happen, whether I see it or not.

When it seems that her clients are doing nothing to help themselves—when she is working harder at change for them than they are—she has to fight discouragement. She says she has to "lean back" into the grace of God, remembering all the times God has given her second chances when she resisted change in her own life.

Questions to Ponder

1. Myria's career has been a path from working with vulnerable children to vulnerable adults. As she describes her work, what do you think she brought from her work with children that was an asset in working with older adults?
2. As you read about the work Myria did at AAA, what skills did she need to work with senior adults whose anxiety was expressed in hoarding?
3. Imagine Myria's work at AAA, particularly with Ms. Trevon. What do you think would be especially meaningful for you? What would be especially difficult?
4. Myria attended a pasta party with Ms. Trevon and her friends. Was this a dual relationship? Or part of her professional relationship? Or both? Do you see this as appropriate social work practice—or not?
5. Myria briefly described her work with Ms. Murphy and her fear of being officially "old." Although she does not talk about religion and faith, what role might you envision for the integration of the faith and religious beliefs—for either the client, or the social worker, or perhaps both—in this practice situation?
6. Myria's path has been shaped in many ways by forces beyond her as much or more as the choices she has made. What are those forces? How do you understand the interaction of life circumstances and your own choices in shaping your own path?
7. Think about Myria's image of "leaning back" into the grace of God when she is fighting discouragement. What is your own picture of the relationship of faith and discouragement and frustration?

Communities and Congregations

Adam Bennett
Executive Director, Serving the City Ministries

A hurricane hit the coastline on Adam Bennett's second week on the job. He was the new executive director of Serving the City Ministries, and although he had been shadowing his predecessor for a few weeks, he was still finding his way. Now telephone poles were down; there was no electricity; and the roof on the three-story apartment complex across the street from the ministry's office had collapsed, leaving dozens of people frightened and homeless. Adam said:

> The City came at 3 a.m. and told everyone in the apartment complex they had to get out of the building. The landlord was nowhere to be found, and the police were telling them to get out. It was very tense.

Adam and one of his staff members, a woman who had been with the ministry four years, were there at the time, offering space in Serving the City (which had escaped undamaged), food, and clothing, but no one was really listening to them.

> Finally one man—one of the fathers that my coworker knew—came over to us, and I told him, 'We're willing to do whatever we can.' He's 6 foot 3 inches tall, the biggest guy around, and he bellowed, 'Hey, these are the guys who love on our kids in the summer!' Next thing we knew, we had about 40 families storing their stuff in our building.

No one that night knew Adam, but they knew his coworker and the investment she had made in their children and their community. Developing that trust is pivotal in community work, Adam says:

> When I first got here, I was the only Anglo in many situations. The community is predominantly African-American, and I did not know anybody except my co-workers. So I just started hanging out with people, getting to know the community. Most of our work is relational, and it's done by people knowing and trusting us.

The ministry Adam leads offers several programs for children, youth, and adults, including summer camp, after-school programs, an internship program for junior high-age youth, a leadership youth program for older teens, and community events for families such as festivals, monthly community meetings, and weekly summer cookouts. The agency's mission is "to offer hope, opportunities, and resources for individuals and families."

> Everyone I had talked to had good things to say about this ministry and its programs, but that night, hearing that father yell that affirmation, that cinched it.

Living and Working in the Inner City

Many inner-city neighborhoods in the United States are plagued with the consequences of poverty—high crime, drug trafficking, prostitution, high teenage pregnancy rates, substandard housing, abandoned properties, schools with low standards, and high drop-out rates, unemployment, few amenities like safe playgrounds and good grocery stores—and hopelessness. The barriers to human thriving are complex and interrelated.

> I have been doing inner-city work since my undergraduate days. It is a long-term commitment for Andrea and me. We see the need, the opportunity to be able to serve a group of folks that truly do struggle and that many people don't see. The chance to bring justice and quality of life for folks is a driving force for us. I see how smart and loving and caring these neighborhood kids are—and what potential they have.

Adam has dual graduate degrees in social work and divinity. He became involved in inner-city ministry as a college student, working with a nonprofit agency in the inner city not far from his university. He met Andrea at school and they married; together they have worked and lived in urban settings ministering to the people struggling with the outcomes of multigenerational poverty. They lived first in a northern city and moved to this coastal city eight years before we talked.

Agency in Transition

When Adam first arrived, the agency was in transition, and it was his job to lead it through that change. He and Andrea had been assigned to the agency as missionaries from a national denomination. The denomination had founded the agency in the mid-1990s to work with people in their city who had been diagnosed with HIV/AIDS and were homeless. At that time, the city had 12,000 to 15,000 people homeless on the streets, yet the city's services to that population were sparse. The agency reached out with a free meal program in a downtown church; the meal was followed by an optional worship service. One of Adam's initial responsibilities was to serve as pastor in that worship service.

Serving as pastor gave Adam the opportunity to develop relationships with the people whom they served; the church had other pastors and services for the "regular" church members. The agency's ministry for persons who were homeless included a worship service, free breakfast and lunch, showers, and fresh clothing. An average of 500 people ate one or more meals with them each week, and 100 of those people stayed for the worship service.

> We didn't require that they have to come to worship in order to eat, but for a lot of them this was their church. They felt welcome, whether or not they smelled bad or were hung over. They found acceptance here.

Adam says they had several men who were homosexual who came regularly to the church service. They were not homeless; they came because they felt welcomed. One man who dressed in women's clothing always sat in the back. Adam tried to encourage him to sit farther toward the front, but he always refused, saying, "No, no, I'm not worthy to do that." Adam told him:

> God loves you just as He loves me. There is no distinction in God's eyes.

The man never moved forward, and Adam became even more determined to communicate welcome to those who felt that they had no place in the church.

Adam recalls those early years fondly:

> It was very challenging and rewarding for me. My goal was to be in relationship with folks other people did not want to be around. The folks who were coming were chronically homeless and struggled with major mental illness. A lot of them did not want to go to a shelter or into rehab. So I saw my role as being there with them.

A Shift toward Community Organizing

In the years just prior to Andrea and Adam's arrival, the agency had narrowed its focus to one neighborhood in the city, shifting from being a congregation for persons on the margins toward organizing the community to tackle the social problems in its neighborhood. The agency had built strong programs for the children and teenagers in the community. After-school and summer programs gave them opportunity to work on their schoolwork, receive tutoring when they needed it, participate in sports, and be a part of fun, self-esteem-building activities with peers and adults who loved them, safe from the violence and isolation of the surrounding streets.

It was Adam's job to provide the resources for the staff and volunteers to do their jobs. "I wear many hats—grant writing, directing and leading the staff, coordinating the strategic planning, and working with the Board of Directors. I work a lot with the finance side and grant administration to make sure that we are on target to accomplish our goals. I also run the vacuum cleaner when needed!"

Despite his professional degrees, Adam found he did not have the business skills he needed to be an effective nonprofit manager. He attended business and accounting classes at a community college to fill in these gaps in his skill set. "I had the people and counseling skills, I could assess and evaluate the needs and the programs, and I had the theological education, but I had to know accounting and how to read a balance sheet."

As the agency moved more into community organizing, it built upon the strong relationships it already had with the children in the community. Adam started weekly summer barbeques for the children and their families. In the autumn, the barbeques became monthly potluck dinners, and everyone brought a dish.

> We asked people what their dreams for the community were, and we explored with them their skills and gifts that could be used to make those dreams a reality. We wanted them to have a sense of ownership from the beginning.

Adam asked the parents to draw a picture of what the perfect neighborhood would look like to them, and he now has these framed and hanging in his office. One of this group's early projects was to help paint a colorful mural on the side of the agency's building. They also cleaned the lot and made a safe place for children to play.

> We now have about 30 parents attend each meeting, and I am encouraged. We are beginning to see the community work together through the parents.

Education as a Priority

In the Serving the City's immediate neighborhood, it is estimated that 80 percent of adult residents do not have a high school education and 69 percent of teenagers drop out of high school without graduating. Typically, those who live in the inner city define success as "getting out" of the community, but the agency is trying to change that mind-set. Adam wants teenagers and young adults to stay and become a part of positive change for the community:

> I see how resilient these kids are. They have been through so many challenges, yet they are pushing themselves, coming to our programs because they believe we can help them accomplish their dreams. We want them to see they can stay and be a part of God's kingdom here. We have had ten years or more of working with these kids, and we are very excited to see what God will do next with them.

The agency programs are designed to give children and youths a vision for what they can do if they stay in school and pursue higher education.

> Young people need help to see that there are other options than being in this part or that part of the drug trade. We want to help them imagine succeeding in school. One kid told me what he really wanted to do was be a valet so he could drive all those cool cars. That's all he saw—the cool cars. He can't even imagine owning one; he just hopes to get to drive someone else's.

What Success Looks Like

A reality of the agency's work is that there are few tidy success stories with happy endings, which can make it challenging for Adam when he meets with donors. Many donors want to see success before they commit their dollars:

> A lot of the folks that we see are chronically homeless, mentally ill, addicted—there is really not anywhere for them to go. We are successful in a different way. We are able to be a part of their lives and care for them and be family for them, even when they continue to struggle. We don't just serve those who can 'make it.'

Adam believes that God calls social workers to care for those who have been beaten up by life and cast aside by society. His caring is not conditional; he communicates care for the people he serves whether or not clients turn their lives around and meet a societal standard of "success." For Adam, Christian faith means that caring for the neighbor in need is how we can best show our love for the God who loves us whether or not we are successful.

In his five years with the agency, Adam's leadership has provided other markers of progress. When he arrived, he was one of three staff members. Now there are seven staff members full- time and four part-time, with additional staff for the summer children's programs. The agency uses an average of 350 volunteers in its programs throughout the year. All this is possible because Adam has successfully sought grants and additional financial support, a priority once the sponsoring denomination could no longer provide full financial support for their operations due to cutbacks. Even with that loss, the agency's operating budget has increased from $260,000 eight years ago to $440,000 during the year before our last interview.

Adam pushes himself and his staff to look for ways to improve their services. He places an emphasis on best practices and research and emphasizes to his staff that making time to keep learning is vital.

> If we are not reading about or searching for other models and other programs that are doing this work well, we are not going to be as effective as we could be.

Personal Life: Ethics and Boundaries

Following their calling to live among and serve persons in poverty has had an impact not only on Adam and Andrea but also on their children; they have two sons. They live in the neighborhood where they work, even though they could have chosen to live in a middle class suburb a commuter train ride away. Adam says that up to this point, the family has experienced more positives than negatives from that choice.

When they use the urban rail system, the family often runs into friends from the neighborhood, friends who are homeless or mentally ill or both. People who are homeless often ride the trains because they are free, air-conditioned, and available any time of the day or night.

> We always see somebody that we know. There was one fellow who is mentally ill and he was hearing voices and talking to himself. He was so happy when he saw us and our kids, because he knows us. It was fun to watch the expressions on other commuters' faces as we greeted each other. You could tell they were wondering how we know one another. To me, that's breaking down barriers, providing relationship and friendship to folks who mostly just get strange looks.

There are challenges, too. Adam reflected on the exchange he had with the man who wore women's dresses in his congregation, a situation that his older son questioned him about later:

> That's when that episode became challenging. How do I explain the concept of transgender to my children? He looks like a guy, but he is dressed like a girl. How do you talk about that? Our older son is very inquisitive and smart. He asks questions. It gives them an experience and a context that I never had growing up. We think they will be stronger for it.

After being homeschooled for several years, the Bennett children now attend a private school outside of the neighborhood. It was a difficult decision, Adam says:

> We'd love for them to be in the neighborhood schools, but it would be sacrificing them; they would wither.

All parents want what is best for their children, and Adam believes that "best" for his boys is in the opportunities and challenging curriculum of a private school, not in the schools in their neighborhood, with their high drop-out rates and lack of resources to challenge students.

The private school also exposes their sons to a way of life quite different from the one they experience in their home and neighborhood:

> Their schoolmates are very, very rich kids with huge houses who have a lot of material things. We have noticed that their parents are happy to have our sons come visit in their homes, but they do not want to send their kids to our house.

Living in the midst of the people whom he serves can lead to challenges in keeping appropriate professional and personal boundaries. Adam has to stop in any given situation and ask himself if he is pastor, social worker, friend, or all three. Those roles are blurred since the agency and the congregation co-exist.

One instance of this occurred when the Bennetts invited one of the teenagers from the neighborhood to live with them. He was a 14-year old who about to be placed in foster care—again—because his family could not care for him. He would grow up in the public child welfare system. Nevertheless, before inviting him into their home, Adam and Andrea had to work through their own concerns: Were they blurring roles? Was it truly in the boy's best interests? Given that they are Caucasian and the boy is African-American, would it create a hardship for him? Adam realizes not everyone would agree with their decision to provide a home for the boy, but for him, it is all about protecting a child. The boy moved in with them.

Adam said he constantly feels as though he is not doing enough and that there is not enough time in the day. He says he often feels like the plate-spinner in the circus—as soon as he gets two or three plates spinning smoothly, two or three others begin to wobble precariously:

That's the part that is hard for me. I want to do everything with excellence, but the reality is I only have so much time in the day, and I have to balance life and family. Those are very important things in inner-city work. If I do not have healthy outlets, I can burn out very quickly and that is very common. It is damaging to the social worker, but it is also really damaging to the work. One of the main community needs is stability. People need folks to see them through.

Adam and Andrea have committed themselves to staying, to being an anchor for the community for years to come, knowing that positive change will take years. They want to be there to see it happen. But Adam admits that living and working in the neighborhood "can be overwhelming," so he and his family spend much of their free time away from it. They go into the city to enjoy activities there and often go to the beach nearby.

Integrating Faith with Social Work

One of his challenges as both pastor and social worker arose over something as seemingly innocent as hot dogs. A committed volunteer in her 70s had been running the church's feeding ministry for 20 years. To get food out more quickly she encouraged volunteers to stack filled plates on top of each other, so that the bottom of a plate touched the food on the plate beneath it, creating potential food contamination. To Adam, that demonstrated disrespect for the individuals being served. As a pastor he wanted to acknowledge the volunteer's dedication, but his social work values and sensitivities also led him to suggest a slower service of plates one at a time. "Without my social work education, I don't think I would have thought about it," he said. The professional challenge was communicating his respect and appreciation for the volunteer even as he pointed out how the volunteer could show greater respect and sensitivity to service recipients.

Sometimes the challenge becomes a struggle, and sometimes one that is counterintuitive by society's standards. Adam remembers a time during a real estate boom that a representative from a large company came to him and said his company wanted to help "the homeless." He offered Serving the City $25,000 down and $50,000 to $75,000 a year. Adam looked into it and found that the company planned to build a multimillion-dollar condominium complex on a site frequented by people who are homeless. What they really wanted was Adam's assurance he could keep the homeless away from that area. Adam says the agency's staff and board were totally supportive when he refused the offer:

> Getting rid of people who are homeless is not what we are about. That was definitely my faith and my social work ethics together making me turn them down.

Another issue involving money came when a union representative offered to purchase $15,000 in toys to give the neighborhood children at Christmas. Adam's agency, though, had a practice of allowing parents to come into its Christmas "store" and purchase, at 10 percent of cost, the toys they chose for their children. The agency purchased the toys for the store with financial donations as well as receiving donated new toys. The toy store allowed parents to give gifts to their children themselves, rather than standing empty-handed on the sidelines while strangers gave the gifts to their children they would like to give. The agency's goal is to strengthen and encourage parents in their role, and that is why the toy store is so important.

Emphasizing the importance of giving parents the opportunity to buy gifts for their children, Adam said:

> Andrea was in the grocery store and she saw one of the kids in the program and his dad, and she wanted to make sure that he knew about the Christmas store. And he said, "Oh, that's great; we need that." His little boy said, "Dad, does that mean you are going to buy me presents this year?" and the dad said, rubbing his son's head affectionately, "Yes, son; I'm going to get you some."

Adam explained carefully to the union representative, suggesting that the union could support the parents by giving toys or money for the toy store instead. But the union representative was not persuaded:

> She told me, "We will triple what you're doing now, but you can't sell the toys." The union wanted the pleasure of giving the toys to the children directly. I said no. She was mad and just could not believe I had turned her down.

Adam believes he also has a responsibility to his staff and the agency to be a spiritual leader:

> Faith is why we are here; it is who we are. Faith informs all that we do. For some, the only way they know how to name that leadership is "pastor."

There was a volunteer in the agency's homeless ministry who unexpectedly suffered a stroke. The doctors did not expect him to live. His long-time live-in companion was at the hospital when Adam arrived to visit, and she greeted Adam by calling him "pastor."

> I wasn't her pastor or the volunteer's pastor, but the relationship that I had with her that next week was very powerful. I was able to be in a role to help her. They weren't going to church anywhere. I was just there, going through it with them.

One question almost anyone in the helping professions confronts at some point is why there is so much suffering and injustice in the world. Belief in a loving God makes that question even more problematic. Adam has been there:

> There are times when my work has caused me to struggle with my faith and to question why God lets this happen—when I see struggle, when I see misery, when I see injustice, corruption over and over and over. At the same time, the struggle points me more toward how God is the liberator and the hope. It colors how I read the Bible and how I relate to God. Watching folks who are homeless care for each other—there is a level of giving that goes way beyond what I do. Like when a guy has one sandwich and he gives half to the guy next to him, even though that is all he has. They look out for each other. They teach me about what faith should be about, about how we should care for each other.

The Rewards

To see Adam playing with a toddler at one of the parents' meetings, or walking to the corner store with a neighbor who is homeless to buy them both a soda, it is clear that Adam is living his faith in little acts day by day, not just in the decisions and strategic planning his role as executive director demands of him. There are many rewards to the way he has chosen to live out his calling, times that, he says, "make me believe I'm in the right place."

There was a call he received in the middle of the night from a man he had not seen in two years, when the man had been homeless. He called to tell Adam that the agency had been there at just the right moments in his life, "giving me the right love. I just wanted you to know that I am doing great. Keep up what you're doing."

There was the teenage boy who hung on the outskirts of the summer barbecues, but would never come across the street and join in. They finally got him to come over and play basketball and have a hamburger. He started attending the agency's teen program:

> He was rough. By age 14 or 15, most teens growing up in the inner city are either entrenched in the drug culture and gangs, or they are not. But he was wavering. After he started attending here, he blossomed and did so well that he became a leader.

Adam muses,

> We know that we are an integral part of positive choices. We are not 'the answer,' but we are a catalyst. We do give opportunity to succeed.

Questions To Ponder

1. What are the reasons the church may have developed a worship service attached to the free meal program and separate from the rest of the congregation's worship? From the perspective of the agency's clients, what were the advantages and disadvantages of having a worship time designed specifically for them?
2. As you think about Adam's work, how do you see the role of pastor fitting with his role of social worker? Are they all one role—a social worker whose service involves pastoring? Or are they distinct professional roles that he balanced, pastor and social worker? Does the population he serves—persons who have HIV/AIDS, who are homeless, who are mentally ill, who are homosexual—influence your viewpoint?
3. In community development, it is tempting to start with all the problems in a community that need to be addressed. How did Adam begin to connect with the adult family members of the children in their activity programs? What was the impact of starting as he did?
4. Adam believed that he was living his Christian faith to welcome people into their programs and worship service who had been marginalized from society and from the church by disease, poverty, sexual orientation, or all three. How do your own beliefs and values as a social worker and as a Christian fit or conflict with Adam's actions as a social worker/pastor?
5. Adam and his wife made the decision to live in the community where they serve but to send their children to a private school outside the neighborhood. They attend worship with the people in the neighborhood, including the man who dresses in women's clothing. What are the values that have led Adam and his wife to make these choices? To what extent are they social work values? Christian values? As you think about where you might decide to work as a social worker, what impact might your work have on your current or future family?
6. What were the social work values and ethics involved in Adam's decision to provide foster care for a child in the neighborhood? How are those values and ethics congruent with or in conflict with Christian teachings?
7. When asked about the integration of faith and social work, Adam told a story about hot dogs. What social work values are involved in this story? What Christian values?
8. What about Adam's work most appeals to you? What sounds draining and difficult? What does that say to you about your own gifts and personal resources for professional practice as a social worker?

Wes McIntosh
Community Organizer, Metropolitan Area Interfaith Organization
Leah Gatlin and Kelsey Wiggins, Co-Authors

As a student in a small Christian university, Wes McIntosh had known where he was going; his plan for the future was set. In his senior year of a degree in biblical languages, he had already accepted a scholarship to a seminary on the West Coast. After seminary, he planned to get his doctoral degree so that he could be a seminary professor and "live in the ivory tower."

During his college years, he had been volunteering in an inner-city ministry, where he developed relationships with the children and their families in the neighborhood. Wes described the ministry as a bunch of White, middle class college students who wanted to help people living in an inner city, low-income, predominantly Hispanic neighborhood, but who did not know what to do. What the college students did know was they needed to build relationships with the children and their families. They developed activity programs to help children with schoolwork, provided healthy and safe recreation, and allowed friendships to blossom with the children of the neighborhood. As his graduation approached, Wes became even more concerned that as much as he had cared, he still had no idea how to help the kids that he had befriended during those four years. It also deeply bothered him that he believed the congregation in these children's neighborhood did not know how to help them either, nor did the congregation seem to care enough to try. A conversation with Daniel, one of the teenagers in the neighborhood, changed Wes's life forever.

Wes and Daniel had known one another for the entire four years. They had become close friends, and Wes knew Daniel needed a friend. Daniel lived with his mother and seven brothers; the boys had six different fathers who were not very engaged with their sons. Daniel's mother struggled just to pay the rent and buy groceries. One Friday night in April, just weeks before Wes was to graduate, Daniel and Wes were "hanging out" on a street corner and talking about Wes' upcoming move to the West Coast. In turn, Daniel told Wes that he was thinking about dropping out of high school and joining the South Side Locos, the city's largest gang. Wes said:

> I thought to myself, "I have no idea how to help this kid; my knowledge of Greek and Hebrew are pointless." It was one of the most humbling moments of my life, sitting on a street corner with a teenager I had known for four years, feeling helpless.

Wes is not one to let a feeling of helplessness discourage him; instead, it motivates him to find answers. The next day—Saturday—Wes realized he wanted to be able to help Daniel and other kids like him in neighborhoods like Daniel's—and so he began looking for what he could do. What professions help kids like Daniel? He came across several jobs requiring an "MSW," but he did not know what an MSW was. He soon learned—Master of Social Work. Due to either coincidence or divine intervention—Wes is not sure which - the girl Wes was dating at the time had a roommate who was planning to attend a Christian university with a dual MSW and Master of Divinity program. Thinking it made a lot of sense for what he wanted to do, Wes cancelled his plans to go to the West Coast and become a seminary professor. He turned in a last minute application to the dual degree program in the university where his girlfriend's roommate was a student and was accepted.

A few months later, in the first weeks of graduate school, Wes heard about community organizing for the first time when he was sitting in his Introduction to Social Work class:

> I remember thinking, "Hm. That sounds interesting. That sounds like something I'd like."

Based on his initial interest, Wes focused on community organizing in his coursework, and when he graduated, the community housing organization where he had completed an internship hired him.

Power

Wes worked as a community organizer for six years in that community housing organization located in the city where he had attended graduate school. Wes' work took him frequently into a large apartment complex called Cityview. There in plain view in the middle of the day, Wes saw people shooting at one another, drug dealing, and gangs hanging out and intimidating the neighborhood. The owners of the Cityview complex lived in another city and did not know or show any concern about Cityview's residents; they made millions of dollars from the rent paid by low-income families all over the United States in complexes like Cityview. Cityview had repeatedly failed state and federal health inspections. According to Wes, the only reason the government authorities had not condemned it was the political influence of the owners.

Wes took on the task of organizing schools, neighborhood associations, churches, and residents to respond to the social hazards in Cityview. He began by having conversations about the community with Cityview residents. He presented the findings to community gatherings. In those gatherings, neighbors came together to list their expectations for what they wanted to see happen at Cityview. These expectations became a scorecard to use in holding the management accountable for life in the housing complex. The scorecard included good and responsive management practices, as well as working with the city police department and its crime-free housing program. Representatives of the community and Cityview management together signed the agreement.

Sixth months later, Wes conducted another series of conversations. As he suspected, nothing had changed; the management had fulfilled none of its commitments. In a subsequent meeting, the building owners made it clear to residents that they would not respond to their demands.

Wes led the newly organized neighbors to consider what they could do next. The group decided to contact the U.S. Department of Housing and Urban Development (HUD) and the city manager, successfully advocating for vouchers to pay the expenses for moving all of the Cityview residents into better living conditions. The group also advocated successfully for the city to condemn and raze the apartment complex. A month after Cityview shut down, crime in the neighborhood went down by fifty percent. Wes still points to the demolishing of Cityview as one of his greatest feelings of success as an organizer, because he was the catalyst for people to organize themselves and together harness their power to pursue a common goal with success.

Wes' greatest victory was sadly accompanied by defeat as well:

> The whole community wanted to replace Cityview with a mixed income development. An editorial in the city paper said it was the most unified group of community members ever seen at a city public hearing. Instead, the City Council contracted with another national organization to build another low-income apartment complex there. So that means that somebody like me is probably going to have to do the exact same work in the future, because it will just return to the same condition.

Wes learned from that experience:

> I learned that the City Council liked me and razed Cityview because it was the right thing to do. But when a business organization came around waving millions of dollars in front of the city, we did not have any power. And power beats influence every day of the week. I just wanted people to like me so they would do what I wanted them to do. Now I am actually trying to build power.

His employing organization was dependent on funding from the City Council. So when they reached a point of impasse with the City Council, Wes' boss told him they could not push anymore. Wes said that it was painful and discouraging. He left shortly thereafter.

Wes now had six years of experience in community organizing. Metropolitan Area Interfaith (MAI), located in a large urban area, asked Wes to move and become a community organizer for MAI. Still stinging from his recent defeat, Wes jumped at the new opportunity. He knew that working with MAI would strengthen his community organizing knowledge and skills. MAI is an organization of institutions, many of them congregations, which work together to address the concerns they share about issues facing their communities. Now married to a social worker who had graduated from the same dual degree program, they moved with their baby so that Wes could begin work at MAI. In the training MAI provided, he was able to analyze the mistakes he had made at Cityview and how he might have been more successful.

Now Wes' work involves organizing a couple of "large actions" each year, rallying neighborhoods to take on the challenges that oppress them. He engages more frequently in "small actions," such as organizing and coaching neighborhood citizens for meetings with a county judge or state legislator to discuss a concern and ask for supportive action. According to Wes:

> Both small and large "actions" often involve demands that politicians do what they had previously promised. Politicians become a lot more responsive when voters from their district are making demands.

Wes spends much of his time talking and thinking about the dynamic of power in human relationships and in the oppression of people who are poor. When talking about MAI, Wes said:

> If people in a community have no power, then nothing happens, so we are about building power so people can successfully pursue change.

The organization of a neighborhood to bring about the razing of Cityview is an example of community power. In his work at MAI, Wes has organized communities that successfully advocated with city government for more police presence on the city streets and good public health care service for persons who cannot afford to pay for medical care.

Wes believes that everyone has power when they act together with others, and his job as an organizer is to bring people together to use the power they have, build even more power, and then network with others to join their power together around the values they share and issues that concern them. Wes tells the story of a woman in her fifties who had never voted in a public election.

I helped her tap into the anger she felt about her son not having health insurance and to realize that others had the same concern about their children. She went from having never voted before to collecting two hundred signatures to support Medicaid expansion and testifying in front of the State Senate's Health and Human Services Committee as a spokeswoman for her community. This woman works as a teacher's aide in a public school; she had not previously been a community leader.

Building Relationships

How does a social worker organize a community to bring about change? Wes focuses his energy and skill on building relationships with community residents and with those who have influence in the community. His work brings together a diversity of people. Wes knows personally the people who gather for a monthly meeting of a neighborhood association Wes had been organizing. They included people of no faith tradition, people with strong faith traditions, Black, White, Hispanic, wealthy, poor, and several faith community leaders. Each of these people was there because they had developed relationships with Wes, and through Wes, with one another—in order to work toward a goal important to all of them. Wes rarely uses surveys in his work. He says:

> Surveys are often a way that we keep ourselves from being in a relationship with each other. I am working with a Catholic church, planning a listening campaign with over a thousand people instead of doing a survey, which is what the church has done in the past. I said to the priest and his leadership team, "If you really want to deepen the relationship of community members with your congregation, a survey will not accomplish that." For example, in Cityview, we gathered pastors, residents, and people in nonprofit organizations and neighborhood associations to start talking about what they would like to see happen in Cityview. The important process was gathering people together who had not been together before.

Much of Wes' day-to-day work involves meetings—meeting people others have suggested he meet, as well as working with people he already knows. In every meeting, despite how casual it may seem on the surface, as Wes learns about people's work and family and daily lives, he is thinking about how MAI can benefit this person and this person's community, as well as how this person can strengthen the MAI network. Each connection Wes makes has the potential of starting several more connections or being a key to mobilizing around an issue.

Wes says he has to be persistent. Sometimes it takes months of consistently calling and e-mailing until Wes can finally meet some community leaders. They have not yet caught a vision of the common ground they share with the work of MAI. Pastors are sometimes the most difficult; many pastors in the neighborhoods where Wes works have full-time employment to support their families as well as their church responsibilities—and talking with a community organizer is hard to fit into their pressed schedules. Wes has been known to visit a Sunday morning worship service, then intentionally hang around until he is "the last person in the sanctuary" so he would have a chance to talk with the minister. He has been trying to establish contact with one influential pastor for five months: "But I'll track him down, because I think he's worth it." His dogged determination requires a healthy sense of himself; he does not take personally the lack of responsiveness to his efforts—Wes loves a challenge.

Another challenge Wes faces is finding financial support for his work. Besides building relationships with influential leaders within the community, Wes must also build relationships with people who have money to invest in MAI and the work it is doing. He solicits donations through his network, as well as developing relationships with private foundations and writing grant proposals to those foundations and to government agencies. While not the favorite part of his job, Wes knows that the work has to have financial support, and the grant writing helps him to gain a clear vision for his work and set specific goals.

In order to build relationships, social workers like Wes often have to get past misconceptions. Wes told a story from his Cityview experience to illustrate. Several city leaders thought that African-American pastors in the community simply did not care about the neighborhood and were doing nothing. Wes learned that one of the pastors had actually attempted to make Cityview better when he first came to town forty or more years earlier, but was unsuccessful. Discouraged, he stopped trying. Wes knew this pastor was working a full-time job as well as pastoring. What others had mistaken as lack of care was actually a lack of time or resources—and a lack of pastors' understanding of their power to bring about change if they collaborated with one another. Over time, Wes was able to engage the pastors with one another and with civic leaders to bring about the changes that were so much needed.

Cold Anger

Wes now is trying to learn to be better at "agitating." Part of his job is gathering people around the same concern to plan for and implement action. He tells a story about a woman who was very angry about her son being imprisoned for a relatively minor crime. Instead of trying to comfort her, Wes accentuated her agitation by challenging her:

> Do you actually want to build power or do you want to keep complaining about how bad things are?

His point was not merely to make her more upset; his point was to motivate her to use her feelings to seek change in the system. Building relationships is not as helpful in organizing if the people are not agitated enough to act.

When asked what keeps him going, Wes responded simply, "My anger." He notes that when most people think about anger, they think about white-hot rage that is destructive and makes others not want to be around it. On the other end of the spectrum is being so angry at one's self that the person cannot do anything and feels incompetent. Thinking in these two terms, people often think of anger as bad or negative. At MAI, they talk about cold anger, an anger that propels but does not consume. Wes pointed to the example of the burning bush and Moses. Flames completely engulfed the bush, but the fire did not consume it. Wes reported that to keep his cold anger going, he thinks about several stories. He thinks about the church in Daniel's neighborhood, which did nothing to help kids like Daniel. Wes is angry at churches that turn their backs on the community's problems. He remembers the days when this anger was white-hot rage; over time, it has turned to cold anger that propels him forward in his job.

Learning as He Goes

Just as Wes learned from the defeat he experienced in trying to replace Cityview with a mixed income neighborhood, he continues to learn and reflect on his previous experiences. Now that Wes has two years of perspective gained at MAI, he realizes:

> I really was not much of an organizer in my work at Cityview. I was a good leader, and I made things happen because people trusted me, but an organizer never does for others what they can do for themselves. An organizer finds talented people and equips them to act in the interest of the community.

He illustrated what he meant with a recent example, in which he organized a group of five hundred people around concerns about immigration policy. He said:

> I was personally responsible for about twenty of those gathered. Instead of my doing the networking, I found those twenty talented people who could network with others and bring them along. I was the one who made everything happen at Cityview. Without me, nothing was going to happen. That has changed. I went on vacation a few months ago, and when I returned, MAI had taken on another issue. They started planning a major fundraiser, and they did that all without me being there. There always needs to be somebody who agitates and gives people imagination—that is my job. But things can also go on for a while without me.

In the months before our last conversation, Wes had organized a meeting of several Catholic priests, Methodist pastors, and lay persons with the U.S. Congressional representative to talk about immigration policy. The congressman treated the group with considerable disdain:

> My priest went back at him and demanded an apology. It was a great moment to see my Catholic priest demand and receive that apology from one of the most powerful Congressional Representatives in the nation.

The group realized that they do not have the power to address immigration policy at the national level. Instead, they reconsidered and have now launched an initiative to address the problem of wage theft in their city. Wage theft occurs when employers pay below minimum wage, do not reimburse for overtime, or do not pay due wages to immigrants whom they know are fearful of authorities and so will not report the abuse:

> Wage theft is rampant, especially in the experience of a Latino Catholic congregation. There is a state law that criminalizes wage theft, but the police are not enforcing it in our county. Now we have built enough power through Catholic congregations to gain commitments from the DA's Office, the Police Department, and the Sheriff's Department to enforce the existing law. We are training people on what they can do and educating law enforcement about how this law needs to be enforced.

The other issue on which Wes is currently working is to legislate water breaks for construction workers:

> A large number of contractors in our city do not allow construction workers water breaks during the day for water and to sit down for a short period. We are working with the City Council to get a Rest Break Ordinance passed for construction workers. There have been challenges; a Councilman actually said to one of our construction workers who speaks Spanish, "If you'd learn English, you wouldn't have to work in the construction industry."

Issues on the horizon are campaigning for living wage legislation and funding for early childhood education. Someday, Wes and his wife want to return to their home state, one of the most conservative states in the nation, to organize communities for change there.

Faith

Wes maintains,

> I didn't choose social work because I like social work; I didn't choose organizing because I like organizing. Deciding to become a social worker came out of my basic conviction that the church should be engaging in the community and should understand the Bible calls for us to do more than preach hell-fire and brimstone.

For him, organizing always comes back to his faith and his beliefs. Because he believes congregations should engage their communities, Wes keeps a cold anger toward those congregations who do not, seeking ways to communicate to them his perspective. Wes often works with church leaders in building the community within a congregation so that congregants know and trust one another— and then work together to seek justice for their neighbors.

Wes grew up Baptist and attended Baptist universities for his undergraduate and graduate degrees. His worldview was Baptist. Then his work brought him into collaborations with Jews, Catholics, Lutherans, Presbyterians, Methodists, and those with no religious tradition. He asserts these interactions have deepened and broadened his faith, particularly learning about Catholic social teachings. His current supervisor is a Catholic Sister. He is establishing working relationships with Muslims. He described a recent day of worship:

> I rapped in an African American Church and, on the same Sunday, led a bilingual AME Church, and then led a training with African American and Latino Catholics.

For Wes, his faith has affected his work and the work in turn has affected his faith.

Wes does not like the word "calling," because it was not used well in the Baptist circles where he grew up. Growing up, he understood a calling to be work to be done for the rest of one's life. He prefers to think now, "Do I feel called to do this today?" Wes gave examples of experiences where he realizes he is really good at what he does:

> Actually, I reflect on a lot of things, but not calling. I think about it now as having a lot of anger, hopefully cold anger, about what happened to my family when I was growing up. When I see a city wasting money on things like a horse park and not spending it on kids, I have a lot of anger about that. I think my calling comes from my anger and how it drives me to do something about the injustices I see. I have the opportunity to do something about that anger with the talents God has given me. My anger is a gift.

I asked about what had happened to his family, and he told me the story of growing up in a sharecropper family, never having enough money to purchase the land they farmed, but always dreaming of owning the land. Wes was never able to participate in school extracurricular activities; he was always working with his parents and brother on the farm. When he was in grade school, despite long years of hard work, his parents lost everything when cattle prices dropped and they could not pay their bank loan.

> The American Dream is that if you work hard, then things are going to work out. That is not reality, and I am angry what happens to families who work hard and still are unable to fulfill their dreams.

No one helped Wes' family—not the community, not the church where they had been faithful members. In some ways, that child in the poor neighborhood Wes met as a college student reminded him of himself. The church in which he grew up and Daniel's inner city church expressed more concern with eternal salvation than with the current suffering of children and families.

Wes reflects that the fuel for anger is pain; it is grief. Grief alone is passive—"I'm overwhelmed and unable to act." But anger seeks to change that which is causing pain. Anger at the church for not caring about children who are growing up in poverty drives Wes as a change agent. He is bringing churches together who have never worked together before to put their faith into action. He says he loves his work and "I can't believe I get paid to interact with different faith traditions and do political work." This work is what he was looking for as a senior in college when he realized he needed to do something to help kids like Daniel in neighborhoods like Daniel's. For Wes, his "calling" was a series of events, rather than a single moment where God clearly spoke to him. In those moments where he realizes he is being successful in his work, he thinks, "Okay, this must be meant to be." The neighborhoods where Wes has found his place are far from the "ivory tower" of academia he imagined as a college student.

Questions to Ponder

1. Which social work ethical principles do you see in Wes' work and his ideas about power? Which Christian ethical principles do you see in his work? Do you see any possible clashes between these two sets of ethics in his work?

2. How might Wes' work be different if it did not come from a Christian or other religious viewpoint?

3. What are some of the ways Cityview shutting down could affect the community, besides lower crime rates?

4. In what ways is tearing down an apartment complex progress? Or not?
5. Wes is a macro social worker, but like most social workers, he finds himself using the skills of working with individuals and small groups as well. Describe Wes' work, as you can know it from this brief case study, at the micro, macro, and mezzo levels.
6. Wes described how he worked to "agitate" a woman complaining about her son's incarceration. How might a clinical social worker have worked with this woman similarly or differently?
7. Wes suggests that pain and grief underlay the anger that drives him. How does that resonate with your own experience?
8. What are some issues or experiences you have had that created "cold anger" or that could be turned into cold anger to propel you forward in your education or your work?
9. How has Wes' story fit with your ideas about power and influence in relationships?

Christina Dobal

Community Advocate
Regina Chow Trammel, Co-Author

It was 5:30 and the staff had closed the doors of Crew Productions. Crew's office building is in the heart of the city, an easy walk from the subway station. Luis, an 18-year-old gang member, had heard about Crew from an ex-gang member he met a few years ago when they both were spending time in juvenile hall. The other boy had become Luis' friend and was now a work supervisor at Crew's bakery, mentoring new employees. Crew Productions had helped him get out of the gang and drug use; he was now enrolled in community college and working at Crew. Luis knocked on the glass doors and tried the knob—locked. He knocked again and yelled through the glass door, "Hello? Is anyone in there? I need help!"

Inside, Christina Dobal, a mental health therapist at Crew, had just packed up her laptop case to head home after a long day. She was tired; the day had ended with mediating a dispute between a client and his pregnant girlfriend. The girlfriend was angry because her boyfriend was too busy at Crew all day to be with her. Christina spent the session helping her client explain to his girlfriend that the changes he was making were going to be good for both of them. The young woman was an ex gang-member herself. She and her family had moved out of the neighborhood and its gangs and violence to make a new start.

Christina heard Luis' knocking as she walked into the lobby on her way home. She opened the door. Not sure if he was carrying a gun or not, she let him in anyway and asked him what was wrong. Reflecting back, she realizes that was a dangerous decision for her to make:

> We are really on the frontlines. There is no buffer between the trauma, the suffering that is going on in our clients' lives, and us. There is no guard. That is great in some ways, but we can also get hurt.

Christina invited Luis into her office and listened as he told her that he needed a new start: "I have had enough; I'm done." If he did not make a change, he said, he knew he was going to end up in prison, and he did not want that to be his life. Christina invited him to tell her about himself.

Luis had grown up surrounded by drug use and violence, living with an aunt and uncle who were members of gangs in one of the city's roughest neighborhoods. He had joined a gang at age 11 as a way to survive the dangers of the neighborhood; he felt safe having a whole group of friends who "had your back." Luis rarely went to school after he joined the gang and dropped out of high school in the tenth grade.

"Why is today the day? What has happened to bring you here now?" Christina asked. Luis told her that it was his birthday; he had just turned eighteen. Now the legal system considered him an adult. Many of his "homies" had been arrested on various charges in the last several days. Luis already had one stint in juvenile detention, and he knew the next run-in with the law would land him in adult jail. The friend he had met while in juvenile detention told him that Crew could help.

Christina had been a therapist at Crew for three years; she understood that Luis needed a place he could connect with adults and peers who could give him hope that he could change the course of his life. For Christina, helping Luis feel accepted and connecting his desire for life to be different with hope and opportunity for real change is her way of living her faith as a Christian. She says it changes how she sees Luis and all the young people with whom she works:

> This person is not just a drug addict. This young man is not just a batterer. This kid is not just a gang member. This is somebody I know. This is somebody that I love. Faith is making that choice for me, the choice to learn to know and love this person. I choose to walk beside these kids through all of the challenges they face.

For more than an hour, Luis' story unfolded to reveal a childhood of hurt, loss, and hopelessness that landed him in a gang he wants to escape but he does not know how. Christina listened to him quietly, soaking in his words, like a sponge holding all he poured out. She told him if he came back in the morning, they could start figuring out a path together. He agreed and went out into the darkening neighborhood.

The night's sleep was short, and Christina pushed herself to prepare for the day despite her weariness, wondering if Luis really would return:

> Luis was either going to show up the next day or not. But if my interaction with him had been accepting and supportive, and if he knows that he is loved regardless of what he has done, then that is faith in action.

A Jesuit Life

Christina grew up in the city. A practicing Catholic, she attended a private Jesuit high school, where she was exposed to the Jesuit ethos that drew her into a life of service. The high school required all students to do community service and combined teachings about social justice with rigorous academic expectations. She credits her Jesuit community of faith as well as her family for her choice of social work as a career. Christina completed a Bachelor of Social Work degree at a Jesuit college. She then went on to obtain her MSW, and three years ago, took a job at Crew Productions, founded 25 years ago by a Jesuit priest.

Crew Productions has since become one of the most comprehensive gang intervention and prevention programs in the United States. Crew is a social entrepreneurship organization, offering job placement and on-the-job skills training, classes to prepare for the high school equivalency exam, mental health and substance abuse services, legal services, and even tattoo removal, so that clients can erase the visual symbols of their gang identity. Crew runs a café, a popular dining spot for the downtown business crowd, serving fresh-baked breads and locally-sourced salads, sandwiches and snacks. They also have café locations in the airport and one in City Hall. Crew produces tortilla chips and salsa, which they sell in local supermarkets. An embroidery and screen-printing business offers custom pens, shirts and more for sports teams and businesses.

All the businesses within Crew help to fund the free social services that clients receive. The ventures also employ the ex-gang members, offering them the opportunity to develop job skills, the dignity of a paycheck, and the social skills training that will help them succeed in the world outside Crew. Christina described it this way:

> Our primary intervention is giving them the opportunity to do an honest day's work and to earn a paycheck. That provides legitimacy with their parole or probation officers. We provide a safe place to be. And while they are working at Crew we surround them with mentors and all these peers and staff members who are working toward goals with them. Crew is a community.

Crew's motto is, "Nothing stops a bullet like a job."

Because her title was "mental health therapist," Christina's clients may not have been aware that she was a social worker. They knew her as the group leader who worked with the teens as together they sort out their lives and encourage and challenge one another. She was their counselor, providing one-on-one support and therapeutic interventions to overcome the trauma, losses, and disappointments that have shaped their lives. She worked with families to strengthen their ability to support their children's fledgling attempts at a new start. Christina also supported and collaborated with other Crew team members—the case managers and the job supervisors.

The Drive to Serve

Each morning, Christina and the other staff members start by meeting together for a time of devotion. Christina has a memorized prayer from her Jesuit upbringing that she recites as the day begins:

> Lord, teach me to be generous; teach me to serve You as You deserve; to give and not count the cost; to fight and not fear the wounds; to toil and not seek rest; to labor and not seek reward; every day knowing that I am doing Your will.

Christina reflected on the meaning that prayer has had for her:

> I did not realize before I went to Crew that all of those things that I am asking God to teach me actually feel wonderful to do. This is not suffering so I will have a reward later. This is in the here and now. Every ounce that I put out, I get back.

She went on to say that social work is not only her work; it is her life:

> Being a social worker is something that I must do. Maybe it is a choice—or maybe it is not a choice. I do not know. I have this drive in me to walk with these young people that is almost out of my control. Yes, I choose to get up and come here every day, but there is a force within that says, 'You are the one to do it.'

While Christina described a force or drive in her to help these young people, which she defines as faith, her own faith and calling are not the focus of her work. "My faith feeds me and fuels me; but none of my clients know I am Catholic unless they ask."

Christina described the vicarious trauma she has experienced in her work at Crew. She believes that social workers suffer. When her clients faced relapse or sabotage themselves she said:

> I suffer, but that's different. The people we love, we see them suffer every day and therefore I suffer. But, I was never angry with them. I get angry at the lack of resources; I get angry about the lack of funding. But the minute I get mad at that kid sitting in front of me, I need to think, okay, something is wrong. Why am I getting mad at her? And it is usually my own pain I am feeling in her behalf. The suffering I experience from listening to their lives is a small price to pay. If I can be a sponge and absorb the hurt and anger for her today, then that is enough.

Law School

At the same time, Christina wants to do more about the forces that create opportunities for gangs, crime, and poverty to ensnare her clients in the first place. She has seen the damage created by the criminal justice system on people's lives, not only those who are incarcerated but also their families, friends, and community. As much as she enjoys clinical practice, after several years at Crew, she decided to go to law school, believing that as a lawyer and perhaps as an elected official, she can work to increase her clients' political power in the communities where they live.

The Jesuits value the three Cs of higher education, Christina says, which are Conscience, Compassion, and Competence. Christina believes that the Jesuit value of serving others through education has shaped her. Whether one is clergy or laity, the Jesuits believe that we all have the same calling to serve others. At the time of our last interview, she had enrolled in a law school that focuses on public interests—on serving human needs.

Christina's vision for her post-law future school is as both attorney and social worker in a community organization. She sees the political process as a means for community-level change and hopes to be employed again at an organization like Crew Productions—this time in the role of advocate. She wants to empower clients in the policy-making process in order to help their own communities: "I can teach them how to access the political process, and not just in voting, which I think is important, but also teach them how to participate in the democratic process."

I asked Christina how she imagines putting her social work profession and her legal profession together. She said:

> I will always be a social worker. I will never be a lawyer with a social work degree; I will always be a social worker with a law degree.

Christina learned at Crew that society had marginalized their clients, but that they could actually really be movers and shakers politically. She wants to create opportunities for folks coming out of the prison system and criminal justice system to harness their political power and to enhance their participation in society. She wants to build a coalition of advocates who will keep clients' perspectives and life experiences at the forefront of the political process.

Her goals feel ambitious, but Christina says that this is her life's work, her calling. She wants to hone her knowledge and skills to equip herself for this work. But ultimately, she reminds herself:

> There is no success; there is no failure; there is only accompaniment.

In other words, her calling is not to be successful as others might define success; nor is it to avoid failure. She is called simply to walk with others on their journey.

Questions to Ponder

1. What do you think Christina should have done when she found Luis knocking on the door after hours?

2. What does it take to love someone, as Christina described, such as a batterer, a gang member and/or drug addict? Whom have you loved that others might consider unlovable, and how did that happen?

3. What role does social work play in an organization with the motto, "Nothing stops a bullet like a job"?

4. Christina talks about being a sponge to her clients and feeling that it is her calling to absorb some of her client's suffering. In what ways is absorbing suffering an expression of social work values? Of Christian faith?

5. How do you view Christina's decision to pursue a law degree in the unfolding of her career?

6. Christina talked about her faith as the motivation that drives her and not the focus of her work with clients, who may not know about her faith. Compare and contrast her view of the integration of faith with social work with your own.

7. Christina's mantra is "There is no success; there is no failure. There is only accompaniment." How does this mantra fit your own theology of calling? How does it fit with professional expectations for demonstrable outcomes?

Heather Quintana
Missionary Social Worker and Pastor
Lori M. Sousa, Co-Author

Growing up in the Midwest, Heather always wanted to live in the snowy mountains of Colorado. She laughs as she thinks about it:

> I never thought God would send me to the tropical jungle where it is hot and full of bugs, but traveling on the Amazon to minister in the small villages that line the river is what makes me most happy.

When I last interviewed her, Heather had been a missionary in Brazil for the past ten years. She received her MSW three years before moving to Brazil, and even though her formal title is "missionary," she refers to herself as a "missionary social worker." Heather believes that her social work training has equipped her to fulfill her calling. As she looks back over her life, Heather is amazed at how everything worked together to prepare her for her work in Brazil. She recalls,

> When I was in high school, I was not exactly sure what I wanted to do. I knew God had called me into ministry and I really loved helping people. As I began to think about my life, I realized that I was happiest when I was helping people.

Heather's decision to pursue social work came after visiting a Christian university, where she talked with social work professors. "I sensed the Lord telling me, 'This is what I want you to do.'"

After completing a BSW from the university she had visited, Heather decided to attend another Christian college for her graduate studies, a program that emphasized integrating Christian faith and social work practice. Though Heather was uncertain about what kinds of employment opportunities she would find after graduation, her dream was to work at the community level. In her graduate program, she gained valuable experience as an intern at a religiously affiliated community development cooperative (CDC) that worked with fifty churches in the city. Looking back, Heather recognizes:

> There were so many skills that I learned that have aided me in my work, particularly the skills of community assessment. It is funny because I remember being so frustrated as a student with learning how to do assessments. I did not like all of the paperwork, but the assessment process has been so valuable for helping me identify the roots of so many individual and community problems in Brazil.

As a graduate student, Heather attended a meeting at one of the churches in the CDC. At the end of the meeting, the minister announced a short-term mission trip to Brazil. Even though Heather was very busy with her schoolwork, she grew excited as he talked about the trip. Her heart was tugging her to be part of the trip—and she listened.

Called to Brazil

On that mission trip, Heather fell in love with Brazil and its people. When she returned to the States, all Heather could think about was going back. She went on two more short-term mission trips, also to Brazil, and she began to sense a calling to live and serve in Brazil. During her third trip, Heather met a Brazilian man who would eventually become her husband and ministry partner, and Heather moved to Brazil to stay.

Jungle and the Amazon River surround the town where Heather and her husband live. Their official titles are "missionaries," commissioned by the Pentecostal Church of God World Missions. Heather says, "I work as a social worker every single day." Heather and her husband started a new congregation eight years ago, which they co-pastor. The congregation that began with 30 members has grown to 250 members and has many ministries designed to meet the social, emotional, physical, and spiritual needs of the people in their community.

A typical day for Heather begins with the morning spent in homeschooling her two children. She prepares lunch for her family, which is the main meal of the day in Brazil. After lunch, she heads to the church ministry office, where she provides counseling for whoever seeks her services. Her clients are not necessarily seeking spiritual guidance, nor are they necessarily members of the church. She works with them in whatever life challenges they are facing. She does a lot of marriage counseling as well as financial planning and counseling. She says, "I do whatever I can to help with whatever problem they are facing; there is no one else to whom I can refer them."

Heather averages two counseling sessions in the afternoons. The culture in Brazil is not as formal as it is in the USA, so people usually just show up at the church or at her house as needs arise. At first, this aspect of Brazilian cultural was difficult for Heather; she worried about the house being "presentable" and whether she was dressed professionally. People would come as early as seven o'clock in the morning or late in the evening. She found herself hiding in her own home, with the lights out. Her Brazilian husband coached her in the culture. She says:

> He said to me: "Heather, they do not care what you look like. They do not care what the house looks like. They just want to talk to you. They just want to have relationship with you. You can continue doing whatever you are doing. You can be washing dishes in the kitchen; just have them sit at the table there as you are washing dishes and let them talk to you. That is okay. And it is okay sometimes to say, 'Can you come back tomorrow?'" He really helped me—and I learned to adapt to putting relationships above all else.

Some of the Brazilians who work in the ministry have told Heather that in the past, they did not like Americans because many of the American missionaries would never allow people to come into their homes. They only met with people if they had scheduled appointments and would not respond to unscheduled knocks at the door. Unscheduled knocks on the door are how most of Heather's work begins, however.

Ministering on the Amazon

Heather says she finds particular joy on the days that she visits the small remote villages that line the Amazon River. Most of the tribal villages are only accessible by boat; the people are deeply impoverished and now live under the protection of the Brazilian government after suffering at the hands of colonizing forces. Colonists came to force the tribes off their land. Well-meaning missionaries as well as doctors, nurses, and sociologists introduced practices that undermined and sometimes destroyed their culture. Heather says:

> The missionaries were sincere and meant well, but there was no concept of cultural sensitivity. They tried to help by making the Indians adopt what they perceived were better ways—USA ways. "Dress like me, act like me, conduct church like we do."

Heather reflects on the current government policies and misdirected activities of the past saying, "In some ways, we are paying for the cultural mistakes of past missionaries and health professionals and sociologists."

The Brazilian government now enforces strict policies designed to preserve and protect the traditional Indian cultures. These policies prohibit Heather and her husband from serving in the designated Indian villages, but not in other surrounding communities that do not live in the traditional indigenous ways. The people in these communities are descended from Indians but not considered part of the protected population.

The villagers whom Heather and her team have served have electricity and a well for water, but they lack adequate food, clothing, and resources needed for basic hygiene. Heather began her work by bringing food and clothing. Heather's social work education and her learning from the past mistakes of others have made her sensitive to and respectful of the cultures in which she serves, trying to teach new ways that fit within their strong traditions. Before she is a teacher, she must be a learner, she says. She must observe and learn their ways. She has learned that people feel honored when she asks to learn from them. Even at the church, she has learned to say, "I have an idea, but I want you to help me know if this would work here."

A Brazilian couple from their congregation, Clemente and Antonia, moved to a village, where they have built a church. The village elected Clemente as President of the Village because he had earned so much respect for the sensitive help that he and Antonia have provided. For example, they have not tried to put running water into homes, but instead to ensure the safety and reliability of the communal well. Running water in homes would tear at the communal culture supported by gathering at the well.

In another example, there is a high rate of childbirth maternal mortality, and Antonia has been able to identify the need for and teach certain hygienic practices that do not replace the ceremonial and cultural practices but give women and babies better odds at life.

Through the influence of a century or more of Catholic missionaries in the area, villagers are largely Catholic, with strong influences from Spiritism, called *Mekumbaria,* that many villagers practice. Heather says that it is a very dark and fear-based belief system, and "many of the villagers report seeing demons." As Heather and members of her ministry began visiting the village, the villagers began to ask questions about their faith because of the stark contrast between Christianity and *Mekumbaria*. Because they are such highly relational people, Heather and her team have taken time to build trusting relationships by listening and learning about their lives.

There are still teams that come to Brazil on short-term mission trips, like Heather did as a student. Heather says:

> It boggles my mind that we will go to these places with a mission team and the villagers will remember specific people who came to visit them. Even after years have passed, the villagers will still ask about certain people. We do not realize the impact of these visits. The villagers are very touched that people would come from so far away to see them.

As a missionary, Heather teaches about the Christian faith to those villagers who want to learn. She believes the message of love that the Gospel offers is one of the greatest gifts she can share with the villagers:

I can give tangible items and encourage people to believe in themselves, but without God, hope is limited at best.

Heather sees no conflict in her teaching Christianity to those who want to learn and her role as a social worker.

On the City Streets

When she is not traveling to the village on the Amazon River, homeschooling children, or providing informal counseling in her kitchen or church office, Heather is leading the congregation's community ministries in their city. Although the ministries receive some support from congregations in the United States, most support comes from Brazilian congregations. A major focus of her work in recent years has been the large population of prostitutes in the city. Prostitution is legal and rampant in Brazil, and from her first visit more than a decade ago, Heather has wanted to help those who have had to resort to prostitution to survive. She began her work with prostitutes right after moving to Brazil:

> I would make cookies, and my husband would drive me to one of the areas known for prostitution. He would sit in the car to keep someone from stealing it, and to watch to be sure I was safe. I would offer the cookies as conversation starters. Many of those I met were men who were transvestites. We became friends. When we started the church, I wanted to involve church members in my work with prostitutes, but I realized church members were not ready to receive these men yet. I just really felt like the Lord was telling me that I needed to put my ministry with prostitutes on hold, and that the time would come when the church would be ready. I stopped going to that neighborhood for a while because I knew I needed a team. I let the men know that I would not be coming back, but that if they needed something, they could get in contact with me.

Heather and her husband made it their mission to prepare their small church, 40 members at the time, to be a place where anybody would find acceptance. Heather says:

> We pounded the idea that the church would be a place where everyone would be welcome and find compassion, regardless of how they looked, what they were wearing, how they made their living, or how they smelled. My husband even said, "If you don't want to be with them, then the door is right there because we're not going to tell them they can't come in."

As a consequence, some church members became interested in the work Heather had been doing and actually asked if Heather would help them start a ministry with prostitutes. With Heather's leadership, the congregation launched the Hosea project. The many volunteers include a psychologist who provides counseling as needed to supplement the counseling that Heather provides to those who seek their help. To Heather's knowledge, there is no other program addressing the issue of prostitution in their city. She has used her community development skills to organize several congregations in the city to work in the ministry. Teams of volunteers go out on the streets with snacks and sandwiches, since many of the young women and men are physically hungry. Eating together becomes a medium for nurturing conversations and friendship:

> We think we honor them by eating with them rather than just watching them eat. Eating together builds bridges. We do not talk about church unless they ask us. They usually do ask; they do not understand why we would come to them with food and friendship. It takes several weeks, and then they begin asking questions such as "Why do you come?" Often, they ask for more contact, "Can I be in contact with you?" Relationships begin to develop.

When these young people say that they want help to escape prostitution, then Heather begins a counseling relationship, meeting them wherever and whenever they can meet with her. She begins by asking, "What's your dream?" For many, their dreams are very limited because life has been very hard:

> One of the dreams I hear a lot is, "I want to go to college someday." I say, "What do you want to do?" "Well I don't know; I just want to go to college." I respond, "You know that's totally possible; I want to hear something that seems completely impossible." They say, "Well that seems impossible to me." I say, "I am telling you that college is possible, and we will help you; but I want to hear, something you think is totally impossible." Then they start speaking about wanting a career or a family.

Heather already sees success; a number of the young women, with their help, have been able to escape prostitution, complete their high school degrees, and obtain employment.

One of the young women with whom Heather has been working, Carlota, actually came to Heather's office, wanting to see the church from which the kind team members had come. Carlota had never had a real job other than prostitution, and she wanted help in finding work. Heather did an informal assessment—she asked Carlota to tell her about her life. Then one of the volunteers who happened to be in the office worked with Carlota on a resume that the church could distribute to help Carlota find an entry level job. Heather left for an errand, and when she came back, Carlota and the volunteer were engaged in conversation with the church's teenagers who were gathering for a worship service and to watch a movie together. Carlota asked if she might stay, even though she came dressed for a night of prostitution rather than watching a movie with the church youth group. The teenagers were kind and welcomed her.

At the end of the evening, Carlota asked Heather, "Do you do weddings here?" Heather responded:

> "Yes, we have lots of weddings." Then Carlota said, "Do you think someday maybe I could get married here?" I said, "I would be so honored if you came and got married here someday." So that to me was just so precious because of where Carlota is coming from and the way she has been treated. In those few hours of kindness and love, she began to really dream about what life could be.

Carlota still does not have a job; she is still a prostitute. With the help of the church, however, she completed her GED, which will make it easier for her to find employment. She is on a new path, even though there is a long way to go.

Heather does a lot of case management as well as counseling. Many of the young women also have children. They need income, but they have no childcare, and so they work as prostitutes at night because that is the only time a family member can provide childcare. Someone has offered the congregation a building and they will use it for a childcare center. That is the next project. Their goal is to provide support for families and a safe place for children while parents are working:

> Recently, the newspaper reported that two small children had died of carbon monoxide poisoning in the night, and the mother was not home. She was a prostitute, and they prosecuted her for neglect. Probably she was out prostituting herself to buy milk for her children. These women prostitute themselves out of dire necessity; she was trying to do the best for her children and then ended up losing them.

The two ministries—one with the Amazon River villages and the other with prostitutes on the city streets—are connected. Traffickers visit the Amazon villages where mothers sometimes are so impoverished that they have trouble affording food for their children. The traffickers offer to take the children to the city and provide them with school. Instead, they enslave children either in private homes as servants or in the sex trade. Several church members had themselves been such children. In addition to working to free children in the city, Heather says to people in the villages:

> If someone comes and promises you that, do not believe them; if you're having problems you need to let us know because we will help you. We do not want you to put your children in those situations.

Cultural Christianity

Heather contrasts the example of Jesus with what she calls the "cultural Christianity" that Americans have exported to Brazil:

> A lot of missionaries tried to make the people become like them. So Brazilian churches are run like American churches with American worship forms, and it just does not communicate in the Brazilian culture. The Brazilians assume that the Western ways in which Christianity came packaged to Brazil is "the right way."

Heather gave an example from an experience she had at a denominational convention in Brazil. The denominational delegates were in an animated discussion about whether or not they should allow a pastor who had changed from their denomination to another denomination to continue to pastor the congregation he had founded. Heather explains that in Brazil it is very unusual for pastors to move around from church to church as they do in the USA. Brazilian pastors usually have started the congregation where they spend their entire life pastoring. Because of this practice, there are not a lot of churches looking for pastors. If the denomination forced the pastor to leave his church, he would either start a new church or have to leave pastoral ministry, and the church would in turn go without a pastor.

As Heather listened to the debate, it was clear the issue had less to do with the current situation facing the church and more to do with trying to make the decision based on the "American denominational model." As the debate continued, Heather stood up and said:

> I have listened to the conversation, and I recognize that you are trying to do this the 'American way.' I am sure that this was introduced to you as the way things are 'supposed' to be done, but the American approach does not work here culturally or financially, and just because it was introduced to you by American missionaries does not mean you have to do it this way.

After Heather spoke, she became nervous at the silence that was the only response. Those presiding quickly decided to end the debate and go to a vote. Contrary to the American denomination rules, they agreed to allow the pastor to stay and continue pastoring the church he started. Heather reflected:

I really think my standing as an American and saying 'the American way is not better,' in some way freed them to do things in a way that was more culturally relevant.

At the same time, Heather and her husband have introduced a cultural shift in their congregation. Many Brazilian congregations are very hierarchical, with the pastor making all the decisions. By contrast, in their congregation, they emphasize equipping the membership for leadership and ministry. The church belongs to the congregation, not to the pastors.

Heather reflected on a young woman who had come from a church with a pastoral hierarchy and began attending their congregation. She was preparing for her wedding. The woman asked Heather to go shopping with her for a wedding dress. In the process of looking at dresses, the store owner agreed to give the future bride a free dress, knowing that she and her fiancé were very poor. Heather went on to describe the experience:

She liked two very different dresses. She looked at me and said, 'I want you to choose which dress I am going to wear'. I paused and then said, 'No, I am not choosing your wedding dress; you need to choose it for yourself.' She said, 'No, no, I can't, I need somebody to choose for me!'" I sensed that it was important that I hold my ground and not make the decision for her. So I said, 'Well then, we are going to walk out of here without a dress because I am not choosing your wedding dress for you!'

When the young woman saw that Heather was not going to budge, she finally selected a dress. Heather talked with her later, and she realized that she had never been given the opportunity to make her own life decisions, even one like choosing her own wedding dress.

Hope in the Midst of Despair

Heather emphasizes in her teaching that the essence of Christianity is love:

We do not say to people, 'We want you to become a Christian.' We say, 'We want to love you; how can I care for you?' Then we try to show that love. That gives us an open door to say, 'God loves you even more than we do.' So many people are so hurt and rejected. They have never had anybody want to love them for nothing in return. We want them to realize that there is a God that loves them and does not ask for anything in return. Once they begin to experience that, they want to love as well. Sometimes we show our love well, and sometimes we fail, but that is our goal.

Heather sees her role as helping the people she serves find purpose and build meaningful lives, so when clients slip back into bad situations, she has to fight discouragement:

> It is just hard when I have poured myself into helping someone who becomes so overwhelmed by the struggle that they give up.

Heather clings to the belief that, no matter what the outcome, she needs to be faithful to God by helping others. Even when there are disappointing outcomes, knowing that people have been touched by the love of God brings her comfort:

> I remember the greatest commandment is love. Love the Lord your God and love your neighbor as yourself. Knowing that I can continue to love people means there is always hope.

Heather believes she is simply living out God's greatest command of "loving God and loving one another," and that is what she seeks to teach her congregation:

> We emphasize that God calls us to love those whom no one loves, who feel unworthy and unwanted. Whoever comes is welcome and we are not going to judge them by their appearance, where they have come from, what they were doing or what they are still doing. We are going to love them because God loves them.

Heather believes she is doing what she has been called and equipped to do as a social worker as well as a minister.

Questions to Ponder

1. Heather believes that her roles as a social worker and as a missionary complement each other. Based on her story, in what ways do these roles fit together or are in conflict with each other?

2. Heather described speaking out at a denominational convention about an issue church leaders were debating concerning church polity. Assess if and how what she did was a social work intervention at the macro level, and how she addressed the cultural issues she saw in the issue.

3. Is going with a young bride in the church she pastors to select a wedding dress and then encouraging her to make the selection herself social work practice? What social work values are involved in what she did, and what you would have done in this circumstance?

4. Heather had described the importance of cultural sensitivity. How does that sensitivity fit with challenging culture in examples such as the one above, in

which a woman in a hierarchical culture is encouraged to make a decision for herself?

5. Heather shares that she initially had a hard time when people in need would show up at her door any time of the day. Do you think Heather made the right decision in trying to adjust to the culture, or is she crossing some important professional boundaries? What would you have done if you had been in her place?

6. Heather mentions several ways her social work skills have aided her in her work in Brazil. What social work skills and/or tools do you see her using in her work?

7. Love is a strong theme in Heather's teaching about Christian faith and in her work as a missionary social worker. How do you integrate your understanding of Christian love with the professional practice and ethics of social work?

Chanphen Yindee
Operations Manager, Rak Lae Pra Pon Foundation
Melissa Ishio, Co-Author

When you meet Chanphen she is likely to apologize for her "not so good English;" her first language is Thai. It is not her use of English that stands out when talking with her, however, but her infectious laughter and passion for her work and her faith. Chanphen is a Christian in a country that is predominately Buddhist; less than 1% of the population in Thailand is Christian. Chanphen first claimed her identity as a Christian when she asked to be baptized as a teenager. She has been claiming her identity as a social worker for most of her adult life. Being a Christian and being a social worker have become the same path for Chanphen.

"And Then I Found Myself"

In college in Thailand, Chanphen majored in commerce. After graduation, her first job was working for a business company. Chanphen remembers sitting in a meeting at work and listening as the manager talked. The entire focus of the meeting was on increasing the profitability of the organization. She noticed that there was no conversation about fairness or justice. Did customers really need the product the company was selling? Was the company asking a fair price for the product? Was the product of good quality? Business meetings never addressed any of these issues. Chanphen remembers wondering how people were valued and supported in an organization with only one goal—making a profit. She remembers thinking:

> What will happen if, when I get older, if I cannot make growing profits for my company?

Chanphen realized she was in the wrong place; her work there seemed meaningless. She quit her job, deciding she wanted to spend her days helping people. She started working as a teacher in a refugee camp for people from Laos, Cambodia, Vietnam and Myanmar. Chanphen saw the struggles and the hardships of their lives:

They had no rights. They had to stay there at the camp. The only thing they could do was to learn from us, so we taught them all that we could.

Chanphen tried to help the people in the refugee camp prepare for the time when they would move to a new country. A year later, an international Christian organization employed her that solicits sponsorships in the U.S.A. and elsewhere. Sponsors commit to making a monthly financial contribution to children to help with food, clothing, and educational expenses, thus indirectly supporting children's families and communities who otherwise live in extreme poverty. Chanphen's task was translating U.S. sponsors' letters into Thai to give to children they were supporting, and also translating children's letters into English to give to their sponsors. She hosted sponsors when they came to visit children and worked on projects such as finding additional funding for school uniforms for children and helping to improve their educational opportunities.

Chanphen was finding her path. She resigned her position to earn another undergraduate degree, this time in Humanities. She studied English as her major language. After graduation, she worked for a decade for the United Nations in Thailand.

In 2004, a devastating tsunami hit the coast of Southeast Asia, including Thailand, with massive destruction and the deaths of more than 230,000 people in fourteen countries. The tsunami destroyed whole communities as ocean waves more than 100 feet in height inundated coastal populations. Chanphen felt God calling her to respond. After much prayer, she quit her job and went with a group from her church to help victims of the tsunami. Soon a Christian organization employed her to coordinate all tsunami relief programs in Thailand. Now she was working directly with people, and she says, "This work was what I had been looking for my whole life." As committed as she was to the work, she felt that she lacked the skills she needed, and she knew she was making mistakes. Therefore, Chanphen left Thailand in 2007 to enroll in a Master of Social Work program in a Christian university in the United States.

"Change Needs Courage"

Chanphen graduated with her MSW in 2009; she returned to Thailand and took a position with a privately funded shelter that works with law enforcement and social services to help rescue children from abusive situations. Three years later, she moved to an American Christian humanitarian organization where she is still employed, Rak Lae Pra Pon Foundation, which means "Love and Blessing." The agency engages congregations from Thailand and around the world in community service and development projects.

As a student, Chanphen had analyzed this organization for a research project. One of her professors, listening to her critique of the organization in a presentation she made at a conference, had challenged her to go back to Thailand and change the organization. Now she is there.

Chanphen's research had explored the organization's culture and proposed changes that she believed would strengthen their services. When Chanphen arrived, the organization had no guidelines for implementing a new program, managing a project, or using finances. Thai culture values hierarchical interpersonal relationships, and so, from a cultural perspective, having no written guidelines and relying on managers to make decisions was culturally congruent. Chanphen determined to change that culture as only a member of the culture could do.

Chanphen's educational experiences in the United States and her work with international organizations had provided her with a perspective new to the agency. Without guidelines and accountability, there is a risk of drift from the organization's mission to the interests and focus of a single leader and even the dangers of corruption. Trying to find the best way to introduce this different perspective was a big challenge for her. In addition, she wanted to implement ongoing program evaluation and strategic planning processes.

Chanphen attempted to implement these changes by beginning with her own team. She loves the people on her team and did not want to change who they are; but she did want to change the way they think about and organize their work together. When Chanphen arrived, the mode of operating was to work on a project, finish it, and then move on to the next project. The only evaluation of their work was counting the number of people served who had been converted to Christianity and baptized. Chanphen developed evaluation policy and procedures for her team that added additional ways of evaluating the impact of their services on the community. These changes have been challenging; Chanphen laughed and said:

> I have support from my coworkers, especially the director who is also my supervisor. But change is not easy. Change needs courage!

Role modeling is one way in which Chanphen is teaching her team how to make decisions. She says, "Every time I make a decision, I also explain to them why and how I made that decision." Chanphen led her team in putting together a statement of organizational mission and standards. The ethical standards that she led the agency in adopting include thirteen statements, beginning with these three:

> We shall perform our duties with mutual respect and with the determination for the common good.
>
> We shall perform with best competence, knowledge and skills in development and aids work to support and assist individuals, groups, communities, local churches and society at large to promote their physical, psychological, emotional, and spiritual wellbeing.

> We shall treat individuals, groups, and communities in need who are beneficiaries with respect and recognize the dignity and worth of a person in accordance with biblical values.

Chanphen says:

> I am trying to 'be the paper for my staff,' to be an example of living the policies and values that we have written together. I don't just want to hold on to those values because I have to; I want them to be a part of my nature.

That she is using her relationship with her colleagues to model new ways of working fits the Thai focus on relationships and hierarchy, even as she modifies the organizational culture.

The staff begins each day with worship and sharing. Although she is a relatively new member of the staff, she says, "They are listening to me; some of the things I talk about they have never heard before. Each day, Chanphen prays that God will help her prepare for the experiences she will face at work; she believes that she is only able to be effective at her work because of divine intervention. Chanphen has also found some like-minded people in her organization, particularly a friend in another department.

> If I have a burden, sometimes I go to her office after work, and I share with her. She knows where I am coming from: that I am a social worker, that I studied and lived in the United States, that I trust in God, and that I trust in praying. So we pray together, and we hope that change is coming. After we pray, things are better and move along, gradually. So prayer is a part of change too.

"Not Jesus Inward But In Action"

One aspect of her job that Chanphen particularly enjoys is being able to show Christ to people. She says, "I enjoy being able to share, not by words, but by action." Chanphen tells her team:

> When you go to do a project, do not just do the project. Stop and look at the people and look at the individual need. If you notice a need in a house or with a family, stop and talk to the family about the need. When Jesus went places, he stopped and looked at people. He saw their needs. He stopped and talked.
>
> I think our job is not so much about talking about Jesus, but it is about talking with people, talking about what they need. We need to empower the church to do the same. It is not just about evangelizing. We need to listen to people's needs. When Jesus fulfilled people's needs, they were able to realize His love.

Chanphen's construction team went into a remote Thai village to help build indoor toilets for homes in that community. Chanphen had just talked with her team about stopping and looking at people. One of her team leaders told her about a young teenage boy in one of the homes whose legs were paralyzed from a gun accident. Even though the team finished the project in that village, Chanphen told the team leader to go back, "Talk with the boy and his mother and see what they really need."

The team leader found out that the boy had been thinking of suicide. He had been a strong, confident boy before, but after the accident, he had become more and more hopeless. So Chanphen and her team member offered him a chance to receive inpatient services in a rehabilitation center where he could learn to be more independent. The people in the village helped the mother get the boy to the rehabilitation center, putting him in the back of an old pick-up truck and driving four hours on dirt roads.

Upon arrival at the rehabilitation center, the boy's condition was very serious; he was malnourished and had many infected bedsores. Chanphen and her team visited him regularly, prayed with him, and arranged for his mother to visit. They also raised funds to help with his medical bills.

The boy now wheels himself everywhere in a new wheel chair. He has learned to transfer from his bed to his wheel chair without any help. He learned to play the guitar and now he plays the guitar and sings Christian songs. He and his mother asked to be baptized. Chanphen says, "That is Jesus in the community—not Jesus inward but in action!"

Assessing Impact

Before Chanphen arrived, much of the agency's work was the provision of services without first assessing the strengths and needs of the communities they served, nor afterwards evaluating the impact of the services provided. For example, a large program of the agency has been the building of water wells with the active engagement of many church volunteers. When Chanphen arrived, she learned that there had been no prior work with communities to determine their own sense of need for water wells, nor was there any maintenance program after wells were built. Consequently, more than 30% of the wells the agency had built had fallen in disrepair. Chanphen took the staff on a tour to evaluate their work. They found that even the placement of some wells had been wrong, too near canals that polluted the wells, creating health hazards.

It took patience and persistence, but Chanphen changed the program, beginning instead with building relationships between the churches that want to build wells and the communities they believe they are serving. More than half of the churches that are currently working with the agency have come on board in the past year, attracted to the new focus on community participation, clear-eyed assessment, and attention to impact. Chanphen praises God for the change.

Organizational Challenges

Chanphen uses the listening and empathy skills she learned in school to come alongside her staff to understand their perspectives rather than just telling them what to do. There have been times, however, when Chanphen has had to confront people. A Christian organization is not immune to the challenges of people misusing their roles and power, of people acting badly. Once she found out that a member of her staff was trying to use his position for personal gain. Chanphen talked with him about the problem and later rated him down in his performance appraisal. When the organization's personnel officer asked her to explain the performance evaluation, she told him he did not need to know this information. She believed the staff member needed a second chance, and that had she told the personnel officer, the staff member would have been dismissed. The personnel officer was not happy with her refusal to share the information, but Chanphen believed she was taking the right path in this situation.

Chanphen says that she thinks she has to be honest in these types of situations but she also needs to be gentle. Confrontation is hard for her; sometimes she goes home and cries because her responsibilities as a supervisor have meant she had to speak honestly to a member of her team in a way that they experienced as hurtful—and that is painful for Chanphen. She thinks that sometimes God lets her feel hurt so she can understand how others feel.

When I talked with Chanphen 18 months after the first interview, there had been some significant changes in the organization. The director is now working on a degree in management and communication, and she likes to talk with Chanphen about her application of what she is learning. Chanphen finds herself providing guidance for her director as she considers ways to create change in the agency.

They do this consultation quietly, because in Thai culture, if Chanphen openly collaborated with the director, others would think she is trying to gain a promotion. As part of their work together, they conducted a communication audit to assess the communication dynamics of the organization from the staff's perspective. Those dynamics are complex; the staff includes Americans, Filipinos, Thai, Chinese Thai, and tribal peoples. Each brings cultural differences.

The communication audit revealed the challenges that Chanphen has been trying to identify for her supervisor. Chanphen experiences this as an intervention from God; now her supervisor is open to learning from Chanphen, and Chanphen is finding opportunities to use what she learned in social work school about management theories. For example, the agency implemented a staff identification system that uses a scanner to identify staff by their fingerprints.

Without conversation or explanation, the agency simply installed the scanners. Chanphen says that the staff has hated the system, but there was no avenue for expressing their concerns. Now the director is asking, based on what she is learning from Chanphen about inclusive management.

And the Future?

Chanphen now has another job offer to direct an organization and she is pondering what to do—it is located in a region of Thailand that she feels called to serve. At the same time, she does not feel God has finished with her in her current work. She is restless and uncertain, saying:

> I am not the kind of person to stay anywhere long; I like to start something and then move on; that is my personal calling. At the same time, I want to be sure that the changes I have helped to implement can be expanded.

Someday, Chanphen would like to form a small organization to bring about community change that can be replicated by congregations.

> My goal for my work is to really exemplify Jesus' ministry in this world. Make it real, but not by myself. Just like Jesus, I want to work with a team. He had a team that impacted the whole world. They did not always have to do big things. Sometimes they did small things with small impacts.

She believes that a smaller group does not need as much funding as a larger organization, but a smaller group does need a big dose of faith. Chanphen believes that God will help her find members for this new group that will not present themselves as experts, but as learners—walking alongside the people they are serving and listening to their needs. Chanphen's goal is not to bring people to Jesus, but to bring Jesus to people. As Chanphen says, "This is how we will bring Jesus to them, and then they will want to come to meet Jesus!"

Questions to Ponder

1. Chanphen had been working for almost 20 years before decided to pursue an MSW in the USA. Put yourself in Chanphen's place and think about moving alone half way around the world to study at a university in a second language. What similar challenges have you faced as you follow your calling? Or might you face as you consider next steps?
2. What changes has Chanphen been able to make in her organization? What change principles has she used in her organizational interventions?

3. Chanphen talks about being able to show Christ to people by actions instead of just by words. According to Chanphen, what do some of these actions look like?

4. Chanphen has helped the agency to evaluate the impact of their services. What is the value of program evaluation from a social work perspective? From a Christian perspective?

5. Chanphen makes the statement, "That is Jesus in the community." What does she mean? What does that statement mean to you?

6. What do you think of Chanphen's dream of forming a group made of people who will present themselves as learners instead of experts? How does the idea of presenting oneself as a learner fit into the helping process?

7. Chanphen has been on a journey in her social work career. What can you apply to your understanding of your own calling?

Physical Health, Illness, and Disability

Martha Ellington
President, Prism, An Adult Day Health Center

Martha Ellington graduated with her MSW in 1993, finally ready, she thought, to pursue her calling to church ministry. All her childhood and teenage years, she had actively engaged in missions in her congregation. She reflects now on the importance of volunteering to help with the Special Olympics and visiting the nursing home as a representative of her church—her first encounters with persons with disabilities. She attended a Christian college, and now she had a graduate certificate in theology and an MSW. She was ready to be a minister in a congregation doing community outreach, and she was excited.

Her first job out of graduate school was as executive director of a church food pantry staffed by volunteers; she thought it was a perfect fit of how she envisioned the church serving the community, the kind of work she wanted to do. Soon she learned that many of the people the pantry served returned repeatedly in need of food to feed their families. These families were chronically "food insecure," unsure of where they would next find adequate food from one month to the next, and many families were trying to raise children in the face of this basic uncertainty. Martha began to ask herself and her volunteers the question, "Why were people having to rely on peanut butter and canned tuna handouts in a country where food is abundant?"

Martha began to challenge the whole concept of emergency food assistance provided in the form of bags of groceries. She thought:

> Why do you have a food pantry, when you can go to the grocery store and get $20 food cards to give people? Why should I give you what I think you want to eat, hoping you like tuna and thinking I know what is best for you, instead of trusting you to

take the card and buy what you like? If I needed help with food, what would I want—someone else to decide what I am going to cook for my children—or the money to buy what I believe they need?

Martha knew that one of the reasons that the church gave bags of food instead of money or gift cards was that they did not trust the clients they served to buy healthy food instead of using the cash or gift card for cigarettes, beer, and junk food. She considered that lack of trust to be judgmental and paternalistic.

She wondered about the source of the problem of chronic food insecurity. Were people eligible for government aid like Food Stamps but did not know how to apply for that kind of help? Or were they not budgeting well and indeed buying expensive junk foods instead of more nutritious and less expensive foods? Martha believed it was her responsibility to push the volunteers with whom she was working to think through how they could address the underlying issues of food insecurity.

Martha was young and as she looks back with twenty-five years of perspective, she believes she tried to create change too quickly. Her suggestions that they switch to gift cards and provide case management services to ascertain the underlying causes of client food insecurity created controversy and challenged deeply held assumptions about poverty, hunger, and ministry in the face of human hunger. Martha was not prepared for the controversy that erupted. "I decided ministry was not for me."

Leaving what she thought would be an ideal position to do what she was called to do did not just create uncertainty; it created a crisis of faith. Suddenly, her future path did not seem as clear as it once did:

> It was hard to regroup. I thought I was doing what I had been called to do—and then I wasn't.

Two More Paths Tried

Twenty-eight at the time she left the community ministry position, she became a job coach in a social service agency, serving people with chronic mental illness such as schizophrenia. Once again, she found herself looking beyond the immediate problems people were facing—needing to become employable so that they could support themselves—to larger systemic problems that were keeping the people she was serving from being able to cope well with the life challenges they faced.

The odds were stacked against her clients; their illnesses were so severe, and the side effects of medication created more challenges, that being able to maintain steady employment was almost impossible. If they were able to find a job, it was often at a low hourly rate, making it difficult to afford housing yet still too much income for them to be able to keep the Medicaid benefits they needed for ongoing treatment of their illness. With no benefits, their illness would quickly undermine even their limited ability to work. Even the stress of the job application process sometimes caused her clients to experience psychotic episodes. They felt hopeless, and as she felt herself caught up in their spirals of chronic illness and poverty and lack of adequate resources to face these challenges, so did Martha. She thought:

> The fact is, there are always going to be people in our communities who are too ill to work for a period of time and perhaps for their whole lives. Do we define people's worth by their holding a job? And if they can't work, then what? Do we just abandon these people to live on the streets or in institutions designed to remove them from our having to care?

Disillusioned and discouraged, Martha quit her second job. She went through the phone book, calling agencies to see if she could find employment. She took a job as a medical social worker with a home health agency, expecting to be a case manager making home visits to clients with chronic or terminal illnesses. The day after she began, the woman who led the program resigned:

> So, my first day on the job was not making home visits. I was thrust into managing the program—and I had to figure out what that meant. 'Figuring it out' is often what social workers do.

The agency served 60 clients. One of those clients was Linda, age 24 at the time. Linda had severe cerebral palsy and the intellectual capacity of a 9-month-old infant. She required total care, and she had been cared for all day every day of her life since she turned 18 by her mother, Bonnie, because no adult daycare program existed for clients with the physical and intellectual challenges that characterized Linda's life. Her mother was facing alone more than 35 years of 24 hour a day care for her daughter, seven days a week.

Once again, Martha found herself trying to serve clients who were trying hard but faced life obstacles that were bigger than they could handle on their own. Surely there was a program somewhere where Linda could be cared for during the day so she would not be isolated at home and her mother would not be trapped by caregiving.

No such program existed. In their whole city, Martha could find no program of day care services for persons between the ages of 21 and 60 who had diagnoses of developmental disabilities, brain injury, multiple sclerosis, or a combination of these challenges. There was Medicaid funding available for people in this age group to receive adult day health services, but no organization was providing them. The only existing option for Linda was a nursing home. There were lots of day care services for children and teens, but they 'aged out' of service provision when they turned 21. There was nothing. Shocked, Martha realized that Linda was not an isolated case:

I looked at my caseload and I had 19 clients who would soon be in the same situation—they, too, were about to become adults. Their working parents were going to have to quit their jobs, and some of them go on welfare, to stay home and provide in-home care 24 hours a day for their adult children. Or they would have to place their child in a nursing home because the parent had to work to live. Nursing homes are not only expensive, but also no parent wants to place their child in a nursing home when that child could be home with them.

Martha could not put this gap in services out of her mind. Even if she had tried, Bonnie, Linda's mother, would not let Martha forget. She called Martha almost daily asking, "What are you going to do to help me find an adult day program for Linda?" Bonnie was caring for Linda 24 hours a day, seven days a week. Linda's world was limited to her mother and the television set.

Bonnie would not give up. She called the State Capitol and then called Martha back and said, "Here are the steps you have to take to open up an Adult Day Center." Bonnie mapped out for Martha what she believed needed to happen. With Bonnie's encouragement, Martha decided to act. She called together owners of home health agencies in the area and explained the need for an Adult Day Center (ADC) for young adults. Everyone agreed there was a need, and the group planned a second meeting to discuss it further. No one came to the second meeting—except Martha.

Somebody Should Do Something

Martha had found a significant gap in services and had concluded that "somebody should do something" for Linda and other young adults who need day care services; surely one of the existing home health agencies would decide to bridge the gap in services. But no somebody stepped up, so Martha decided, "that somebody was me." She talked her life partner, Laura, into joining her to start their own day treatment center. They named it Prism. Laura had experience in the banking industry and so could lead the business side of a new organization. Prism opened thirteen years ago, and Martha laughs, saying, "I had no idea what I was doing."

Two clients came on the first day they opened. They had hired a nurse, and three assistants, two full-time and one part-time. By the second day, they had five clients. In less than a week, they were serving 12 clients each day. Many of those first clients are still with them.

Many of the clients Prism cares for are medically fragile as well as challenged by cognitive and physical disabilities. Most have very limited mobility and some have no ability to speak, although they communicate in sounds and gestures that those who know them have learned to understand. Some cannot feed themselves or control their bodily functions. Martha points out that they all are God's children, as valuable and beautiful as any other of God's children, and worthy of the best care and opportunities to flourish that we can provide. That is her mission.

Benny was a special client in her life—although they are all special to Martha. Severely mentally retarded, he was nonverbal and could only communicate with his eyes. At age 34, he weighed only 38 pounds. He was living with his grandparents, now in their 80s and attending Prism each day. When his grandmother died, an aunt wanted to "put Billy away" in an institution. Benny and his grandfather loved one another, however, and they both loved Prism, so the grandfather arranged for a home health care agency to help him in the evenings with Benny's care so that they could continue to live together. When the grandfather died, Benny had to move to an adult foster home. He contracted pneumonia and died shortly after the move. Martha believes he lived as long as he did because of the love of his grandfather and the care of Prism.

The movement away from large institutions where those with cognitive and physical challenges lived their whole lives away from mainstream society began in the 1960s. President John F. Kennedy made improvement in the care of persons with intellectual disabilities and their families a top agenda of his administration in the 1960s. In 1963, Kennedy signed the Maternal and Child Health and Mental Retardation Planning Amendment to the Social Security Act, as well as other legislation that provided for research into the causes of intellectual disabilities, prevention programs, and community-based centers for persons with developmental disabilities (John F. Kennedy Presidential Library, 2014). It was the first time that families had the hope of any option other than placing a disabled child in an institution or state hospital, often at considerable distance from their homes and, often, for a lifetime. It took years, however, for federal legislation to bring about both (1) changes in attitudes about appropriate care for persons with physical and intellectual disabilities and (2) the development of community-based services—like Prism—that allowed people with disabilities actually to receive care in their communities so that they could live at home. Some of the early clients coming to Prism had come from institutions where they had lived for decades. Martha remembers those early clients:

> They were the forgotten ones. Nobody had worked with them. Nobody had talked to them. Nobody had touched them, and they were now in their forties. They could not walk, talk, or do much of anything. Just exist. We watched them come alive because we loved them, talked to them, and worked with them in occupation, physical and speech therapy.

Passing the Test

It soon dawned on Martha that this federal legislation was just being formulated and passed when many of the clients Prism first served were being born, and for those like Linda who had been born with significant disabilities, their parents had few options.

> Everyone, including the medical professionals advising them, assumed that they would put their children in an institution; so the families we were serving were those who had bucked the system. They had made advocacy for their children a central focus of their lives. They had fought long and worked hard to keep their children with them, at home.

These families were strong advocates for the best possible care for their children and fiercely protective of their wellbeing. Martha became their ally.

About six weeks after Prism opened, Martha says a parent who brought her daughter to the day center asked Martha to dinner. She proceeded to drill Martha with questions, taking a long list from a folder she had brought with her to the restaurant. "Who are you? Why are you qualified? Who's backing you? What's your Plan B?" Finally, satisfied, she put her list aside and told Martha her story. "For 10 years, since my daughter graduated from high school, what you do at Prism is what I have wanted for her."

Martha laughs, remembering that encounter:

> I guess I passed her test because she got on the phone and put the word out. 'This place is OK. Give this woman a call.' We went from having 12 or 13 clients a day to a waiting list. Evidently, these parents had all been home with no relief from taking care of their child, with television as their only outside contact, child and parent completely trapped.

Prism Today

Prism, now with 67 staff members, serves 125 clients every day, five days a week. They have vans to pick clients up from their homes. The staff calls their agency "a factory of smiles." Because their clients are all medically fragile, the staff is keenly aware that every day might be the last day for one of their clients—and they want to be sure that it is the best day it can be. No one sits in a wheel chair in front of a television or parked in a hallway. The staff fills the days with activities—therapeutic program activities from arts and crafts to music and exercise. And there are parties for any and all occasions. The agency serves nutritious snacks and meals individualized to dietary needs. There are always nurses in the center, as well as occupational, physical and speech therapists. The average age of their clients is 36 and the most common diagnosis is cerebral palsy.

Although none of the clients they serve are likely ever to be employed, many make progress. Clients have learned to walk for the first time, to communicate more effectively—and to smile a lot. To illustrate, Martha told us the story of Ruth, who had recently graduated from high school and had aged out of the day care program for children with cerebral palsy. The vocational rehabilitation service had given Ruth an electric wheelchair, and the mother was anxious to find a day treatment program for Ruth so that she could continue working to support the family. When Martha asked the mother why Ruth needed a wheelchair, she said, "If Ruth is in the living room and I can't get to her quickly, she just crawls to the kitchen." Martha asked the mother when Ruth had last had physical therapy, and she just shook her head and said, "first grade." Martha recognized that if Ruth could crawl, she had potential for greater mobility than an electric wheelchair would encourage. Through the physical therapy services at Prism, Ruth learned to walk with assistance. Martha reflects:

> She may not be able to walk as well as some people, but she can walk; we have to give people a chance.

Prism also provides counseling services to clients' families in their homes and case management services. Martha knew from the first families they served that by caring for these adult children, they are caring for their families. Martha explained:

> We have to address the needs in the family that the child's challenges have created or complicated. Our program is unique because 82 percent of our clients are living with their families; only 18 percent live in group homes. The trend in other programs for clients like ours is that 75 percent live in group homes, where there are several clients who are together cared for by paid staff members, not their own family environment. Families must deal with the impact of having a medically fragile and intellectually challenged member on the lives of other children, on careers, and on marriages. Parents face the reality that their child may well outlive them—how can they provide for their ongoing care? Prism provides social workers to walk with them through these life challenges and decisions.

Her Daily Work

Martha loves the challenge of taking a difficult, if not seemingly impossible, reality and turning it on its ear. She is a big-picture, macro thinker who admits her management style is "chaos and disorder." Hiring a manager to take over the hour-to-hour details was key to the center's success.

> Getting it open and up and started and operating—that really has been my expertise as a social worker. That is what I'm good at in my career. I love to take a problem and focus on what we are going to do to fix it. I like to get it up and running, but that is when I am finished.

As the staff grew and other specialized positions were filled, Martha was able to transition into a new role of advocacy and the one she thinks is her gift—that of "agitator," as she says. Agitators are people who sow seeds of discontent when there is too much comfort and complacency with the status quo. She spends a great deal of her time these days with legislators, fighting the hard fight with state government to maintain funding for the populations Prism serves. Martha explains:

> Currently in our state, 19 percent of our dollars for long-term care go to community-based care, and another 81 percent goes to nursing homes and institutions. We would love to see it be 50/50. That has been our whole philosophy, to rebalance long-term care expenditures. It is less expensive to help people live in their own homes, and that is where they are happiest. We just need to provide the supports that families need to keep loved ones home and not in an institution, if that is what they want.

Challenging the status quo is her new vocation. She learns the reasons given behind policies and challenges them. Who made that rule? Who says it has to be this way? Since the Supreme Court upheld the Americans with Disabilities Act's "integration mandate" in the Olmstead decision in 1999, Martha and others fighting for the rights of individuals with severe disabilities have firmer ground from which to battle. The Olmstead case began when two women, Lois Curtis and Elaine Wilson, both with mental illness and developmental disabilities, were voluntarily admitted to a hospital psychiatric unit. After their treatment, and after mental health professionals stated that they both were ready to be moved to a community-based program, the hospital continued to confine them for several years, until they filed suit under the Americans with Disabilities Act for release. In 1999, the United States Supreme Court held in *Olmstead v. L.C.* that unjustified segregation of persons with disabilities constitutes discrimination and that public entities must provide community-based services when such services are appropriate and clients desire such care (United States Department of Justice, 2014).

Martha describes her work:

> I make sure the stories I live with every day get told. Linda's mother told me that when her daughter was born, the doctor put the infant in her arms and said to her, "She's a 'Mongoloid.' You should go ahead and put her in an institution now." Her mother went on: "That was 43 years ago. I didn't do it then and I don't

want to do it now. But now I'm tired and I can't get home health service." The rules of home health care did not allow her to receive the services of an in-home caregiver. All she could afford is an occasional babysitter as a companion—someone who just took the daughter to the mall to let her sit all day. Until Prism.

Martha came to a time that she thought she was finished and wondered what to do next. She had moved from being the Executive Director to being President of the Board and less engaged in the daily work of the agency. Prism was humming along, heralded by parents and state legislators alike as a model program. She had mentored Teresa, the agency social worker, to assume a leadership position; Teresa is now the Executive Director.

As she wondered where her path would lead next, leaders in other communities began asking if she would help them replicate the Prism services in their cities. She has become a popular speaker on the topic of community-based services for persons with disabilities and often preaches in congregations, thankful for the opportunity to use the combination of her theological and social work education and her lifetime of experience in walking alongside persons with intellectual and physical challenges and their families. She is hopeful that her speaking and preaching will inspire others to develop adult day health centers. Most communities have adult day health centers but are more focused on moderate level care for seniors, not on adults who are medically fragile and with developmental challenges. Martha believes that it is just a matter of time until Prism is replicated to provide services for adults with disabilities, veterans with war-sustained brain injuries, and persons with multiple sclerosis.

Social Work as Ministry

She defines "community ministry" differently than she did in 1993, when she first started out with her new MSW degree. She says:

> I remember in class one of the professors saying, "You don't know when or where or what, but you'll find your calling. For some of you it will be the homeless, for some seniors, but you'll find it." I don't think I really grasped that until now. I think I found an amazing ministry. This is my passion.

Recently Martha shared with me the rest of the story of Linda, whom doctors recommended institutionalizing as a baby born with Downs Syndrome. Martha said, "I'm not sure what you will think about what I did as a social worker, but I just did what I thought I needed to do." She went on to tell me the story:

> Linda had a massive heart attack and they were waiting for her brother to come before they ended life support and allowed

her to die. Linda had been with us since the beginning week of Prism, and Bonnie, her mother, has gone to the State Capitol with me countless times to testify in behalf of persons with life challenges like Linda. At the hospital, Bonnie said to us that she was ready to let Linda go and talked about how much better Heaven would be with Linda coming in. I told about how she has inspired me and I have told Linda stories in the workshops I do. The mother is a saint; she has been taking care of Linda for 48 years. Her husband was killed when Linda was five years old, so she has carried on alone.

When we got ready to leave the hospital, I reached for Bonnie's hand and she grabbed on tightly. I asked her, would she like us to pray? She said 'Please! Please, Martha.' And so I did. It felt like a privilege to hold this saint's hand and tell her how much I loved her and Linda and I don't know what all else I said, but just to hold hands and cry was a gift to me. I had been Linda's social worker for 24 years, half her life.

Later the family asked Martha to give a eulogy at Linda's funeral, which she did, including the story of heaven being happier with Linda there, a reading of John 14:2, in which Jesus said that he was going to prepare a place for us. Martha ended by leading the congregation in singing the hymn "When we all get to heaven." Martha shared later that if Linda had been placed in an institution 48 years earlier, she never would have lived such a long and full life. She is in awe of the fierce love and dedication of her clients' families, and of the gift of sharing life with them.

Recently, Martha was speaking at a conference about her work with families. She describes the work as being an agent of hope—social workers can provide hope to families imprisoned by the disability of a member. She said a hospice social worker came to her in tears afterward, saying she had been doing the work for 30 years, and she needed the reminder of what it is she is supposed to be doing. Martha is an agent of hope not only for families, but also for social workers who, like she was in her early jobs, seemingly trapped along with their clients in systems that create hopelessness rather than hope.

Martha wants to help congregations minister more effectively to persons like her clients and their families. Some of her families have told her that their congregational leaders have taken them aside and told them not to bring their adult child back to church because others found their presence disruptive and interfering with worship. Consequently, they have lost their church at a time, Martha believes, they need community most.

Yet there are signs of hope. One congregation in her city offers a "Friday Night Life" program for adults with disabilities—three hours of fun activities, staffed by professional employees and volunteers—giving their families an evening of respite care. Other congregations have found ways to embrace and include; one of the residents sings in her church choir every Sunday, recently wearing a hat she had made at Prism in an art activity.

Martha believes her calling is figuring out how to develop programs to address needs; for her, that is a way of "sharing the good news." In reflecting on how her career and ministry as a social worker have unfolded, Martha recalls what she described as "the best sermon" she's ever heard in which a chaplain referred to a man she had met who was homeless and said, referring to the man, "I saw Jesus today." Martha told me:

> Visitors come through Prism and are impressed by what they see. They say 'God bless you for what you do. They look at Prism participants and all they see is problems and brokenness. That is because they do not know them. When I look at one of my program participants, I see a God-created human being, and I know each one of them—what they love and what they hate, and how to make them smile. I see Jesus everyday as I see them. Every day I get to worship and minister as I journey life with these program participants and their families. And I walk through the grief with families who lose their precious ones. This is my calling.

Questions To Ponder

1. Martha believed God had called her to missions as a leader in a congregational setting—and yet her "ideal" first job came to a disappointing end. If you were Martha, how would your belief that you were pursuing your Christian calling impact your reaction to such a disappointment?

2. Have you been a part of a congregation that had a food pantry or something similar? What kind of reaction can you imagine in that congregation to the idea of using gift cards rather than bagged groceries for emergency assistance? What are the social work values that are at play in determining the best way to help with human needs like hunger?

3. In Martha's second job, she asked rhetorically whether persons' worth is defined by their employment. What are the implications of a Christian response to her question? Of a social work response?

4. How do you see Martha's early experiences in social work practice—at the food pantry, the employment coaching for persons with mental illness, and the home health agency—preparing her for her founding and leadership of Prism?

5. What do you imagine the professional relationship is like with families and clients whom Prism has served for years? Martha describes a mother taking her out to dinner. How do you imagine professional boundaries and professional relationships to be different in this kind of practice setting as compared to a setting like an emergency room where clients may only be seen once? What are the advantages and disadvantages of those differences?

6. How would you map the relationship between Martha's direct practice with clients and her role as an advocate, organizational designer, and macro-practitioner?

7. Martha uses the term "program participants" rather than "clients" or "patients." What does the use of terminology communicate?

8. Martha expressed uncertainty about how other social workers would evaluate her decision to hold hands, pray, and grieve with Bonnie, Linda's mother. What is your perspective on the role of social worker as minister and friend with service recipients?

Courtney Barrett
Hospital Social Worker

Part of Courtney Barrett's job as a clinical social worker in an outpatient clinic for senior adults was to check the "Death Board." Daily, the names of patients in the clinic who had died in the previous twenty-four hours were added to it. After three years in her job, Courtney said she had still been amazed at how quickly the board filled up.

She had experienced the reality of the death board in her own life—not once but four times, losing all her grandparents in rapid succession. It was the loss of her "Memaw" that was the hardest for Courtney. "She was the third grandparent I lost in a year, but she was the one who was like a parent to me; she raised me."

When Courtney was a child, her mother, a single parent, worked long hours to provide for her family. Courtney stayed at her grandmother's house until her mother remarried when Courtney was 6 years old. "I didn't go to daycare. I went to Memaw's house."

During her grandmother's last year, Courtney's aunt took the primary responsibility for her care, but Courtney went one weekend a month to give her aunt a respite. It gave her the opportunity to experience "the other side" of her practice, i.e., the hands-on caregiving and, ultimately, the death, she says.

Courtney has no doubt she is right where she needed to be, caring for the people she needs to care for, to which she credits her grandmother. "She is absolutely the reason I chose to work with older adults as a career. I am doing really good work because of her inspiration in my life."

Although she grieved the loss of her grandmother, Courtney learned to cope with the realities that face many of her clients of diminished health and death. Her clients' names were sometimes on that death board. She loved working to make the last season of life for her clients meaningful and joyful.

Courtney decided as a student that she wanted to work with older adults. She learned that social workers provide case management and direct services to older persons and their families across a wide array of community settings, from nursing homes and hospice to in-home services. They also administer long-term care agencies, develop new programs, and insure that the voices of older persons shape organizational and public policy. Empowering older adults who are vulnerable to neglect because of their ill health or poverty, recognizing an individual's unique assets, and strengthening bonds between generations are the unique contributions of social workers with this population group. In sum, social workers walk alongside adults in the second half of life as they encounter the opportunities and challenges of longevity and life transitions.

A Day in the Outpatient Clinic

Courtney was one of two social workers in the senior outpatient clinic in a state teaching and research hospital. Between them, they tried to meet and offer their services to every patient who came to the clinic, which usually meant that Courtney consulted with five or more patients in the clinic each day. Courtney worked particularly with patients with chronic health issues, especially those who have received a diagnosis of early stage dementia. Courtney also provided support for patients with terminal illnesses as well as their caregivers.

Courtney's work usually began with an assessment of the patient's psychological and social wellbeing. Courtney was especially watchful for signs of depression or anxiety, both common in the face of health challenges. Sometimes she met with patients alone; often, however, she included caregivers—spouses, children, whoever was providing the patient's daily care—to discuss her assessment as well as other diagnostic information. Courtney provided a professional relationship and environment where the patient and family could ask questions and explore what they may have been too emotionally overwhelmed or confused to ask the physician: "How will this disease progress?" "What will this the condition and treatment mean for how I live my life?" "For my family?"

> When I see a patient, I also check for other needs beyond the medical aspect. Do they have nutritious meals available? Do they need Meals on Wheels or home health care services? Can they afford their medical insurance and medications? Many patients do not know what services are available or how to gain access to services that are offered. Medical needs cannot be separated from all the other aspects of life that influence health and wellbeing.

Given the issues her patients face, Courtney knew that she would not have opportunity to develop long-term relationships with some of them. The life expectancy for a majority of their patients was not long, she said, and many were referred to hospice, which means, sooner or just a little longer, she knew she would see their names on the Death Board.

Working Collaboratively

Courtney was a member of a team that provided clinic patients with mental and physical health services. Others included geriatricians (physicians who specialize in the care of older adults), psychiatrists, psychologists, dietitians, physicians' assistants, nurses, and physical therapists. The pace was too fast for a set meeting time, so they have "fly-bys" in the workroom, in which team members communicate an immediate need with one another. The physicians' schedules varied and some were only in the clinic a few days per week, so Courtney made sure she flagged patient needs for the physicians in the electronic medical chart. Her days were filled with her work with patients and caregivers and the seemingly unending work of recording notes and completing other paperwork like letters and forms for the physicians.

Courtney appreciated being a part of the cutting-edge medical care that her teaching hospital provided. She helped initiate a palliative care clinic, which focuses on easing the patient's experience through serious illnesses, because she saw the need for that kind of care for patients with chronic pain and terminal conditions. Courtney worked with those patients on a more consistent basis.

Not all physicians understand the importance of the social worker's role in holistic health care, Courtney said. Some seem to think that social workers are primarily counselors who can help when there is an emotional crisis. Courtney recognized that it was her job to educate the physicians on the ways she could help the physicians help their patients:

> I spent a lot of my time intentionally building relationships with physicians, so they will remember I am here to be used; those who are successful in providing holistic care and meeting social service needs are the ones who make social workers an integral part of their team.

Least Favorite Part

Without a doubt, the part of her job Courtney liked least was wrestling with how billing guidelines control the kinds of services they could provide. Courtney says Medicare guidelines are often difficult to interpret and do not adequately consider how social workers interact with patients and/or their families. The guidelines did not allow her to bill for social work services with a patient if it did not take place on the same day of that person's visit to the physician, for example. Medicare also does not provide reimbursement for work with families apart from the patient.

Courtney gave an example:

I had adult children of a patient call me to set up a family consultation, and I was excited because I knew they were trying to provide the best care for their father, who had been diagnosed with Alzheimer's Disease. But they did not want to bring their father with them because they thought our conversation would be too overwhelming for him. I pondered what to do, and I met with them anyway, even though the hospital could not be reimbursed for my time.

Ethical Challenges

The number one ethical challenge Courtney struggled with was the client's right to make their own decisions versus their safety, and she believes that the right to self-determination is a challenge for anyone who works with the elderly. Patients have the right to make their own decisions and ethically, social workers must allow them to do so. However, Courtney has found it is a fuzzy line and one that often conflicted with what she believed was the best course of action for a patient. She gave an example:

> If a patient is a hoarder and has filled their home with so much stuff that there are only narrow paths through the rooms, and the home health provider refuses to go into the house because it is so dirty, then I call Adult Protective Services. If Adult Protective Services does not believe the patient is in any immediate danger and takes no action, then I have to talk with the patient. If she does not want anything to change, and she does not want to leave her home, then I have the responsibility to allow her to decide for herself, even though I believe she is unsafe and may even die in that environment.

Courtney described another patient who was rapidly failing physically. She lived alone and her siblings, in their 80s, were trying to take care of her. The patient was deaf and could not tolerate hearing aids, and so she could not use the telephone. She had four adult children, and Courtney said she asked the patient repeatedly to allow her to notify her family about her failing health. Finally, the patient agreed that Courtney could call one of her sons. Courtney left three messages for the son but none was returned. The woman died a week later in her home.

> That's where she wanted to be. That was her decision. My opinion was she should not have died alone, but she made her decision and I honored it. Things like that happen daily. It is tough. That is why it is so important to find constructive ways to deal with my own emotional reactions. Sometimes I just go home and cry, but

that does not happen very often. More often I try to find positive ways to process my feelings and rejuvenate myself.

Other Challenges

Courtney also experiences anger and frustration that she cannot do more to help older adults who suffer abuse physical, verbal, and financial abuse by family members or caretakers. Sometimes the abuse is physical or verbal—actual physical assault or emotional cruelty. Sometimes the abuse is financial, when caregivers take the older adults' financial resources for their own purposes. Courtney referred about 20 cases a year to Adult Protective Services. She did not believe any of them resulted in any action being taken, however. Investigations would conclude that the allegation of abuse was unfounded, because older adults in poor health were often reluctant to report mistreatment if they feared being taken out of their homes.

> It is really hard to not think about what will happen to them when I walk out the door at the end of the day. I do what I can, but it is still hard, knowing a patient is going to be back in the situation where they may be hurt. I believe the system has failed them. If they were 6-year-olds, they would be removed from the home and placed in foster care, but because they are 86, no one seems to care.

Faith and Practice

Because Courtney worked in a state hospital, there was limited, but still some, opportunity for her to initiate conversation with patients about religion and faith. She would ask patients what they draw upon for strength in times of adversity, and many told her about their religious faith—whether that is Christianity, Islam, Buddhism, or something else. "I try to help my patients use their faith to draw strength for what they are facing."

Courtney credits a lot of who she has become as a social worker and the essence of who she is as a person to being a Christian. Her grandmother's influence on her life as a young child set Courtney's life course:

> My grandmother was a faithful Christian and believed very strongly in helping people, and I grew up wanting to be like her. My faith is the reason that I do what I do. I want to be the hands, the feet of Christ—to do what I believe I'm called to do.

Courtney draws on her faith and her Christian beliefs to strengthen her for the work, just as she helps patients draw on their faith for the strength they need to face the health challenges before them.

On most mornings, Courtney arrived before the rest of the staff, and she used that time at her desk to pray for her patients, her co-workers, and for the strength and wisdom for the work she would do that day. "It's my way of entering into the still before the storm," she says.

She draws from one particular passage of Scripture to keep her centered:

> Therefore we do not lose heart. Though outwardly we are wasting away, yet inwardly we are being renewed day by day. For our light and momentary troubles are achieving for us an eternal glory that far outweighs them all. So we fix our eyes not on what is seen, but on what is unseen. For what is seen is temporary, but what is unseen is eternal (2 Cor. 4:16-18, NIV).

She said:

> That is my focus on my practice. What I do may not be outwardly seen or rewarded, but I am doing good work for the right reasons. If am doing the best I can, then that is all that God expects from me.

A Career Change

Even with the frustrations, the Death Board, the challenges of Medicare, and circumstances that cannot seem to change, Courtney was unwavering in her belief that she was doing exactly what she was meant to do. Yet after four years at the clinic, and two years after my first interview with her, she left what she still calls her "dream job." The administration changed, and Courtney clashed with her new supervisor, who Courtney says did not understand the role of a social worker in a medical clinic, especially when Courtney's services could not be fully reimbursed by patients' medical insurance. Courtney says that she delayed leaving for two months because she wanted to be sure that her patients "were treated the right way." But when a job at the Veterans Administration (VA) hospital was posted, Courtney applied and was hired as a medical/surgical social worker.

Courtney now works with veterans who come to the hospital for neurological problems and vascular or gynecological surgery. The neurology patients are usually older adults dealing with strokes and their complications, Parkinson's disease, and amyotrophic lateral sclerosis (ALS), often referred to as "Lou Gehrig's Disease." Courtney's helps patients and their families cope with difficult diagnoses and end-of-life issues, often connecting them with needed resources for coping at home after they leave the hospital.

A Day in the VA Hospital

Courtney's workday begins in meetings with treatment teams where they review scheduled surgeries, patients' progress, and discharge plans. Courtney then visits each of the patients scheduled for surgery that day to identify any concerns they may have that she can address. Her next set of rounds is with patients whom the hospital is discharging. Courtney makes sure that they have everything they need—from transportation to medical assistance at home—to cope with the medical challenges they are facing. Courtney then proceeds to doing the same kinds of psychosocial assessments she did at the outpatient clinic with any patients newly admitted to the hospital. She muses that the work she does is very much a continuation of her work at the outpatient geriatric clinic; the only difference is that all of her patients are veterans, most are male, and not all are older adults.

When I asked Courtney to tell me about one of her more recent patients, she told me about Mr. Smith, who came to the hospital with vascular disease that resulted in an amputation of one of his legs below the knee. The surgical team asked Courtney to help prepare him emotionally for the upcoming surgery, which Mr. Smith had not expected. Courtney says:

> Like most of the patients I see, he is a little rough around the edges and does not talk about his feelings. I just went into his room and joined in watching football on TV with him and tried to develop rapport. The next day I talked to him and told him he would be going to surgery the following day, and asked how he is dealing with that. He talked about how much he wants to be sure he receives a prosthesis.

Courtney knew that the physician does not think Mr. Smith would be a good candidate for a prosthetic device, doubting that he would follow through on the rehabilitation that would be required. So Courtney began counseling with Mr. Smith, preparing him for the emotions of an amputation and the hard work of rehabilitation. She also arranged transportation, so that Mr. Smith could actually get to the rehabilitation clinic to do the work needed to obtain the prosthesis that is so important to him. Courtney said, "It's a lot of phone calls, a lot of coordination."

Despite the seriousness of the work of a hospital, the days are also full of laughter. Courtney says:

> These guys are funny; they are not pretentious. They have seen things that I don't ever want to see, and they have a wisdom about life and death. They joke, and sometimes their humor is very inappropriate, but it is their way of coping—and it helps us cope, too.

Courtney still reflects wistfully on her previous job. There she was able to develop deep relationships with many patients from the time they first came to the clinic until their death. At the VA hospital, patients are much more likely to leave in a matter of days, and Courtney has too much responsibility in the hospital to follow up with patients after they return home. Consequently, Courtney does not receive the appreciation from her patients that she had received in the geriatric clinic, but she says she does not need those shows of appreciation as much as she did earlier in her career, when she was fresh out of school and still uncertain of herself. She now is confident in her role and that she is doing what she needs to be doing for her patients.

Years had passed since my interview with Courtney when she was working at the geriatric clinic, and with the job change, I wondered how she now viewed the relationship between her Christian faith and her professional work. She said to me:

> It is still why I do what I do. I did not choose social work for the money. I do make a good living; I own my house and vehicle, and I can buy pretty much anything that I need. Because of the emotional toll social work costs, I have to be doing it for a more compelling reason than my salary. I want to be Jesus to the least of these. I want to make a difference in people's lives like Jesus did.

It Has Changed Me

Courtney reflects on how the work has changed her. A 38-year-old female veteran had come into the hospital three weeks before our interview, still alive but with an artery bleeding into her brain that had robbed her of the ability to communicate or walk. She did not do drugs; she had not done anything to cause the freak medical crisis. Another patient had come to the hospital with mild stomach pain that turned out to be an aneurism, and he died. The families were shocked and grieved, and Courtney grieved with them:

> It is difficult for me to see people who are struggling and broken; it is not a happy job. Yet I find it fulfilling. I help them cope, even as they suffer; I am doing what I was called to do.

Dreaming a Future

Although Courtney loves her job, she has plans in the future. She would like to start an agency that will help support older adults who want to continue to live independently but who need help to do so. She knows that many adults could continue to live at home if they just had a wheelchair ramp—but they cannot afford to build one:

The VA provides that for veterans, but if older adults are not veterans and cannot afford to build a ramp, they are either captive in their home or find themselves in institutional care.

Her family shares her dream. Her brother can build ramps for those who need but cannot afford them. She wants to match older adults with people who are willing to meet their needs to stay independent, and she wants to do it as a tribute to her grandmother. Perhaps there will be another section to this chapter in a future edition.

Questions to Ponder

1. Courtney's experience as a child with her own grandmother influenced her decision to work with older adults. What experiences have shaped your own journey thus far as a professional social worker?

2. Given how Courtney chose to work with older adults, would you call her work a Christian calling? Why or why not?

3. What are your reactions to the Death Board? What social work values and ethics might be related to this feature of clinic staff communication?

4. Courtney describes her struggle with allowing patients to make their own life decisions, such as when they need to move into a care facility instead of staying in their own homes, or what to communicate to their children about their illnesses—especially when Courtney believes they are not making the best choices. In fact, social workers with all population groups have to come to terms with how to respect client self-determination in the face of their belief that clients are making poor choices. What, if anything, makes this struggle especially challenging when the client is in declining health?

5. Courtney calls those she serves "patients." What other terms have you read thus far for what social workers call those with whom they work? What influences—and should influence—the terms we use?

6. Given that Courtney viewed her first job as her "dream job," how has she made sense of her career journey to a new position and how has it shaped her dream for the future? What are the common threads in the previous, current, and future practice settings on Courtney's path?

7. How are Courtney's faith and professional journey related?

Kara Terry
Nursing Home Care Manager
14

As an MSW student, Kara imagined herself doing social work at the macro level. So after graduation, she took a position with the public health district. She supervised the diabetes education program, overseeing diabetes education in different locations around the city. She also led groups herself on the topics of nutrition and preventing heart disease and cancer wherever she was invited—often social service organizations and senior centers. At the senior centers, she also added topics such as living with arthritis.

As much as she enjoyed doing the research to develop the educational programs and then developing the programs and delivering them, Kara missed having relationships with individuals and families as ongoing clients. She found herself feeling bored. She began a Ph.D. program, but right after she enrolled, she learned the delightful but unexpected news that she was pregnant. Her daughter was born the next semester, and she dropped out of doctoral studies. She told herself that someday, when her daughter is a little older, she will return for the doctoral degree. In the meantime, Kara began looking for a job.

When Kara had been an undergraduate student, her grandmother had a surgery that required physical rehabilitation; she had spent a few weeks at St. Theresa, a nursing and rehabilitation center. Kara remembers being struck by the warm and supportive atmosphere, by how helpful a social worker had been to her family. That experience had actually drawn Kara to social work. So when someone in her life group at church told her that there was a social work job opening at St. Theresa, Kara jumped at the chance. "I just felt like the universe was conspiring to put me there," Kara reflects.

St. Theresa Center is part of a Catholic organization, Trinity Health Network. At St. Theresa, Kara is the social worker responsible for the care of a hundred patients on the two nursing home floors of the four-floor facility. The floors Kara serves provide long-term care; the other floors serve patients with short-term rehabilitation care. St Theresa is home for the foreseeable future for Kara's patients, who are mostly older adults. She loves her work with the patients and their families—"I look forward to going to work everyday."

Kara feels honored to serve her clients, especially those who are in crisis after the death of a spouse or facing their own terminal illness. For example, Mr. and Ms. Myers were both residents at St. Theresa, but he was living on the fourth floor and she on the first floor, which is the unit serving those with memory loss. Ms. Myers was in the early stages of Alzheimer's disease. She had been receiving hospice services, but she had rallied and her health actually improved. Then Mr. Myers became terminally ill; once again, hospice services became involved with the couple.

Mr. and Ms. Myers had only one another; they had no children, only a nephew who occasionally visited. The loneliness was even worse, however, because Mr. Myers' declining health meant he was no longer mobile enough to make the journey from the fourth floor to the first floor to visit his wife. After decades of living together, they were hopelessly separated from one another. Ms. Myers was aware that her husband was dying and was extremely anxious and upset. Learning of their predicament, Kara advocated successfully for them to be moved into adjoining rooms. Mr. Myers died just three weeks later. They were able to be together for those last three weeks, and Ms. Myers anxiety diminished. Mr. Myers died peacefully, though Ms. Myers was bereft at losing him. Kara spent time with Ms. Myers, just sitting with her and listening to her as a way of supporting her and communicating that though she was lonely and grieving, she was not alone. Kara stays very busy, with more the 100 patients and their families for whom she is responsible. Those quiet times sitting with Ms. Myers had to be carved out of a busy schedule, and her patience in listening is a skill she has had to nurture in the press of demands on her time.

Kara uses the word "honor" to describe her work with her patients; "I am honored to do this work with them; it is not just a job."

Kara reminds herself frequently that she is working in their homes, and so she seeks to treat them as she would want to be treated by someone working in her home; when she walks into their rooms, she recognizes that she is a guest and they are her hosts. Taking the role of guest gives her relationship with her clients a more equal relationship than if she takes the role of medical staff treating patients in a medical facility. This simple shift in role encourages more client agency and self-determination, more engagement in the decisions and choices that have impact on their daily lives.

Kara recognizes how lonely some of her patients are who have few family members or friends nearby; some have outlived everyone dear to them. Kara's goal, therefore, is to create connections with others—other residents or volunteers—and to create as comforting and comfortable a home environment as possible in a medical facility.

Like so many other social workers, the burden of paperwork and progress notes is the least favorite part of her work, but she even sees the paperwork as important—it gives her a focus for her visits with the residents. Every three months, she must complete a mental health exam, a depression screening, and update the social history for each resident, so the paperwork actually organizes her work.

She reflects back to the social worker who helped her family when her grandmother was a resident on the rehabilitation floor. Kara comes from a well-educated family. She remembers how surprised her parents were at how difficult they found it to navigate the health care and elder care systems. They simply could not have done what needed to be done for Kara's grandmother without professional help—education and income did not protect them from needing a social worker. Kara remembers how kind the social worker was, how calm and patient; she guided them as they navigated the bewildering systems and decisions that faced them. Now Kara looks at the rehabilitation floor where her grandmother received care and realizes what a fast pace there is as people are admitted and discharged on a daily basis, and what a press of responsibilities that social worker must have been carrying—but none of that interfered with her presence and care for Kara's family. Kara is trying to be that kind of presence in the lives of the residents and families she serves.

A Normal Week at St. Theresa

Two days each week, Kara begins her morning with a brief staff meeting, followed by care plan meetings that include the social worker, the dietician, the floor nurse manager, the floor activities director and, whenever possible, the resident and the resident's family. Together, they consider the current care plan to see if it needs to be changed in some way to better meet the needs of the resident. Care plans are developed when a new resident is admitted, and then are revisited every three months. In addition, whenever there is a change in the resident's condition—a new diagnosis, a significant loss of weight, the development of pressure ulcers from being in bed or wheel chair, or a change in their mental status, the staff meets to change the plan. Kara makes sure that families know that they do not need to wait for a scheduled care plan meeting; if they are concerned about an issue, they, too, can call a meeting. Kara enjoys these meetings, which often last more than an hour; it is fascinating to see how the web of different disciplines works together with the family.

One afternoon each week, Kara participates in a meeting with all the physical therapists, occupational therapists, and speech therapists. There they discuss the care of all their patients. Kara spends the remainder of the day documenting the meetings of the morning and working on social histories with her clients. On one day each week, Kara retreats to write other reports that are required. Although she enjoys the busy days of meetings and interaction with clients, she also enjoys the quiet and sense of satisfaction that comes from finishing those reports.

Whatever meetings are or are not scheduled, Kara responds every day to the emerging needs of residents. On the November day we talked, she had made several dental and hearing referrals and arranged for the repair of a motorized wheelchair. Later, she and another social worker and Sister Martha, a nun who is the vice president of the health care network, were planning a Christmas shopping trip for those residents who do not have family. Kara is proud of how St. Theresa watches out for the needs of clients who have no nearby family and friends, even down to providing Christmas presents.

There are daily frustrations along with the satisfactions. One of Kara's clients, Ms. Williams, needed new hearing aids. It took almost a month and an estimated fifteen hours of Kara pushing through systems until Ms. Williams finally had her new hearing aids. Ms. Williams says she is very happy but still, Kara says, many days she does not wear them.

> Of course it is her right to wear them or not wear them—I believe in self-determination; but I wonder why she wanted them so badly if she wasn't going to wear them.

Kara said a friend who is a social worker in another agency asked her what it is like to work with a large medical organization's administration, assuming that Kara would be frustrated by red tape and regulations. Kara told her friend that, quite the contrary, she has had a very positive experience. She finds the agency's administration to be extremely caring and committed to the welfare of St. Theresa's residents. The executive director makes time to visit and form relationships with virtually every resident.

Kara told me about Ms. Pointer as an example. Ms. Pointer is a resident in stage four renal failure, receiving dialysis every week and suffering with stage four pressure ulcers. Kara shuddered, "those ulcers are the worst of the worst—they will never heal," she said. As a consequence, Ms. Pointer is in constant pain. Kara talked about the advantages of hospice care with Steve Pointer, Ms. Pointer's son, who has her medical power of attorney. But Steve Pointer refuses to accept that his mother is dying and so he will not agree either to hospice services or to a Do Not Resuscitate order, nor will he allow her to discontinue dialysis. Kara knows that Ms. Pointer's pain could be managed better by hospice, and it would be such a relief to Ms. Pointer not to have to get out of bed and into a wheelchair to be transported across town for dialysis, where she has to stay all day hooked to the machine. Because of his relationship with Ms. Pointer and his knowledge of the family and the situation, the executive director called a meeting with the medical director to see what could be done to honor the wishes of the family and, at the same time, make Ms. Pointer more comfortable. As a consequence of the medical director's intervention, Ms. Pointer received more potent pain medication that brought relief. Kara was proud of her agency, where the top administrator knows the clients and cares that their needs are met.

Kara reflects that she found herself becoming defensive for Ms. Pointer in her work with Steve Pointer. Therefore, she imagined herself in Steve Pointer's place; if Ms. Pointer had been her mother, how would she react?

> It must be so difficult to have to make those kinds of decisions, and people are just trying to do their best in terrible circumstances. Steve Pointer lives more than two hours away, so it is hard for him to see the daily suffering. When he came recently for a visit, Ms. Pointer was asleep; his visit was too short to see her awake—and in pain. Although Ms. Pointer can still talk, her mental condition is increasingly deteriorating because of the renal failure and the effects of medication. She is dying, and she is dying in a great deal more pain than she has to, from my perspective. But she is his mother, and he does not want to let go.

Kara says that the choices Steve Pointer has made would not be her choices, but she recognizes that what she would do in the same situation is not the issue. Ms. Pointer is not her mother, and every situation is unique to the family going through it together. So she is trying to honor his wishes and still provide a level of care for the resident so that she could be more comfortable. Still, Kara was in tears after talking to Steve on the phone and trying to communicate the situation to him in ways that were realistic and also compassionate.

Meaning-filled Days

Kara came into this work knowing that she would be dealing with life and death issues, working with families who are in conflict with one another, who are going through terrible circumstances, and who sometimes see the decisions and choices before them differently than she does. When there is nothing further she can do—when Steve Pointer makes decisions that are not what Kara would choose if she were in his place—Kara prays. After she finished the phone conversation with Steve, Kara went to Ms. Pointer's room. Ms. Pointer was asleep, her only real respite from the pain. Kara had planned to visit with her and hold her hand. Instead, she sat down beside the bed and prayed for peace for Ms. Pointer and her son. No one knew she was there, but she says that it helped her, and she prayed for God's help for this suffering family.

Kara appreciates Viktor Frankl's logotherapy (1969), a theoretical approach that focuses on how people can find meaning in their lives through love and work, and even in suffering. She learned about logotherapy in graduate school, and it has shaped her own worldview. Kara finds meaning in helping her clients make the transition from this life into the next with the least suffering possible; there is nothing else she can do. It is enough; she finds peace in doing all she can do and praying her clients into God's care.

Just the day before we talked, Kara had talked with one of her grieving residents. Her twin sister had just died, and now she was the last surviving member of her family—she had been one of ten siblings. Listening to and honoring her grief, Kara felt a meaning she could not put into words—"It is a profound experience; it has given me a sense of awe at the human life cycle." She goes home each day from her nursing home residents, some of them terminally ill, to her two-year-old daughter, growing and learning and stumbling over herself with energy.

Sometimes she and her colleagues laugh instead of crying. Toileting seem to be a focus of attention at both ends of the life cycle. Kayla's daughter is beginning the transition out of diapers. When we talked, Kara had just had a long conversation with a hospice worker about how one of the residents is more alert and communicates better on the days she is able to evacuate her bowels. So they agreed that Kara would call the hospice worker for a visit on the days the resident has had a bowel movement, so the hospice worker can visit when the resident is alert. Kara said:

> We just have to laugh or we end up crying, knowing what it would feel like to be that resident if she knew that other people are discussing her most private bodily functions.

Some of the residents with memory loss find comfort in holding baby dolls. Some do not want to take a bath or eat—holding on to some vestige of self-determination in the same way Kara's toddler daughter asserts control in whatever way possible. So Kara laughs a lot—and prays a lot.

Our Work is Our Prayer

Kara's Christian faith is the foundation of her honoring life in all its stages, including life's last stages and the people who are traversing that stage. Christian practices that she believes she is living through her work are hospitality—giving people comfort—and service. She thinks of what she wants for her own parents, and it is not to end up as residents in a nursing home. As proud as she is of the services of St. Theresa Center, Kara has resolved to keep her parents in their home, or in her own home all the way to the end of life, using in-home nursing care if needed rather than moving them into a medical institution.

St. Theresa is a Catholic organization, and one of the organizational core values is service to the poor. That has implications for the kinds of clients Kara sees:

> St. Theresa absorbs the costs of care for many of our patients who cannot afford health care. Many have never had access to health care and health care systems, much less an inpatient setting. They come from such difficult circumstances, and I find working with them really rewarding.

She described Mr. Moreno, who had been homeless before being hospitalized with a leg infection. Upon discharge, he was sent to St. Theresa for therapy. He was a construction worker, but the infection had interfered with his ability to walk, much less do construction work, and he lost his job and then his apartment. Homeless, he had a hard time walking from one place to another to find food and shelter.

> He was here for a few months. We got that leg back in shape, and that meant that he was able to get a job. When we released him, he moved into the Salvation Army shelter, but he would ride the bus over here to volunteer to help other patients. He is not volunteering anymore because he is working during the day, but it is so rewarding to see him doing so well. Now he has an apartment. He has this sense of dignity that we did not see when he first came to us.

Many of Kara's clients are virtually alone in the world, sheltered away where society never sees them. They never leave. Perhaps a family member comes for an occasional visit, but they never go out—unless it is to the dialysis clinic across town. Kara quotes Jesus in calling them "the least of these" (Matthew 25: 30); they are marginalized and ignored. They are the ones whom Kara believes Jesus called his followers to place at the center of concern.

Four times a year, the St. Theresa staff holds a nondenominational Christian memorial service in the chapel for all of the residents who have died in the previous three months. Some families attend; some do not. At the last service, at the chaplain's request, Kara read the names of each resident who had died, and as she did, a candle was lit to symbolize the life lived.

Kara appreciates work in a Christian non-profit organization because she has the freedom to initiate conversations about clients' spirituality and faith practices. When she works through a psycho-social assessment with clients, she includes questions about their faith practices, and then she ensures that clients are able to practice their faith while they are patients at St. Theresa:

> Some of my clients are going through really difficult situations, and when I know them well enough to know if it would be helpful—or not—I ask if they would want me to pray with them. They always seem so grateful and so appreciative of the opportunity for somebody to talk with them about their faith and how are they making it through this rough time.

Mr. Butler was only forty years old when he had a stroke. He came to St. Theresa almost completely paralyzed, with minimal use of his hands and difficult speech, unable to walk. He asked Kara for a Bible:

> I brought him a Bible, and then he was trying very hard to get the Bible open a particular place. He was getting very frustrated, and he kept on dropping it. I could not understand his speech, and he could not tell me which passage he was looking for. So I asked him, 'Would you like me to read a couple of my favorite passages?' He nodded, and I read the Twenty-Third Psalm and then the Beatitudes, and he said, 'Thank you.' There were tears in his eyes. There are a lot of places of where that would not be appropriate for me as the social worker, so I am grateful to be in a place where reading the Bible is appropriate if it is what a client needs and wants.

Kara does not have to pray with her clients or read scripture passages to them for her to be living her faith through her work. She says:

> My work is my prayer, and my prayer is my work.

Kara thinks about grace a lot, she says. She sees the grace of God in the lives of patients who go through such suffering. She has a better grasp of how all of God's children, regardless of their differences, experience pain. She preached in the worship service in another nursing home in the city, one next door to her congregation, which provides worship services in the home twice a month. She spoke about being the Body of Christ:

> I used the example of the frequent Bingo game, the favorite activity on the nursing home long-term floor. It is comical, because new patients are unsure, coming from conservative Christian backgrounds that frown on gambling. I reassure them that there is no money involved and so they end up joining in. Some residents have sharp minds but have lost their fine motor skills, and so they have difficulty marking their Bingo card. Some are virtually deaf, but can still see well. And we have people who are virtually blind but can hear well. So Bingo games can take awhile, but it is fascinating and touching to watch as they all help each other to make sure that they haven't missed a spot on their card—whether because they can't hear the calls or can't see the cards or can't mark the little boxes. Some can see, and some can hear, and some can mark cards, so they pool their abilities. They are community even in Bingo. They are being an example of helping each other and the different gifts that each of them have, and how they use those in service to their neighbors. It is an honor to see that.

Next Steps

Kara loves her work and loves working in this organization, with these clients. She is the only licensed social worker, and she is now talking with the director about the fact that a psychologist who has been coming in to provide counseling services will soon be retiring. Kara would like to take on more clinical services, so that she can work more in depth with some clients than she can as she serves as care manager for a hundred residents.

> Residents often have situational depression, in response to the move to nursing care, which they believe to be a final home. Their whole lives, they had been able to do what they chose to do when they chose to do it. Now they have to eat at a certain time, and eat what someone else decides they need. They have to shower at a certain time. They have to wait until an aide comes to take them to the toilet. Some struggle with these restrictions more than others.

There are also the family dynamics that complicate the lives of some residents. Kara believes she has the compassion, knowledge, and skills to be helpful to residents if she had time in her workday to provide clinical services. She is looking forward to this change in her responsibilities.

Kara says she is exactly where she is supposed to be, at least for now. She thinks she is providing her clients good care, and she looks forward to going to work every day. She is struck again and again by what an honor it is to serve people in their home, in their final years.

Questions to Ponder

1. Describe the frustrating first years for Kara as a social worker after graduate school. Imagine what your first years might be like if the path is not immediately clear; how do you understand that kind of struggling? How might you cope with lack of clarity and having to change paths, as Kara did?
2. How does Kara manage the heavy responsibility for paperwork that shapes her work life? What do you see to be the advantages of Kara's approach? The disadvantages?
3. Give examples of Kara's commitment to self-determination and the dignity and worth of the individual as you see examples in her work.

4. Kara talks about the skills of listening and presence in her work. Think about those from a Christian perspective. How do you see those to be expressions not only of social work values, but also of Christian values?

5. Karen uses the following terms in talking about one of her clients—dialysis, Do Not Resuscitate (DNR), renal failure, medical power of attorney, and pressure ulcers. Define each; search the Internet if they are unfamiliar to you.

6. Kara hopes never to have to place her parents in a facility like St. Theresa Center. Imagine what it is like to work in a place day after day where you hope never to be a client. How has Kara come to terms with that reality?

7. Kara combines laughter with awe and prayer as she sees the meaning in her work and her own family life. In what ways do you identify with how she makes sense of her life and work?

8. How does Kara lace prayer through her work? How do her approaches to prayer resonate with your own?

Jon Black
Hospice Social Worker
Emily Bibb Mosher, Co-Author

Jon Black describes the family in which he grew up as very religious and very conservative. Many of his family members were ministers in a Pentecostal church. Jon started his education at a two-year community college and then searched for a university where he could complete his degree.

He was looking for a professional degree program that would prepare him to help people in some way, that would be a way to serve God through his work, and that would give him lots of flexibility. Doing the same job for the rest of his life, especially if he got bored with it, sounded miserable. He wanted "options," to be able to shift and do something else when he became restless. The more he learned about social work, the more it seemed a great fit. His family knew he wanted a job either in ministry or another field where he could help people, so they encouraged his decision to pursue a social work education. After completing his undergraduate degree in social work in a public university, he decided to go on to pursue the Master of Social Work degree. This time, he searched for and found a program in a Christian university, because he wanted to figure out how to integrate his faith with his profession service, a topic not explored in his undergraduate program. He said:

> So much of what social work does to help people seems like what Jesus did when he was on earth so, for me, social work is continuing Jesus' work.

That was the kind of social work he wanted to do.

In addition to finding his place in social work, graduate school also helped Jon find a new sense of belonging in his Christian faith. It was during graduate school that Jon allowed himself to face the realization that he was gay. He was distraught; his worldview told him that he had to make a choice—either he could be a Christian or he could be gay, but he could not be both. But his social work classes and conversations with faculty exposed him to a greater diversity of thought; he learned that not all Christians believed that Christianity and homosexuality are mutually exclusive. He found a book written by a social worker that examined the issues of sexual orientation as addressed in the Bible and the doctrines relating to sexual orientation of various Christian denominations. As a result, he says, he came to understand that he could be gay and also be a Christian.

> That was life changing; I don't know that I would have come to that understanding if I weren't a social worker.

During his graduate program, he had an internship at Grace Hospice Care. When he graduated, he went to work for a year in a nursing home, and then Grace called him and offered him a social work position. Jon jumped at the opportunity, and he has continued to serve as one of the social workers at Grace for the past six and a half years. In his time at Grace, he has worked in a variety of positions. He first worked as a field social worker directly caring for patients and then moved to the referral department. Now he serves as the compliance coordinator and medical records manager, a position that allows him to implement better policies and procedures at Grace so that the field social workers have more time to spend with their patients instead of doing paperwork.

The Admissions Team at Grace

Hospice services are available to patients who have a terminal disease and a doctor who has certified that they have less than six months to live. Medicare and most insurance plans cover the costs of hospice care, which include medications, needed medical equipment, around the clock access to care, and support for loved ones following death. When Jon worked on the admissions team, his days began with sorting through the referrals that had come the previous day from case managers, nursing homes, and hospitals. He then called families to have a first conversation about providing a referred family member with hospice care.

Jon said that these calls are often "delicate;" hospice can be a scary concept and families often do not understand what a referral to hospice means. He began by telling them that their physician had referred them and he was calling to see if Grace Hospice could be helpful to them. Jon would ask the patient or family to tell him about the current situation that led to their doctor's referral. He explained that the hospice staff works as a team, with nurse's aides, nurses, physician, social worker, and chaplain all working to make sure the patient is comfortable in every physical, emotional and spiritual way possible during the end of life. The team provides support for the family as well as care for the patient.

Grace does not have an in-patient facility. Instead, the team goes to wherever the patient calls home, whether that is a house or apartment or an assisted living facility—or even under a bridge. Jon arranged with the family for a nurse from the agency to visit them and discuss the various options available through Grace Hospice. Jon sometimes went with the nurse if he sensed that there was a need for a social worker to engage with the family as they entered care. When the family or patient needed services that Grace did not provide, Jon made referrals. Jon assessed the family's situation, made an initial plan with them, and then provided that plan to the care team that would provide ongoing services to the family.

There were times that "under a bridge" was the reality—Jon had hospice patients who were homeless. Sometimes he visited those patients at the rescue mission, or even at a fast food restaurant. One of the biggest challenges with homeless patients is providing the pain medications they need without making them a target for theft, since the drugs that treat pain are popular with prescription drug abusers. Jon arranged for the rescue mission to provide a locker where Grace can stock a few days of pain medication so that the patient can access it.

Jon's goal and the goal of Grace is to prevent needless suffering, whether physical, psychological, or spiritual—that goal is what he loves about the work. Sometimes it is a concrete service; when someone was in pain and had no transportation to a drug store, Jon would drive to the pharmacy. At other times, his work was as simple and profound as being a compassionate presence to a patient who was lonely and frightened.

Jon remembers one of their patients in a local nursing home, Mr. Matthews, who was in pain and silently crying when Jon arrived. Jon promptly went to the nurse to ask that Mr. Matthews receive his pain medication. She replied she would be right there. Jon returned to Mr. Matthews' room to wait with him, holding his hand. When several minutes past and no one came, Jon returned to the nurse, saying, "I know you are really busy, but he is in real pain." Again he returned to Mr. Matthews' room and waited, and again no one came—and so Jon repeated the whole scene again. This time, he told the nurse that Mr. Matthews was crying with the pain, and she replied "Oh, he does that all the time." Jon stood there, clearly waiting on her to act, instead of returning to the patient's room. Irritated, the nurse retrieved the medication and took it to Mr. Matthews.

After the situation had calmed and Mr. Matthews had settled into a more restful state, Jon returned to talk with the nurse before he left, expressing his concern as a colleague that she seemed overworked. She told him how overwhelmed she was. Gently, Jon was able to insert into the conversation the philosophy of hospice, which is to provide medication at the very first sign of need to get ahead of the buildup of pain, making it easier to manage. Hospice does not advocate attempting to decrease the pain medications over time, which might be the approach with non-terminally ill patients. Providing medication at pain onset would make patient care easier for the nursing staff as well. Jon's goal was to ensure more effective nursing care for Mr. Matthews when Jon could not be there with persistent pressuring.

With family members, Jon helped them focus on living life rather than awaiting death. Often families were reeling with the news of a terminal diagnosis, still in a state of disbelief or even outright denial that a loved one was dying. For them, to choose hospice meant "giving up" the fight to live. Jon's role was to help them and the patient to understand that choosing to work with hospice does not mean that death will be coming "right now." Instead, his task was to help them live life to the fullest for as long as possible and "letting nature take its course."

Compliance and Medical Records

Recently, Jon moved out of the admissions and referral department and into his new role as the compliance coordinator and medical records manager. One of his responsibilities is working with the management team to draft and implement new policies and procedures. Jon knows this may not sound like social work or as fulfilling as working directly with families, but he enjoys making changes in this area so that the field social workers can spend more time with patients at their bedside. For example, when Grace admits new patients, the team assigned to the patient has a long list of information they need to collect, including such diverse issues as spiritual concerns and medical power of attorney. Because of the sensitive nature of admitting a patient into hospice care, this is not always the ideal time to ask all of these questions, and so the staff would leave parts of the document incomplete as they attended—rightfully—to the immediate needs of the patient and family. Jon helped change the paperwork process so that instead of the document immediately going into the patient's chart, it goes to the primary team so that they can follow up within a couple of weeks. Due to this change, the teams now are thoroughly completing the document while still being sensitive to the needs of the family.

Jon also is developing a training program for social work competencies specifically for hospice care. Jon primarily will use this curriculum to teach important medical social work skills like discharge planning, case management, or pain and symptoms assessment to the social workers at Grace. He plans to have an annual training for basic competencies, followed by trainings throughout the year on specific topics, such as telling the difference between grief and depression.

Learning Grace at Grace

I asked Jon how working at hospice is related to his own religious beliefs and faith. He responded,

> My world view before graduate school was very narrow; the doctrine in my church taught that I was right and everyone else was wrong.

Jon's social work education and the experiences he has had in hospice work have taught him not to make snap judgments of others, that there is a lot he does not understand.

> I want to learn more about the person, more about what motivated their choices, what influenced their life and understanding who they are—that can totally change my understanding of a person's situation. I feel like I've learned more about God's grace.

Jon went on to say that both his profession and his faith affirm people's basic right to choose their own path, and that at no time should that be more the case than at the end of life.

> Even if I think the choice a patient is making is not the best one or what I would do, it is their right to make that choice. Who knows? They may be right and I am wrong about what is the best path for them.

When Jon first began his work at Grace, he was "very scared for people who were dying if I didn't think they were saved." His perspective has changed; he has come to the place of recognizing that, though people cannot control death, they can control how they meet God. It is not his to judge:

> I am present to them and I try to show God's love through that presence. Being that presence is what God calls me to do. It is between them and God about the rest.

His work has exposed him to a diversity of faiths and worldviews. He has come to extend grace to himself, that he does not and cannot have answers to all of the big questions of life and death.

> I do not understand everything there is to understand and that is okay. I know what I believe and if someone else believes differently, well then, that is okay.

Restless

When Jon first started at Grace, he had the feeling that anyone could do his job as a member of the admissions team. In fact, two other people had responsibilities much like his, one a nurse and one with no professional education at all. Then he realized that both of them were relying on him to help them navigate their responsibilities. He began to realize how his professional education had prepared him for the work. Even though his work ended with the admissions process and the assignment of a care team, families came to him at patient memorials to express their gratitude, and he realized that what he was doing mattered.

Just a few weeks before our first conversation, one of Jon's colleagues asked for help with an admission. She was not sure the patient was capable of making his own decisions, and she did not know what to do, so Jon taught her how to assess his mental capacity. It turned out that, indeed, the patient had cognitive impairment that was severe enough that he could not provide an informed consent for services, and so Grace had to involve the family in the process of securing the legal right to make decisions for him. As a for-profit agency, there is some pressure at Grace Hospice to admit an established quota of patients, but, with Jon's advice, his colleague stopped the admission. Jon supported her decision because it was the right action for the wellbeing of the patient. "I felt honored that she came to me for advice in that situation."

The pressures of working on an admissions team where supervisors evaluated his work by the number of admissions made Jon restless. He enjoyed his role as coordinator because, in addition to working directly with patients and their families, he was also supporting six other staff members who were in turn helping patients. He liked the feeling of his efforts multiplied through them. That multiplicative effect was what drew him to his current position in management.

The restlessness in college Jon says motivated him to choose a profession that would allow him to change directions along the way; that restlessness continues to shape his decisions. He has moved from direct care to management, and someday, he says, he would like to work with the International Hospice and Palliative Care Foundation. He would like to advocate for legislation that would increase access to hospice care on medical insurance plans. Thankfully, Grace has financial resources that allow them to take patients who are not able to pay and have no insurance. Still, he says, many people who are terminally ill do not even think to ask about hospice because they believe they cannot afford it.

Jon would also like to do more community education about hospice and the end of life. "I also have this desire—it scares me that I have this desire—but I also have this desire to work in pediatric hospice." He thinks it would be a lot more difficult work than he is doing now and for some reason, he thinks that it would be even more rewarding.

New Beginnings

While Jon has undergone several changes in his job at Grace, even more significant have been the challenges and changes Jon has faced in his personal life. A few years ago, he went to the emergency room with pain in his lower right abdomen, but while scanning for appendicitis, doctors found something else. The doctors did a biopsy and learned that Jon was in stage four of Non-Hodgkin's Lymphoma. Over the course of three years, Jon went through several rounds of chemotherapy. Jon is thankful to be in remission now, but he still can recall the trauma of the experience very vividly. He remembers one time during chemotherapy when he started having severe pain in his ribs but the pain medicine was no longer working. While Jon was in pain, he said:

> A friend came over and just sat with me. There was nothing he could do. There was no other medication to give me. All he was able to do was just be there, and in that moment, it was like

he was holding some of the hurt with me. That now is one of my best memories. I understood the power of just being with someone, of the compassion there is in that, and how it does not take the pain away, but it helps. I have used that experience to influence the care I provide when I see patients, and when I do trainings for new employees, I share that story.

Jon realizes that this experience has allowed him to understand his patients better. He used to doubt the impact that simply sitting with someone can have, but now that he has felt its power himself, he no longer feels weird sitting silently with a patient.

Jon's struggle with cancer affected more than just his ability to understand his patients, however. It also affected how he views himself. Jon explains that the combination of graduating school, telling his family that he is gay, wrestling with what it means to be a gay Christian, and surviving cancer "made me feel like a new person." Looking back on the person he used to be and even reading what he wrote in his journal before these experiences shows Jon how much he has changed. Whereas he used to be "hard headed" and needed a "black and white" answer to what was right or wrong, now he understands that questions do not always have a clear answer. Some people told him that he developed cancer as God's judgment on his sexual orientation. At first, Jon did not know how to respond and even wondered if they were right, but later he remembered that even his grandmother, "the matriarch of the family," had cancer. Other friends told Jon, "that there isn't a good reason this happened; it just did," and they would be with him through it. As Jon emerged from these experiences with a new outlook on himself and the world, he felt that his old name no longer captured who he had become. Jon had an official name change, a marker of his new identity.

Though Jon's perspective and even his name have changed over the years, his faith remains a significant part of his life and his work. Jon sees God at work in the lives of his patients at Grace. As an example, he tells the story of a patient who was very close to dying one Friday:

> I came back to work on Monday, and he was still alive and struggling and a still small voice in me said, 'Call the chaplain.' So I sent the chaplain an e-mail, and she said, 'I'm just around the block; I'll be right there.' She walked into the patient's room, and prayed with him, and he was able to let go. He died ten minutes later.

Jon believes that voice was God at work in him, being present so that he can meet the needs of those he is called to serve.

Questions to Ponder

1. Jon tells how his social work education changed his understanding of the relationship of Christian faith and sexual orientation. What can you imagine were the implications of this worldview shift on his work with clients?

2. Jon describes how his work in hospice has made him more curious about people's experiences and less ready to form judgments of them. He connects that shift to a shift in his religious beliefs, to learning "more about God's grace." How do you see being more curious and less judgmental of others as related to religious beliefs such as grace?

3. How did Jon navigate the ethical decision presented by his colleague about admitting a patient who seemed not to have the mental capacity to make his own life decisions? What social work ethical principles were involved in this decision?

4. Jon has moved from direct practice with clients to management. What made management an appropriate career change for him?

5. Jon has struggled in his personal life with issues of sexual orientation and physical illness. Trace how he has integrated those personal experiences with his understanding of faith and social work practice.

Mental Health and Mental Illness

Raelyn Greer
Clinical Social Worker and Assistant Program Director, Department of Mental Health

Bethany Parrott, Co-Author

16

Raelynn Greer rides the Metro across the city to work. As she travels each day, she passes by countless people who look like they are having hard times, many apparently homeless. Raelynn aches for their suffering, yet she does not have the helpless feeling she used to have when she saw people who were homeless and perhaps mentally ill. Now she is doing something to help people like those she sees from the windows of the Metro.

Raelynn grew up knowing she wanted to be a social worker. Her parents and grandparents were strong advocates for human rights, including rights for people who are gay and lesbian, in an area of the country and during a time when very few shared their views. Raelynn's sister struggled with mental illness, and as a consequence, her family members were strong supporters of mental health services and advocates for the de-stigmatization of mental illness. She also married into a family supportive of her interest in social work; they encouraged her to consider a dual MDiv-MSW degree program. The program seemed like a perfect fit, so Raelynn enrolled, finished her MSW first, and then worked in a residential child treatment facility while she completed the MDiv degree.

Clinical Practice with Children and Families

Raelynn joined the staff of New Start almost five years ago. New Start, a nonprofit mental health agency, works with many recent immigrants from Central and South America. The State Department of Mental Health funds the agency. New Start provides short-term therapy for people experiencing a mental health crisis that is impairing their ability to function normally. The agency works to stabilize people until they are able to function effectively in their environment, usually about six months. They then refer clients to other agencies for ongoing services. There are always others waiting for services.

A couple of years ago, a much larger agency, Hope Center, offered Raelynn a position doing virtually the same kind of work but with a significant promotion to Assistant Director, and she took the position. The State Department of Mental Health also funds Hope Center, although in an even rougher area of the city than New Start's neighborhood. Hope Center's surrounding neighborhoods have the highest levels of poverty and violence in the whole metropolitan area. It provides community-based mental health services at eleven sites in this large urban area. The clients of Hope Center are about 60% African American and 40% Latino.

There is much more gang activity around Hope Center's sites than there was around New Start, and depending on what is going on in the neighborhoods, Raelynn sometimes closes down service areas that are too dangerous. Staff can then not do field work in the area until the gang activity abates, although they can phone and clients can come to the agency. Hope Center works closely with the police, who provide safety training for Raelynn's staff.

Raelynn works specifically with children and families. In addition to mental illness, many of her clients are experiencing other crises in their home life: homicide or suicide, threat of eviction or homelessness, gang involvement, criminal activity and prosecution, family violence—and often a combination of crises. Many speak only Spanish in an English-speaking world.

One of the families with whom Raelynn is currently working includes two adult brothers, their wives, and four children living in a one-bedroom apartment in a neighborhood controlled by gangs. Their worries include the basics of physical safety in a violent community as well as finding steady employment so that they can pay the rent and purchase necessities. On top of those challenges, they are trying to cope with trauma they have experienced in leaving behind a rural Central American home and family, a dangerous border crossing, and then adjustment to city life in the U.S. These experiences created an emotional overload for one of the brothers, who has had a first diagnosis of schizophrenia.

The reality is that within the limitations of the agency's work, Raelynn will never be able to help her clients eliminate the problems they face completely. But then again, she says, who ever completely eliminates all problems? Her goal is to help her clients cope more effectively with their illness and other life challenges than they were coping when they came to her, and to find hope that the tomorrows will be even better.

> The clinical work that we do is difficult because 85% of our clients have had a history of sexual abuse, physical abuse, domestic violence, school violence, community violence, and/or poverty. Every one of our kids has been traumatized in multiple ways.

Raelynn told the story of a teenager sent by the high school because he was defiant and insisting on carrying a gun to school—when he attended, which was sporadic. As Raelynn worked with him, she learned that he had a realistic fear of gang violence. Raelynn understood that in his neighborhood and school, he needed a weapon to feel safe. She considered it a success when she helped him switch from a gun to a knife as his protection out in the neighborhood and at least to say that he had stopped carrying weapons to school, although Raelynn was not altogether confident in his truthfulness, given that the school did not check for weapons.

Another client, a 15-year-old immigrant girl, was suicidal after being raped twice at the border crossing. Raelynn explains that it is common for their clients to have traumatic experiences during the border crossing. Raelynn uses cognitive behavior therapy as her usual approach to helping clients cope with and recover from the trauma they have experienced.

Leading and Supervising

When she first began working with New Start, Raelynn was the Program Manager in charge of two crisis intervention programs that operate 24 hours a day, 7 days a week. One program provided intensive services for clients in crises; the other program served persons with mental illness that needed more long-term services. Raelynn not only administered the programs; she also worked directly with clients.

A couple of years ago, shifts in state mental health policies required more emphasis on evidence-based practice (EBP) involving a more structured treatment approach, and it fell to Raelynn to lead the agency in making this shift. The government funding supports only those research-tested interventions it has approved; all of the programs are for prevention and early intervention. Raelynn said:

> These approaches are great when a client has experienced a traumatic episode, or is struggling with an adjustment to a single life change. But our clients experience a pile-up of crises and traumas. We had to adjust for our clients. A lot of these EBPs are created in Seattle with their population in mind. We have found some things that work with families in Nebraska or Minneapolis do not work for families in our city. We had to translate materials for our immigrant population.

Raelynn has taken on learning the EBPs, adapting them for their agency's population, and then teaching the adaptations to their staff. For example, a program developed in the Northwest is very effective in working with children with disruptive behavior—children with Oppositional Defiant Disorder, Attention

Deficit Hyperactivity Disorder, Obsessive Compulsive Disorder, or other challenges. For example, young boys manifest depression by being irritable, and that irritability lands them in trouble. The curriculum is designed for groups of children and also for groups for their parents. Raelynn said:

> It is an amazing program. It was created for people that are English speaking and are White and that have had minimal battles with socioeconomic issues or community violence. I am glad White middle class people have this resource. But we have parents who have just come over from the border who speak no English, and their children were born here, and there is culture conflict in the family. Child Protective Services would consider their ways of disciplining to be abusive—and they end up with someone reporting them on a hotline. So I have had to do a lot of adapting.

The resulting program, dubbed Bear School, is working for their clients, but there was a lot of work on Raelynn's part to make it so. Carlos, a five-year-old boy, had participated in The Bear School for 12 weeks when his teacher asked Raelynn, "What medication have you put him on? He is doing so much better!" Raelynn grinned as she told her that there was no medication; Carlos was participating in the Bear School and meeting with a case manager—and he was making the changes himself.

The curriculum calls on parents to spend individualized time with their children. Raelynn pointed out that for many parents, that may simply be impossible:

> How do I tell a single mother of five kids whose husband beat her and then left her, that for her kids to be better, she has to spend ten minutes a day with each of them individually? She barely has ten minutes to breathe. Some families are ten people living in a one-bedroom apartment. They simply cannot have "individual" time. So we explored what we could do instead. I have a single mom with three kids all under the age of six, all three in the program for their disruptive behavior. I helped her learn how to speak to each kid individually even while they are all together. She can encourage, validate, and play with them individually even though the siblings and maybe other family members are in the same room. I would say, "Tell Jonny this," instead of saying "All you guys are doing great." I helped her think about what she could say to each kid that was different from what she said to the others. That is one small example of how we changed the curriculum.

Raelynn supervises the other therapists, working with them to match treatment modalities to client needs, such as her choice of cognitive behavior therapy with the young girl who had been raped and was suicidal. Raelynn meets regularly with each therapist, and she leads clinical supervision groups, where therapists can learn from and support one another. When therapists are stuck, Raelynn steps in to brainstorm options. She has always loved teaching others. She believes she is skilled in training, supporting, and caring for her staff; those skills are important because their jobs are difficult, and her staff is at risk for frustration and discouragement. Considering the nature of the work and the situations these therapists deal with daily, support is essential.

Raelynn is a cancer survivor; she had just completed chemotherapy when we talked first. One of the reasons she made the move from New Start to Hope Center was that the work hours were shorter and less stressful. She was working sixty or more hours a week at New Start, and she was very much in charge. Now her hours are limited to forty each week, and it is a much larger organization so that the clinical direction does not all fall on her. She is learning from colleagues rather than feeling responsible for a more unidirectional learning process, with her the educator. Being a cancer survivor has also given her a new perspective on the work:

> I think before cancer I would often be swept up in anxiety created by notes not completed on time or government changes that would affect our work. Since my cancer treatment, I have not been so easily stressed by minor challenges; I know now what a real crisis is. I think it made me a better supervisor; I can help my staff evaluate what really is a priority.

The support Raelynn provides to her staff also comes back to her as well—they support and encourage her. She depends on them, and she knows she can always reach out for help. Support includes pointing out ways they can improve their work. As hard as the work is, Raelynn believes that their services are effective. They have more successes than failures.

She had just trained a new staff member, Linda. One of Linda's first clients was a teenager, Myla, whose father had sexually abused her over a number of years. Myla had initially resisted being involved in therapy, but she finally had connected with one of Raelynn's staff members—the staff member Linda had replaced. Raelynn said,

> I was certain we would lose Myla when I transferred her to Linda. I met with Linda yesterday, and she said she had a wonderful session with Myla, and that Myla is willing to stay and try. And what I mean by wonderful is Myla did not cuss Linda out and leave. She actually stayed. And to see Linda feeling good about what she had accomplished, that made for a good day.

Success sometimes means simply holding on, and support may be celebrating such a victory with one another.

As Assistant Director, Raelynn is involved in every aspect of the agency. The last time we talked, she had just spent three hours in a budget conference call with the agency leadership, a weekly meeting in which they check revenues, expenditures, and staff time allocation. Raelynn is responsible for the hiring and dismissal of the entire clinical staff, and she provides them with group supervision. She also provides clinical backup for her staff when they are away sick or on vacation—or when they are stumped and need help. She is also certified to hospitalize patients who are mentally ill when they are not willing to admit themselves.

Raelynn also thinks it important that the staff have fun with one another. Once a month, there is a potluck lunch, a party, or a movie afternoon. The week before we talked, they had "hat day," and everyone wore hats. Next month will be a "plaid shirt day."

Faith and Practice

The staff does not discuss religious beliefs and faith practices, since their organization is a public agency funded by the State Department of Mental Health. But for Raelynn, social work is how she lives her belief in a loving God. Her job allows her to help those who cannot help themselves and to support her staff colleagues as they provide help to people in need. She believes she is following what Christ did and taught.

Her faith gives her strength and motivation to serve others, but it is not part of the treatment process. Raelynn learns about the religious beliefs and practices of her clients, and she incorporates those beliefs and practices when they can be helpful in the treatment process. The majority of New Start clients are Catholic. Raelynn says that, though her own Christian beliefs may vary in some ways from those of her clients, still, her faith makes her more sensitive to how faith and hope can be strong foundations in the healing process for her clients.

Raelynn said that when clients come from desperate situations, their faith and hope for healing are all important:

> Families who have to take three buses and spend an hour and a half in travel time to get to their therapy session show their faith.

Raelynn and her staff have learned that their faith and hope for a better future motivates families to try new approaches to the challenges they face.

Raelynn believes she is called to social work. She never heard an audible voice saying "Be a social worker," but she says that she knew God called her to social work because it fit her so well. It is simply "who I am." She said:

> Social work is helping those that cannot help themselves. That is what God has called us to do in this world.

The work has challenged her faith as well; she has been frustrated and angry, and she has challenged God to explain how God can allow the experiences some of her clients have faced. One of her clients is a young child who was kidnapped, tortured, and sexually abused by several gang members. Hearing about what her client had suffered was traumatic for Raelynn; social workers do experience secondary trauma from their work with traumatized clients:

> Here was this sweet, cute, outgoing boy with a curly head of hair who told me what he had endured, and it made me physically ill to hear it. How can God allow this to happen to an innocent child? Where were the people who were supposed to help him?

She still does not understand, but she has come to a point of peace with her understanding that God gave people freedom, and that freedom includes being able to make bad choices and to do evil in the lives of others. Understanding that does not make her work any easier, however. Raelynn stopped watching the evening news on television because of how overwhelmed she is by terrible events happening elsewhere in the world. She has "enough terrible" right where she is.

At the same time these realities fuel Raelynn's belief that God called her to protect those who need to be protected and to help those that need help;

> If we would all do that, then the story of this kid who was tortured and will ever be scarred might never have happened.

Raelynn works in one of the most violent communities in the United States. As a consequence, the image of Christian witness she chooses to describe her work is "passing the peace." In many Christian worship services, individuals turn to one another and recite the phrase "The peace of Christ to you," which is answered with "And also to you:"

> That is what we should be doing on a daily basis, in our activity, in our behavior, as we live our life—passing the peace, doing something good for another person, trying to help, trying to make this world just a better place. That is what God calls Christians to do. People can do that in all kinds different professional fields. For me, though, this is where I need to be. This work is how I live my faith. I get paid poorly by the Department of Mental Health. My hours are long and tiring, and I am cussed out on a weekly basis by parents that want literally to kill me. I have to be careful driving to work because of all the gang violence. But I leave each day knowing I have tried my best to do something to help another person. I do not know that I would find that in any other field. So this is 100% where I need and want to be.

Questions to Ponder

1. Raelynn says that she knows that God called her to the work she is doing because it is such a good fit for her. How do you think about God calling us to that which fits us?

2. Raelynn describes the secondary trauma she has experienced as a result of hearing about the experiences of her clients. How does making herself vulnerable to trauma fit with your understanding of Christian calling?

3. What are the ways you hear Raelynn coping with the stress and secondary trauma of her work?

4. How does Raelynn describe the role of clinical services with clients who have experienced multiple and ongoing crises and trauma?

5. What skills do you think Raelynn has used in adapting treatment methods for the client population she serves?

6. What does Raelynn enjoy about her role as supervisor? What would you like about her style if you were her employee?

7. Describe the role of peace in Raelynn's own life, as well as her sense of calling to "pass the peace."

Sunshine Parker

Therapist,
New Beginnings Treatment Center

Myria Bailey Whitcomb, Co-Author

As a teenager, Sunshine Parker had looked for someone she could talk to about her life, and as an adult, she wanted to be that person for other teenagers. She thought she would become a child psychologist. She never considered social work as a profession. She understood a social worker to be someone who took away children, who is nosy and telling others how to raise their children—"just not a person you want to have in your life."

After graduation and exploring the avenues open to her for working with children, she realized her understanding of social work was "just flat wrong." She went to social work school, and she quickly realized that it was the right choice. During her first semester, she read a case study in a text book and thought, "That could be my family." It was the story of a young teenage girl whose mother had to work long hours to support the family and was too overwhelmed to see the girl's loneliness, her sense of not fitting in and not finding her way in school. Sunshine wanted to be the social worker in a community-based teen program that reached out to that girl, helping her find her way and grasp a vision for her life.

Covenant Care Ministries

Following her dream to work with adolescents, Sunshine took a job with Covenant Care Ministries when she completed her MSW. Covenant Care Ministries is a Christian foster care and adoption agency, working through and with congregations across several states to recruit and support foster and adoptive families. Covenant Care first employed Sunshine as a caseworker with children and their families. Most of the children had experienced neglect or violence in their birth families and public child protective services had removed them from their homes. The state agency then contracted with Covenant Care to provide these children with foster homes and social work services while the state agency worked with the biological family. It was Sunshine's job to help children to feel safe and to form attachments with foster and adoptive parents.

Sunshine worked with foster care families in an area one hundred miles in radius, so she traveled a lot to see all the families on her caseload at least monthly. Many of the families lived in small towns scattered across a largely rural region. Sunshine supported foster parents with all the creativity she could muster, helping them to find the resources they need to work with the traumatized children in their care. She listened to foster parents and helped them find ways to deal with challenges. She provided in-home supportive counseling to children. She went to court with children where they learned that their parents were too immersed in drug addictions to be able to parent them responsibly. When children had difficulties in school—and most did—Sunshine went with foster parents to school to work out strategies for helping children function better in the school environment.

One eleven-year old client, Brian, had been so severely abused by his father that he had to be hospitalized. After his physical wounds healed, the state agency placed him in one of Sunshine's foster homes. Brian was withdrawn, not talking, not engaging in play with other children. Through her work with Brian, Sunshine helped him to feel safe in his new home, and in a few months, Brian had joined a football team. Sunshine said that when he looked at her in one of their sessions together:

> I saw that God was looking at me, telling me that I am in the
> right place, doing what God called me to do.

The work was not easy. She had to explain to children happy in foster care that, if the court has ruled that their parents are now able to care for them, they would have to go home, even though they would rather stay with the foster parents. Sunshine also walked with foster parents through the wrenching separation of sending children they had come to love back into uncertain family environments.

Sunshine reflected on her work with one group of three siblings who had lived with their grandmother. The grandmother had custody of the children because their mother was addicted to drugs. The grandmother had a car accident and was subsequently arrested for drinking while intoxicated with the children in the car. The police called Child Protective Services (CPS) telling the story of the grandmother's arrest and saying, "Come pick up the children." The CPS worker contacted Covenant Care, who placed the three children in one of Sunshine's foster homes. Thomas was age six; his two little sisters, Maria and Doreen, were ages three and four. When Sunshine first visited the children, they were frightened and worried about their grandmother. Thomas was wetting the bed at night, and Sunshine could tell that he had some developmental delays that had not been assessed.

Sunshine served as case manager for the foster family and referred to another agency for individual therapy. Later she would learn from Thomas' therapist that he had been sexually abused. She was frustrated; she wanted to be the one providing therapy. Still, she knew her support for the foster parents was critical.

She encouraged them, listened to their concerns, and helped them find ways to communicate safety with these three traumatized children. She also spent time playing with each child each time she visited, so she could know the children and assess their progress.

Covenant Care promoted Sunshine to be the foster parent trainer, teaching new foster parents how to understand the experiences behind the behavior of traumatized children, how to understand and manage the behavioral challenges these children present, and how to provide a home environment that is safe and supportive for both the children and the foster family. Her message was, "We cannot give up on these children; they don't have anyone else but us."

Sunshine's identity as an African American was important in the work she was doing with Covenant Care. Because many of the children and families they serve are African American, Sunshine was attentive to whether or not agency policies and procedures created a cultural respect and sensitivity in the services they provided. Sunshine believes that all child welfare agencies need more African American social workers:

> Though they don't say it, it matters to a child and it matters to a family if they think you understand their situation because you look like them.

Moving Up

Eighteen months after she joined the staff of Covenant Care, Sunshine was promoted again, this time to a supervisory position, in which she carried responsibility for evaluating and suggesting improvements in the agency's services. Sunshine was surprised that when she told the families on her caseload that she would no longer be their caseworker they were really upset. Several said to her that they really felt a connection to her, that she cared about them and about their children—and of course, that is true.

In her new position as Quality Improvement Supervisor, Sunshine worked nationally to review and create policies and procedures, with a special focus on risk management. Sunshine's work with families and children had prepared her to look at the agency's policies and procedures with sensitivity to their experiences and needs. It is not always easy to balance the needs of children and families with agency realities such as licensure laws.

Sunshine developed policies designed to ensure the safety of children, families and social workers. Social work can sometimes be hazardous, especially when the work involves visiting families in their homes and helping them deal with the challenges and stresses of normal family life compounded by the past experiences and insecurities of children who have experienced abuse and neglect. Although it does not happen frequently, social workers have on occasion been verbally and even physically assaulted in their offices or in home visits, and the profession increasingly is making safety of both social workers and their clients a top priority (NASW, 2013).

Working with children who are often wary or distrustful of adults and with families stressed by the challenging behavior of children wounded physically and emotionally is not easy. But neither is being a supervisor responsible for policies and procedures—and there are fewer experiences in an administrative role of seeing God in the face of an eleven year old who has been abused by his father. Developing policies and addressing accreditation issues is not glamorous; staff are not always excited and grateful for the evaluation of their work that was Sunshine's responsibility.

Sunshine was the youngest person on the national office team, and one of two African Americans, and she said she sometimes felt overwhelmed with the responsibility. She tried not to allow herself to worry about proving her professional competence to her colleagues. She said has found herself praying, "Lord what are you doing with me?" Several months into her new responsibilities, her supervisor told her that the agency leadership had seen in her the potential for leading an agency like Covenant Care, and they wanted to be sure that she had the experiences to prepare her.

Sunshine loved her work at Covenant Care. Her supervisor, Pat, was like the father figure she never had. Although Sunshine's father lived with her mother and provided financial support to their family, he was not a part of Sunshine's life. She would learn later that he had "side families" that he was also supporting—other partners, other children. Her friends were surprised when he came to her high school graduation; they thought her mother was a single parent. So Sunshine was drawn to Pat's warmth and his mentoring.

The work also fit her; she was comfortable at Covenant Care. She said, "There was nothing really left for me to learn." She compared herself to a high school senior football player who is highly esteemed and plays a central role on the team—but who is afraid to go to college and be back at the bottom. Yet, Pat was encouraging her to dream bigger—"You have too much to offer; you need to be considering where God is calling you next."

Sunshine listened, but she would not consider a move. Sunshine was working closely with one of the foster mothers, Liz, who had a particularly challenging child; Liz was herself a social worker. One day, Liz also said to her, "What are you doing? Is case management the best use of your gifts?" Liz suggested that Sunshine come to work with her at the New Beginnings Center, a publicly funded residential treatment facility for adolescents. Sunshine said to Liz, "I can't do that; you people are so good at what you do." Sunshine did not think she had the clinical skills she would need in an intensive treatment environment. Still, Liz persisted, "You are making a mistake; just come for an interview."

Sunshine agreed to an interview and told Pat, who responded, "Good! Go, go, go!" Sunshine interviewed at New Beginnings, but the agency hired someone else. The agency director called her personally to explain that they really wanted to hire her, but they had only one position. So Sunshine told Pat, "I tried; it didn't work. I'm staying here." Still, he persisted, "This is not where you're supposed to be." Sunshine was relieved, however. She was comfortable, and she loved the supportive relationship with Pat.

Several weeks later, the New Beginnings Center called her again; they had an opening and they really wanted her to apply. She agreed to an interview, and Pat's response was, "Go do it; you've got it."

A few days before the interview at New Beginnings, Pat's wife called her to tell her that Pat was in the hospital with a bacterial infection and was not doing well at all. Because Pat and his wife were also foster parents, she asked Sunshine to come to the hospital and take the children home. Sunshine herself provided care for the children overnight; Pat died the next day. Sunshine was devastated to lose him from her life.

The week after Pat's death, Sunshine went to the interview and New Beginnings hired her. Sunshine thinks that God knew that she did not have the strength to leave Covenant Care because of her attachment to Pat. It took losing him for her to take her own next step. He was her inspiration and the reason she made the bold move to leave the comfort and security of Covenant Care to start over at New Beginnings.

The Next Step

Sunshine had been on the staff of the New Beginnings Center for more than a year when we last talked. There she functions as a therapist, working with the ten girls on her residential unit as well as with their families. The treatment approaches they used include crisis management, behavior management, and cognitive behavior therapy. Most of the girls have been in treatment before; New Beginnings feels like "the last stop" for them; they cannot function in the emotional intensity of a home environment such as foster care. There is no place to refer them if New Beginnings cannot help other than a state hospital. Sunshine reflects back on her message to foster parents in training at Covenant Care, that "these kids don't have anyone else but us." Now she realizes she is the "anyone else" that remains in these children's lives.

There are days when she longs for the comfort she felt at Covenant Care. She thinks, "This is crazy; I can't help these girls." She remembers, though, that she *has* helped. Jasmine, age 16, was one of her first clients at New Beginnings. Jasmine handled her emotional pain by cutting herself, and the cuts were deep. Sunshine almost despaired of reaching Jasmine, who had closed herself from others, a sad and dark soul. Jasmine ran away from New Beginnings but came back scared; she had cut herself so deeply that she had lost a lot of blood and needed stitches. Sunshine had no idea what to do beyond having her physical wounds treated, but she stubbornly kept meeting with Jasmine, sitting with her in silence, being available. Jasmine was frightened enough by her own behavior to recognize that she needed help. She agreed to work with Sunshine to find other means of coping with her emotional pain than cutting—to use her words, to not allow what others had done to her to define her. Sunshine said:

> When she left New Beginnings, she was a completely changed person; she is very funny and has a great sense of humor. She wrote me a letter when we finally discharged her. She said I saved her life because I actually cared. I did not try to fix her. I just cared. That is when I knew this is where I needed to be even though it is going to be really hard.

Sunshine says that the last year has held the best and worst experiences of her life. She has had to learn a lot fast; the clinical knowledge and skills she needs for the work are beyond what she learned in graduate school, beyond what she needed at Covenant Care.

> Even though I have helped some, there are also some kids that don't give a damn about what I say or what anybody else says, and they're going to do whatever they want to do, and I cannot fix it. I have to be okay with that. Still, it feels like I'm failing and I am giving up on them.

She is determined to find ways of reaching each child in her care. She thinks of Pat every day, believing she is living into the potential he saw in her. She also remembers his words to her when they had to send children back to parents whom they knew were probably abusing drugs, and who might well once again abuse their children:

> Sunshine, God will always take care of His babies. We are just called and placed here to help them through their journey. In the end, God will always be there to take care of them.

Her Faith

Sunshine depends on her family, her friends, and her church to keep her balanced and centered. When she is overwhelmed, she stops to pray, "Lord, I don't know what I am going to do, but I know you've got my back." She knows that her mother prays for her every day. She lives her faith by being a consistent presence in her kids' lives, "even the girl who calls me a bitch every day and has to be restrained because she is hitting other girls." Sunshine believes she is called to mirror God's presence and love for these children, even when others find them unlovable. Sunshine says that for her, being a social worker is her ministry.

God has called me to be in this field and to work in it wherever God puts me. It isn't just my work. I am always a social worker and always a Christian, wherever I am, whatever I am doing. I am a social worker because I am a Christian. Being a social worker is more than the work I do; it is my life.

Questions to Ponder

1. Describe the role mentors have had in defining Sunshine's sense of personal and professional development.
2. She describes her relationship with Pat, her supervisor, as a father figure, and her relationship with Liz, a foster parent, had a personal dimension. How might you think about these relationships from the perspective of professional boundaries with colleagues and clients?
3. Pat's advice to Sunshine was pivotal in the career move she made from Covenant Care to New Beginnings. What role do other people have in shaping your own journey?
4. How has Sunshine learned to cope with the uncertainty and sadness of her work?
5. How does Sunshine's sense of calling resonate with your own? With other social workers in this book? How is it different?

Diane Tarrington

Senior Director of Social Services and Commissioned Minister, Volunteers of America

Angela Dennison, Co-Author

18

Like many Baptist college students, twenty-year-old Diane was spending the summer school break doing "summer missions." The denominational missions agency assigned her to work with a Baptist congregation in a suburb of Washington, DC, and with international students at a nearby university. She was doing many of the usual activities college summer missionaries did in the 1980s—holding day camps and working with Vacation Bible Schools. It was good work and she enjoyed the children, whose childhoods were much like her own experiences had been, but she became intrigued by what two other student summer missionaries on her team were doing in a community center in the impoverished inner city. They were working with families in poverty and leading activity programs with their children, whose lives were very different from those in the congregations of the middle class suburbs where Diane was located.

Diane shared her interest with her supervisor, who was the congregation's Minister of Education. Next came what Diane calls "one of the most pivotal nights of my life." Her supervisor knew Diane was from a rural Midwestern area of the country, and so he took her for a drive through areas of the nation's capitol city, off the tourist maps, that he thought she needed to see:

> I saw what life in the big city was like; with all the urban issues and the problems that were going on. That was the first time I ever saw a homeless person. It took my breath away. It actually hurt to think about someone not having a place to be that night. I could not wrap my mind around it. I had no mental compartment in my brain to file that piece of information.

Diane said she could not sleep that night:

> I could not come to grips with it. I spent time in prayer and concluded that we *shouldn't* come to grips with that! We should address it!

Diane began looking for a profession that would allow her to work with the people who were struggling with poverty. She enrolled in an MSW program that focused on preparing social workers to lead and serve in the missions and ministry of the church and that included a graduate certificate in theological studies for social work students. Integrating ministry with social work to address the issues of homelessness and poverty would be the focus of Diane's career for the next 25 years.

Twenty-five Years at the VOA

When she completed her graduate studies, Diane took a position as the case manager of the Family Emergency Shelter, an agency of the Volunteers of America (VOA). The VOA is a Christian church that develops and supports social service organizations like the Family Shelter. In addition to housing and homelessness services, the agency operates substance abuse treatment programs, outreach and support services for persons who are HIV positive, and veteran's support services. The agency still employs Diane today but her roles have shifted through the years. She says:

> My whole career has been dealing with homelessness in one way or another; either in preventing it or addressing it.

She moved from being a case manager to Assistant Manager, then Manager, then to serving as Director of Homeless and Housing Programs. Most recently, she became Senior Director of Social Services. In her new role, she is developing and expanding programs and evaluating the agency's wide array of services.

Diane finds inspiration in the hard work and extra efforts of her colleagues. She tells of one staff member at the shelter for homeless families who places the pets of homeless children in "foster care." It is challenging to organize a network of veterinarians and other folks willing to temporarily care for strangers' pets, but this staff member does it so there is not one more great loss—the loss of a beloved pet—in the midst of all the other losses homeless children suffer. Diane says that is not part of the staff member's job description, but she does it anyway because she cares enough to imagine what life must be like for children living in a homeless shelter, worried about their beloved cat or dog.

This sensitivity to the needs of their clients, taking the time to know and understand the people they serve, is part of the culture of the VOA. Diane reflected on a recent experience that she said "might seem silly in a way, and I don't know if it is the best example of social work practice, but it really was a great day." One of the subsidized senior housing complexes asked her to come to deal with a complaint by an angry tenant. The resident was threatening to file a formal grievance because the agency's maintenance department would not fix her malfunctioning freezer. Several of the other tenants were rallying around her cause as well. The maintenance man for the property told Diane emphatically that the freezer was working perfectly. He said that the tenant, whose hands tremble with Parkinson's Disease, was spilling the water from her ice trays, and that explained why she never had ice cubes and had a mess in the bottom of her freezer.

Diane went to the woman's apartment and after talking with her for a while said, "I know this might seem silly, but will you show me how you put your ice trays in the freezer?" The woman agreed. Diane spotted the problem—the plastic ice trays were cracked and the water was leaking from the bottom of each square. The tenant's failing eyesight prevented her from seeing the problem. Diane went across the street and bought $2.00 worth of ice cube trays and solved the problem. Diane said:

> People can become so entrenched in their struggles, and blame each other, and blame systems, but sometimes we can solve problems by just listening and observing and seeing the world through the eyes of others.

A Culture of Caring

One of Diane's responsibilities is overseeing a training institute that brings in guest professionals to train her staff. Some of the topics have included trauma informed care, group therapy, setting and maintaining professional boundaries, HIV and AIDS, and family violence. Her goal is to keep the agency's finger on the pulse of new research, so that they are prepared to provide the highest quality of services to their clients.

As an administrator, Diane sometimes engages in direct services as well. One such time involved an apartment complex of the VOA that serves adults with chronic mental illness. Diane was spending her evening in the apartment complex's office to provide any support the residents needed. She had posted her hours: 6:00 PM to 10:00 PM. At 9:55 PM one evening, she was shutting down her computer when she spotted one of the residents heading down the sidewalk to the office. She said:

> I was so frustrated. I thought, "I have been here for four hours! Why did he wait until now? I am so tired. I cannot believe he is coming over here at the last minute!"

When he got to the door, Diane asked him if it was an absolute emergency or if it could wait until she was back later in the week. He said, "Oh, I just wanted to make sure you got to your car safely and it started ok." Diane said she felt guilty for having been so frustrated moments before. She says:

> Of course, it is not a client's job to take care of us and we should never expect that; it would be unethical to do so, but that mo-

ment was evidence of God's grace and an acknowledgement of our common humanity. We all want to be useful, and we want our care for one another to be mutual.

Sometimes former clients want to "give back" to the agency that has helped them. A young mother, an army veteran, had been a client of the Family Shelter several years before. She had lost her job, moved in with relatives, and then hid in the relative's former apartment after the relative had moved away. She and her son would ride their bikes to a friend's apartment to shower and stay during the hot summer day, but go back to the vacant apartment to sleep at night, always avoiding the maintenance workers and hoping the apartment would not be rented before she could find other housing.

Finally, she was able to get into the Family Shelter and eventually into the agency's transitional housing program. The staff referred her to a program that allowed her to move into a house. After one year of successfully paying rent monthly and work on the property to improve it—called "sweat equity"—the program gave her a no-interest mortgage. She went from being the head of a homeless family to being a homeowner.

At the request of the VOA, she spoke about her experiences to the City Council, advocating for the creation of an Affordable Housing Trust Fund. Diane says watching her speak passionately to the City Council to help the agency and other homeless families, and later attending a cookout at the woman's house to celebrate her becoming a homeowner, were among the happiest moments of her career.

Caring about clients can also be painful. When asked what she likes least about her job, Diane said in working with government housing programs, it sometimes became necessary to terminate client services. She says:

> I know sometimes there is no way around it, but it is always painful to for me, and I pray for the people I have to evict because they are using drugs or in other ways breaking the rules of the housing program and are unwilling to be evaluated by a chemical dependency counselor or seek needed treatment.

She is also pained when she hears people, especially Christians, who are apathetic about people struggling in poverty and homelessness, or who blame the poor for their distress. She believes that the Bible teaches that every Christian has a responsibility to care for people who are poor.

From Ice Cubes to Advocacy

Diane also serves as an advocate. She is an introvert, so her love of advocacy has surprised her. When I talked with her last, she was working to establish a City Affordable Housing Trust Fund, which would cost each taxpayer the equivalent of what it costs to buy a two-liter bottle of soda every month. That would create a dedicated revenue source of more than ten million dollars to build affordable housing in place of abandoned buildings that blight the city's neighborhoods.

The city houses 9,000 persons in homeless shelters each year, and that does not count the many who were living in their cars, on the streets and below underpasses because the system stays filled beyond capacity. Just the week before we talked, there were sixty homeless families that had to be turned away. The fund would be used to rehabilitate abandoned buildings and rent them to homeless families at an affordable rate. If a family makes every payment, then the rent becomes payment on a mortgage and a home ownership opportunity. As Diane says, everyone would win. Currently, there are 25,000 families in the city—almost 90,000 people—waiting for subsidized housing, at risk of homelessness because they are having to pay too much of their income for housing. These families would be paying back the trust fund so that the funds could be used for other families.

Diane's coalition has documented research that it is better to provide housing for homeless single adults who may be alcohol or drug addicted than it is to leave them on the streets, where they end up in emergency rooms, jails, and hospitals at much higher cost than providing subsidized housing. Diane remembers that when she began in the field of homeless services 25 years ago, the practice was to require clients to stop using alcohol and drugs before providing them with housing. Since then, research has shown that providing persons with addictions with housing first—before they are able to achieve sobriety—enables an "incremental scaffolding approach." That is, clients enjoy living in an apartment instead of on the streets and so become hopeful and motivated to make change. Some can cut down from seven drinks a day to five, and then to three. Diane says:

> Not all of them, but some of them; and some is a whole lot better than none. We have had great success in putting people who have been on the streets for years into permanent supportive housing apartments, where a social worker comes to them and continues to work with them, and they become willing to look at changes to improve their health. How much better for them to be in an apartment, even if they are continuing to drink or use drugs, than out on the streets where they may very well die, or in the emergency room or jail.

It is both a kinder and a more cost-efficient approach to substance abuse and homelessness.

Diane and others in the coalition are seeking to influence the City Council members to vote to establish the fund with new tax dollars. They conducted a "power analysis," determining who knows whom that can bring influence on the council members. The challenge is that some people are opposed to the idea of any additional tax. Diane also cited examples of the two elderly properties and a twenty-unit apartment complex for severely mentally ill persons that the VOA has managed well and are appreciated by the community. Diane says:

> I think of the homeless kids that we serve in our family shelter, and I wonder who the person is who is not willing to give up the cost of a two liter so that kid could have temporary shelter and then a home. Surely there is no one like that.

Just three weeks before our last conversation, a 12-year-old homeless boy was with his mother. She had taken him out of school early that day so that they could pick up his father from work—they were living in their car because the father was not making enough money to afford housing.

While the boy was playing in the park while waiting for his dad, a homeless young man with mental illness lured him into the woods and murdered him. That tragedy further drives Diane; that boy should have been in school, and the young man with mental illness should have been in housing and receiving services:

> We can spend all day long talking about what could have been, but I do believe if either one of these individuals had been in stable housing, this might not have happened. These kinds of risks come just by virtue of being homeless. What is the worth of one human life?

Diane's voice was filled with passion and even anger. The introverted case manager of 25 years ago, because of her experiences with homelessness, has become a strong and convincing advocate.

Diane also has happy stories about her work. In 2007, Griffin, a fifth grader, and his older brother Shawn, age 15, lived in the VOA family shelter for several months. Griffin's mother had died with cancer when he was six years old, and the father and boys had been homeless for much of the boy's lives since then. They left the VOA to move to Florida, in an apartment an aunt had rented for them.

While the boys were in the VOA shelter before their move, they participated in the VOA Study Buddies program, a two-hour after-school tutoring program Monday through Thursday evenings. One of the tutors has been volunteering for almost 25 years and has worked with hundreds of children over that time. In 2014, the volunteer saw Griffin, then age 18, on the Good Morning America television show—and she remembered him and recognized him. The show had dubbed him the "Homeless Valedictorian"; he was about to graduate as valedictorian of his high school class. He was living with his girlfriend's family until the end of the school year, so that he could focus on homework; his own family was homeless yet again.

In the interview, Griffin talked about staying in a hotel room with no food. Diane realized that this homelessness must have taken place in the months right after his move out of the Family Shelter, and that the rented apartment had not lasted. Griffin had been in middle school and again homeless. Middle school is a time that many kids, especially kids with the challenge of homelessness, go off the tracks, skipping school and using drugs. Instead, Griffin said in that interview that he had resolved that when he entered sixth grade, he just had to do his homework and make straight A's so that he would not have to be homeless anymore. That resolve must have developed while he was in the Family Shelter and participating in Study Buddies. Semester by semester after that, he kept his resolve.

The show underscored that as hard as he had worked to succeed in school against the odds, he did not have sufficient funds to go to college. Someone started an independent fundraising campaign for him and raised sufficient support so that he had enrolled in the university as a civil engineer major. His older brother had also graduated from the university.

One of the staff members talked to Shawn, Griffin's older brother, and asked what they remembered about the VOA Shelter. Shawn said three memories stood out for Griffin and him. First, they remember that the spaghetti was the best they had ever eaten. They asked the chef what made it so good, and she told them that she puts brown sugar in the sauce. The boys had experienced real hunger, so food mattered to them; when it was good, they wanted to know why. They also remember playing baseball in the VOA parking lot and a nearby park. They both loved baseball. Griffin wrote in the brim of every baseball cap he received, "Never Give Up"—his message to himself. And third, they remembered that they were in that Study Buddies after-school program every time the doors were open, two hours a day, Monday, Tuesday, Wednesday, and Thursday. It was there they grasped that education was their way out of homelessness and instability.

Diane said she has been doing research on how to build resiliency and buffer children from the impact of adverse experiences like homelessness, substance abuse, and family violence—often, the children they serve have experienced all three. Griffin had experienced the death of his mother and chronic homelessness and yet grabbed hold of a vision to put homelessness in his rearview mirror and resolve his adulthood would be different. Diane wants more of her clients' stories to have such happy endings.

Social Worker and Minister

The VOA has its roots in the Salvation Army, although it became a separate Christian church and organization in 1896. Today, staff members who have been with the agency for at least a year can choose to become Commissioned Ministers, which Diane has done. She was recently ordained at the initiation of the church, in recognition of her spiritual leadership. Diane coordinates all the ministry activities of the agency, such as Bible study groups and worship services.

Commissioned Ministers take on duties above and beyond the scope of their specific jobs within the agency to be engaged and active in the ministerial aspects of the organization's work. They may lead Bible studies, collaborate with affiliated congregations, and preach or lead music in the agency's bi-monthly worship gathering. These worship opportunities take place in a congregation within easy walking distance of many of the agency's programs, so that clients, who are invited, have a clear choice about whether to participate or not. The ministers also gather each month to pray for and plan the ministerial the work of the agency. Staff or clients who wish to submit prayer requests can do so and the ministers of the agency pray for these concerns.

In her work in the housing programs of her agency, especially the senior adult facility, Diane has the opportunity to help residents deal with their grief after the death of a fellow resident. She holds what she calls an "informal time of remembrance" a day or two after the funeral. She may bring a candle or a bouquet of flowers to serve as a focal point, and ask the gathered residents to share things they remember about the person who has passed: what were their habits, what did they love, what were the things that made them unique? Sometimes this can bring much laughter along with some tears and can be very therapeutic. After a time of this kind of sharing, Diane takes a break and invites those that wish to return for a more religious service with scripture, hymns, and prayer. There is a clear line of demarcation so that persons who do not wish to be present for a religious service have an opportunity to excuse themselves.

Diane ends these remembrance gatherings asking if anyone can think of a way that they would like to honor the life of the person who has passed. Recently at one of these gatherings in the senior adult facility, one of the residents said, "Gloria was so hospitable. She was always cooking for us and having us over. I am going to cook a meal in her memory and have anybody that wants to come. She was such a good cook, (long pause) except for her brownies. They were awful." With that the whole room howled with laughter and someone said, "Yes, they were terrible brownies, but we loved her for making them anyway." Diane says these times serve an important function; funeral services often do not offer the space for these moments of sharing life stories.

The agency is careful to give clients the freedom to participate—or not—in any of the agency's religious services. Diane says even apart from the requirements to separate worship from the social services they provide using government funding, it is the right thing to make sure no clients feel compelled to express a certain faith perspective or to even have any faith perspective at all. She notes:

> We have to make sure our social services to clients of different faiths or no faith identity are absolutely of the same quality with the same level of care and their needs are met just like we would with a client who does share our faith.

She notes that many clients may not even know the organization is religiously affiliated, especially when they first receive services. Additionally, while administrators apprise prospective staff members of the religious heritage and current identity of the agency, staff members do not have to profess a particular faith perspective either.

Diane thinks both the social work profession and the church have a responsibility to enter into the dark places: poverty, homelessness, grief, crime, and abuse. She says:

> I see this as not an opportunity, but a mandate. When my daughter was six, she asked me, 'Why do you want to work with sad things all the time?' I do not remember exactly what I said to her then, but I do believe it is where Christ would be fully present were He here in physical form. Christ would be walking down those long dark places with people.

For eight years, while working full-time in the homeless and housing programs at her agency, Diane also served on a local church staff as the Minister of Church Social Work. She says:

> Because the local church is part of the fabric of a community, often people will seek help there; they won't go to a therapist or a social service agency, but they will talk to a minister.

One of the older women had expressed skepticism that her church really needed a social worker when the church first considered hiring Diane. Then the woman's husband died. Tears would well up at church even as she fought to keep her emotions hidden. Diane reached out to her many times, always with the woman politely refusing conversation, saying she was "fine." Finally, Diane suggested that they watch a movie together and she agreed. Diane went to the woman's home, popcorn in a sack under arm, with her copy of the movie *Shadowlands*, the film portrayal of noted theologian C.S. Lewis' journey through the grief at the loss of his beloved wife. As they watched together, finally the woman's tears flowed freely and she shared her feelings and struggles with Diane. While she never publically affirmed that the church social worker had helped her directly, she often suggested to other widows that they should connect with Diane and "watch that movie she has."

Diane offered family life education programs through her congregation, focusing on those "tricky points in the life span" as she calls them—issues like dealing with infants and toddlers, facing the "empty nest," and caring for aging parents while also raising children. She formed a multi-generational women's support group whose participants used creative writing as an outlet for telling the stories of their life journeys.

Diane also supervised social work interns at the church and together they developed a program they named "Covenant Families" for families who came to the church for financial assistance in a time of crisis. In addition to short term financial help, Diane offered to connect the family to a mentor from the church to help with budgeting and other life skills, connect them to vocational and other educational opportunities, and be a friend in whatever challenges they might face. In turn, Diane provided ongoing support to both the family and their mentor.

A Serious Commitment to Hope

When asked how she deals with tough days, Diane replies:

> On some days, what gets you through is a serious commitment to hope that God is there in all of it. Hold on with both hands and do not let go. Let other people see it too where they have not been able to see it for a while.

Diane tells of a time when she held onto hope and would not let go. In 2007, her city, like most municipalities during the height of the recession, was slashing its budget. It had proposed a very severe cut to its funding for the VOA Family Emergency Shelter and other agencies it supports. The city had public hearings for the affected agencies to make a plea for their programs to make a case for restored funding. Diane's colleagues asked her to represent the agency. It makes her tearful to think about it. She says:

> I hate public speaking. Some people are naturally gifted to speak before the Council and the media, but I was really anxious. I had written a speech. I had three minutes to give that speech. I felt like I had put together a good case for our program. I began with, "If we have to tell clients our doors are closing, I don't know where I can tell them to go." I felt like I was really fighting for them, but it was not just me. I felt like I was not alone; I know the Spirit was with me. The City Council restored the funding.

In that moment, Diane felt a power that was not her own; she felt God's presence enabling her to make the case well. As a result, over one hundred homeless families have found shelter in her agency every year since then.

On that pivotal night in Washington, D.C., more than thirty years ago, Diane had been unable to wrap her mind around someone not having a home. Diane still has not come to grips with homelessness; she is still doing something about it.

Questions to Ponder

1. Diane's daughter asked her why she "wants to work with sad things all the time." Diane says she does not remember how she answered her; how would you answer that question?

2. In what ways does the agency context support the integration of faith and social work practice? How do you think the agency's efforts to ensure clients do not feel pressured to participate in religious activities, but does make them available, to be a reflection of Christian values? Of social work values?

3. What do you think of Diane's "ice tray" intervention? Do you see what Diane did as social work practice? Why or why not?

4. Diane would never have seen herself in the role of advocate before she became one. Trace her path into advocacy. What elements do you see that she brings to advocacy for people who are homeless that you think have the potential for making her effective?

5. What do you think about a social worker allowing or encouraging clients to respond with care for or advocacy for the social worker (the client who walked her to her car), or for other clients (the former client who advocated for other clients)? How do you decide what is good, ethical practice—and what is not?

6. If you were doing research on building resiliency in children who have adverse experiences like homelessness, what are the factors in the story of Griffin that would be most promising to study in the lives of children who are homeless?

7. In her role as minister, what steps has Diane taken to integrate her role as a spiritual leader with her role as a social worker? How does she express respect for the religious—or nonreligious—perspectives of her clients?

8. Think about a time you have had a "serious commitment to hope." What kind of circumstances did that get you through? How do you nurture a spirit of hopefulness in the face of working with "sad things all the time"?

Kevin Arroyo

Field Director,
Center for Hunger Solutions

Jeremy Everett, Co-Author

An undergraduate English major in his senior year, Kevin attended a capstone retreat for one of his classes. Students were telling the group about their future plans. When it came time for Kevin to respond he nervously stated, "I just want to help people." He was unsure what this meant for his career path, but he and his wife had mentored two young boys from a low-income neighborhood, and he had grown to realize that helping people who were poor was how he wanted to spend his life.

Kevin and his wife, Eleanor, had met the boys when Eleanor was a summer day camp counselor in their university's summer camp for children in the community. Eleanor befriended one of the children, and she invited him and his younger brother to come with her and Kevin to church:

> We started taking them to church every week and after awhile, the doors opened for us to meet their aunt and uncle, with whom they lived. By taking them to church once a week, we were able to get to know them pretty well.

Through this growing friendship, Kevin began to learn about ways of living different from those he had experienced in his own family. He realized that he was taking seemingly small things for granted, such as bathing every day, since he knew this was something the boys did not do. Kevin mused, remembering:

> Poverty housing was different from anything I had encountered before. They had several cars outside that may or may not have been functional. There were always random dogs around and the inside of their house was cluttered more than our house ever was. If we gave the boys a granola bar, they were so excited because it was very rare for them to have a snack.

Kevin had grown up watching his parents serve in their rural community:

> I grew up in a small farming community where you helped your

neighbors. That was natural and I did not recognize that there was any other way to live. As I got to know the family living in poverty, the lifestyle I witnessed was one I had never experienced. They seemed alone with no one to help. I recognized that changes needed to be made, and I wanted to be a part of that change.

Kevin and his wife were taking the boys to their Baptist church located in an inner-city neighborhood. Most church members were middle-class Anglos; most of the neighborhood was low-income African American and Latino. Several of the members of the congregation had decided to move into the neighborhood where the church was located. Together, they felt called to try to reverse the trend of many predominantly Anglo churches that had relocated to suburban communities when neighborhoods transitioned into ethnic minority and predominantly low-income residents. The church had decided not only to stay in the low-income area but, by members relocating to this area, they could also focus on strengthening a neighborhood that the city's systems and institutions were ignoring. Kevin and Eleanor felt called to be a part of this movement:

> We were moving out of our on-campus apartment and a friend e-mailed me saying, 'Hey I'm thinking about moving and have some ideas of where you guys could live.' Something divine was happening.

Kevin and Eleanor spoke with their friend about the home where she was currently living. Her house was less than a mile from their church. "It is a neighborhood that's not ideal for a starting family; it's not the suburbs," Kevin remarked. Yet Kevin and Eleanor felt like it was the right place for them. The friend that offered her home to Kevin and Eleanor served at the time as their church's mission pastor. She was at the heart of the changes occurring in the church and her house gave Kevin and Eleanor the opportunity to live into what they experienced as God calling them:

> When we first moved in we thought we would change the neighborhood but I think we realized quickly that we are now part of the neighborhood; we are just one of the families that live here. It is all part of living with our neighbors in a Christian sense, and being intentional about the relationships we build.

Seeing a Sign - Choosing Social Work

Kevin regularly looks to close friends whom he respects for their counsel when he is making decisions about next steps in his life. He decided to go to seminary because he had a number of friends who had been students there, and they recommended it. Kevin applied and began studies for his Master of Divinity degree.

Kevin knew nothing about the seminary's dual degree program with the university's graduate social work program. One day walking across campus, he passed by the School of Social Work. Glancing in a window in simple curiosity, his eyes caught on a recruitment poster that read, "Do you want to help people?" "Yes!" he almost said out loud. He veered off course, walked in the front door of the school, picked up a packet of information and left without talking with anyone. Later, he read about the dual degree and discussed it with students he knew and learned were enrolled in both seminary and social work. The more he learned, the more he knew it was what he felt called do. He applied and was accepted into the MSW program.

As he met other social work students and heard stories about their field placements, Kevin gravitated towards grassroots community organizing and sustainable agriculture as a means of addressing global poverty. He planned to do his social work internship at the International Hunger Farm, an organization that trains interns from around the world in sustainable agriculture theory and skills. When he was finalizing his plans for his second year internship, however, the Farm's social worker announced his resignation, and, with no social worker supervisor available, the Farm decided not to take a social work intern.

Kevin was distraught; he thought that the Farm internship was the way to live into his calling. He did not know how to find his way forward. A social work professor called him out of the blue, asking him to lead a class project for the community practice course in which he would be enrolled the next year as his internship. Working with city government, the project's focus would be building a city-wide coalition to address the high poverty rate in the city. Kevin said about the opportunity:

> I'm very introverted and would not want to be in front of the class so it did not make sense that the professor would call me, but I trusted her and so I said yes. I jumped into leading the project.

The experience of leading the city coalition was powerful; the city adopted the agenda the class developed, and Kevin had opportunity to develop and demonstrate skills of leadership and coalition building. The experience made him the right candidate for a new school project that was attempting to address domestic hunger through coalition building. Kevin graduated with a job offer to be the Field Director for the Center for Hunger Solutions (CHS).

Faith and Practice

Kevin sees a call to address poverty and hunger as synonymous with his Christian commitment—Jesus' call to love our neighbors means loving people who are poor and hungry:

> I feel that as a Christian I am called to work for the poor and help do what I can to end poverty. I believe to love God is to live my faith in my actions—to love my neighbor. I cannot do that better than through the work I am doing here at this point in my life.

Kevin reflected that he has seen God moving in his life as he looks back through experiences—meeting and befriending two young boys living in poverty, moving into a low-income neighborhood, the closing of the opportunity with the Farm and the opportunity for an internship with the city, and then the opportunity to work in the Center for Hunger Solutions. When Kevin had first walked through the doors of the School of Social Work, he had imagined working directly with low-income families, but his internship with city government exposed him to work in capacity building.

> When I worked with the City, I did not work with anybody in poverty. I worked with people who *worked* with people in poverty. I realized that this work was an ability I had and I could have an impact on poverty far more broadly than working with individuals. CHS was a perfect fit.

Kevin's responsibilities with CHS have changed considerably over the years. He initially supervised ten AmeriCorps Volunteers In Service To America (VISTAs); AmeriCorps VISTA is a national volunteer program designed to fight domestic poverty. VISTA members have made a one-year commitment to be engaged in community service projects in exchange for a modest living allowance. Eight of the VISTA members Kevin supervised were located in the home offices of CHS; two were based in other regions of the state.

Each VISTA worker was working to build Food Planning Associations (FPAs) across the state. FPAs are community-based coalitions of private and public organizations, congregations, and government agencies. The purpose of the FPAs is to ensure greater access to three healthy meals a day for families in their region who are living in poverty. In the first year, Kevin and his team developed and supported FPAs that served almost half of the state's population. This collaborative model led to increases in access to summer meals and breakfast at school for children who might otherwise go hungry without the school meals they received when school was in session. CHS also increased the number of households living in poverty who received the benefits of the Supplemental Nutrition Assistance Program (SNAP).

State and federal government agencies and foundations were impressed with the effective strategies of CHS. The following year, CHS received over $20 million in multi-year grants and contracts. Kevin's team was about to multiply. He was now managing twelve new regional offices with over 60 staff. His responsibility was hiring and supervising twelve Regional Directors with the help of his new supervisor. Kevin handled his new challenge with trust in God's guidance, just as he had moving into the inner city and taking the leadership role with his internship class.

Capacity Building for Capacity Builders

Kevin developed a methodical approach to supervising the regional directors. Each morning he called one of the directors to talk over the work in that region. He asked that the regional director set the agenda, discussing the successes and challenges of the previous week. Each director was supervising the regional staff, and Kevin encouraged the directors to discuss with him how the staff was doing and any successes and challenges in the supervisory process. Kevin also made it clear that he cared and wanted to hear how the director was feeling about the work and the context of the work in the director's personal as well as professional life.

Once a week, all of the regional directors joined Kevin on a conference call. These meetings were a little more structured; Kevin provided a list of discussion topics for the meeting, giving the regional directors an opportunity to dialogue with each other about their outreach work in the regional offices. In turn, Kevin and another co-worker scheduled weekly supervision training with a Human Resources consultant from the university to help strengthen their supervisory skills.

Kevin spends most of his day in scheduled and unscheduled meetings with his team. As a result, Kevin has been frustrated that he is less able to devote energy and time to strategy development, and developing strategy is his favorite work. Still, he is working with people who are working with people in poverty—and he feels called to this work.

Kevin also enjoys taking on challenges that come with the job. For example, Kevin learned that the mayor in the city where one of the regional offices was located was expressing concern that CHS' organizing efforts could potentially thwart the city's goal to reduce poverty. That seemed counter-intuitive to CHS' stated mission of ending hunger and reducing poverty, so Kevin called for a meeting with the entire regional staff to learn more.

The regional staff explained that much of their focus had been on including in their region's FDA the actual people living in poverty in their city. That seemed right to Kevin; the CHS model is to include everyone in building the coalition—city government leaders, business leaders, representatives from social service organizations, congregational leaders—and community residents living in poverty. The regional director had grown up in poverty in the community where she now served. Because of her own experiences, she had worked exceptionally hard to include representatives of low-income families in the developing FDA, unintentionally neglecting city leaders—including the mayor.

While she was working to build the FDA, in a parallel and unrelated process, city leaders had been discussing poverty in their region. The city leaders were poised to take on the problems of poverty as they understood them. Not only had CHS not included the city leaders; the city leaders had not known or included the CHS Regional Director in their discussion. Now the lines were drawn. The regional director was ready for battle, believing that the city leaders understood poverty to be a consequence of the actions of those living in poverty, not a systemic economic issue beyond the control of those who are poor. According to the regional director, the city leaders were trying to fix poverty in the city by fixing the poor, and their approach offended her.

In response, the CHS staff had called a meeting of young leaders in the nonprofit community to discuss the direction of the city's initiative. Learning about the meeting further threatened the city leaders, even though the CHS staff had not intended to create an alternative to the city's initiative.

Kevin discussed with the regional CHI staff the need to work with city leaders; if the community leaders feel unsupported and threatened, they may be less likely to work collaboratively with CHS' regional staff to support the city's food insecure residents. Together, Kevin and the Regional Director devised a plan for gaining the trust and collaboration of city leaders.

Kevin wanted his staff to feel supported and trusted. He wanted them to know his care for them was unwavering, but he also wanted to push them to new learning, which is often uncomfortable. That push to do the uncomfortable, after all, has been part of Kevin's story. Thus far, his life has been a journey that has required stepping into the unknown and trusting that God is there with him.

Questions to Ponder

1. Kevin and his wife moved into the inner-city neighborhood of their congregation. What are the benefits to social workers living in a low-income neighborhood? What are the disadvantages?

2. Kevin's story is one of discernment of where God was calling him. Is there a formal or informal process you use to discern major professional decisions in life? Is there a process your community of faith prescribes to discern next steps?

3. Kevin graduated three years before the interview and had already moved to a position of considerable organizational responsibility. What do you need to prepare yourself for the possibility of rapid growth in responsibility?

4. Kevin had a dilemma when dealing with one of his regional offices that had not been working in collaboration with city government. What caused the problem? How did Kevin handle this challenge? Should Kevin have met with city leadership to solve the problem, let his regional team take the lead, or taken some other action?

5. What ways, if any, could Kevin have averted the problems that developed in the regional office through his supervision?

6. Kevin is not working directly with people who are poor; he is working at the macro level with systems and organizations. Does his work fulfill Jesus' command to love neighbor—or does Kevin also need also to engage directly with people who are poor?

People Who Are Refugees and Immigrants

Karen Richmond
Refugee Resettlement Social Worker
Amy Butler, Co-Author

Karen started out as a business major in college, but she was restless. "I didn't want my life to be chasing everything for myself; I wanted to invest in the lives of other people." She spent a semester in her university's program in Thailand. After coming back to the U.S. and finishing her degree, she returned to Thailand to teach English. She thought of her time in Thailand as "an adventure—a break from life."

Instead of an aside from life, however, Karen's experiences in Thailand began to define her life path. Thailand confronted her with the global refugee crisis—there were nine camps in Thailand for Burmese refugees during Karen's time there. She wondered what it meant to be a refugee—and why so many? Karen began researching how people come to be refugees, and how the global community addresses the needs of people and families who have to flee their homelands because of war or persecution. Now she understands that through that exposure to the experiences and needs of refugees, God was calling her to serve.

Karen laughingly says:

> If God had ever tried to call me before Thailand, I wasn't listening.

In college, she was always surrounded by a large group of friends, always busy with activities—she is an extrovert and loves people. The time in Thailand was a sharp contrast; when she was not teaching, she found herself alone and even isolated. She was searching, asking God for direction:

> If I had not been asking, I don't think God would have called me—or maybe I just would not have heard.

Still, the way forward was murky. Karen did not know what to do. The time she spent in Thailand had been difficult for her; as much as she loved the culture and the people, she was lonely and she longed for home. After the seven month commitment she had made to serve in Thailand, she returned home to the suburbs of the Midwestern city that had been home to her all of her life. She wanted to work with people who are refugees—to serve them—but she wanted to do it closer to home.

What Karen had not realized growing up in the Midwest is that the U.S. is a refugee-receiving country, and that her very own city has a large refugee community. When Karen learned that, she was ready to prepare for what she perceived was her life calling—to work with people who are refugees. She explored what the requirements were for that kind of job, and she learned about social work. Karen returned to her university, this time to complete a graduate degree in social work.

When we first interviewed her, Karen was a Refugee Resettlement Case Manager. She was the first contact a family who are refugees had when they land in their new home. Karen, or a member of her team, met them at the airport. In the following days, the team helped the family apply for the benefits they could receive from the U.S. government to help them over the first six months until they could settle in and find employment. Karen taught the families to navigate American grocery stores and bus lines—and any other systems new to the family that they needed to survive.

Daily Work with People Who Are Refugees

Karen began each day reviewing news outlets for any events that would directly affect her agency and the people that might be coming her way sooner or later as refugees. Until the pace picked up later in the day, Karen chased the paperwork; there are always a lot of forms and reports to keep up to date since government contracts fund her agency.

Later in the day, Karen taught a cultural orientation class for those who had newly arrived; the students learned basic survival information—everything from the laws of our society that may be quite different from those in their homelands to how to keep a house or apartment clean. Some of the families Karen served have never lived in a house with four walls, a roof, and running water and electricity before—much less an apartment complex.

Karen spent a lot of time in the community. She enjoyed going with her clients to learn how to buy their food in a grocery store, since many had never shopped anywhere but a village marketplace. Everyone else in the world, it seems, uses the kilo and not the pound for measuring; Karen helped them learn to translate. The sheer size of U.S. grocery stores and myriad of choices are overwhelming. Complicating all of this orientation and teaching was the fact that Karen and her clients usually did not speak a shared language.

When a new family was coming, Karen prepared for their arrival. She loved furnishing their apartment, making a nest for them in their strange new environment. She used a small budget to shop for them, finding decorations in the agency's donation center—silk flowers or wall decorations that speak welcome. Karen enjoyed the time by herself, reflecting on the people she served. She had recently prepared for a large Somali family, knowing that they would have many barriers to overcome. So as she prepared the apartment, she prayed for them and committed herself to walking beside them. Those preparations were her favorite part of the job.

On the day she would meet the Somali family at the airport, Karen first went home to her own kitchen, where she prepared a meal to have waiting for them. She spent the whole day in preparations—and then the airport welcome. She said:

> I loved the moment when I would meet them and take them to their new home for the first time; usually they were so grateful and happy—and tired.

Within thirty days, children must be enrolled in and attending school. Some children had never attended a school before, and they were being plunged into a public school in the U.S. without the ability to speak English. Karen had to fight discouragement when she saw how daunting the task was for her clients to make their way in a place so different from their homeland, in a language they often know very little or not at all.

The paperwork seemed endless, and it was Karen's least favorite part of her job. Sometimes, the documentation she was required to do actually interfered with her work with clients. She had actually caught herself debating about whether or not to make a home visit to a client family because she knew that if she did go, it would create still more documentation to add to the pile she had already not completed. Karen found the stress mounting as she sensed the piles of her paperwork deepen.

Sometimes her schedule would fill with appointments and meetings she had to attend but that interfered with the time she needed for her clients. Karen mused that if she did not care so much, she would not be so stressed, and that what she experienced is a common problem for social workers funded by public dollars; there has to be accountability for the resources they use, including her time. Still, it is frustrating not to be able to do all she wants to do with her clients.

Because the work is hard, Karen and her colleagues need to find or create humor in their workdays to ease the stress and the discouragement that can threaten all of them. They do. It was a large and busy office, with more than 60 social workers and other staff, and Karen said that the sounds of laughter somewhere in the office would ring out throughout the day. It made her smile and melted the frustration.

On days when the banter of the office was not enough and she sensed that her own ability to give was running on empty, Karen would dig back into her time in Thailand and remind herself of the experience of God calling her, or her own desire to serve. She also knew that she was not alone; her co-workers felt a similar calling to the work, and they supported one another. She attended a conference of Catholic agencies, where she met with people all over the country doing refugee work. There they were able to share their common struggles and joys:

> I met people who were thousands of miles away in a different city—and they are feeling the same feelings I have; I am not alone; I am not bearing it by myself.

Karen realized the support she finds in relationships with other social workers facing the same challenges she faces also translates into what her clients need. She knew that she could only do so much for her clients; they also needed the community support that comes from other refugees who share their experiences. So a big part of her responsibility was connecting her clients with other people who have been refugees who can be there as community after Karen's work with new families ended.

The Next Step

Karen's goal was to find a healthy balance between her work life and her personal life. She wanted to stay fully engaged with her clients and hopeful for their futures. That meant finding ways she can do this work for the years stretching before her. She was uncertain about how to develop that resiliency. The colleagues she liked the least are those who go home at the end of the day and leave thoughts and worries about their clients at work. Yet she knew she had to find a way to be both engaged fully with her clients, as well as have a life that is not defined by her work. She could put in ten hours every day and still not finish all there is to do. That leaves little time for the professional development opportunities she would like to pursue—polishing her skills in grant writing and taking a class in non-profit management. Moreover, she was finding that the work was increasingly having a negative impact on her personal health and wellbeing.

> I loved the work, but I did not sleep much. I was picking up clients from the airport at 1:00 a.m. It was so rewarding, but it also challenging for one's personal life.

It was not just the demands and the hours. Karen's concern for her clients was slipping into her personal life in challenging ways:

> I would wake up in the night from nightmares of my clients being in the emergency room somewhere or being lost because they did not know where they were or understand what was going on around them. They relied on me to understand everything they need to know about this place that is now their home. The burden seemed heavier and heavier.

Two years before our second conversation, Karen moved from working with the Catholic agency engaged in refugee resettlement to a nonreligious network of organizations that are engaged in refugee resettlement; some are religiously affiliated, including the one from which she came, and some are not. The funding for her new position is the same federal source for refugee resettlement services. Instead of working at the direct services level, however, Karen is now working in the national office located in the Northeast, providing program monitoring and oversight, making sure that the agencies are complying with the government requirements for funding and that clients are being served well:

> I sensed that I had mastered the direct services aspect of refugee work, doing the same core services kind of over and over and over for new families as they come in. I needed a new challenge, so that caused me to look at working for the national office, to develop a larger vision for what we do. Still, I really miss the direct daily contact with clients.

Of course, the move also addressed the struggles Karen was having with feeling the heavy burden of the direct work with families. It was far more than just a way to address her personal needs, however. The new position has given her the sense that she is in a position to influence the services available to families who are refugees across the country, not just her own caseload. Karen reflects back on her business degree and how it is important to her for reasons she could not have foreseen then:

> My work in the national office has given me more opportunity to flex that side of myself, working with budgeting, capacity building, and planning. I am using gifts that were not relevant to direct case management work with a client.

Moreover, she is gaining an international perspective on the work they do. Different countries respond in different ways to the global refugee crisis; the national office has given Karen opportunity to know more about the issues of refugees and cross-nation responses globally.

Life and Faith

Karen thinks her work has strengthened her faith. When she was working with clients, she had the feeling that she was at the heart of what God had called her to do—"Loving the people that God loves, those who are poor and strangers." Her clients were resilient in ways that she could only dimly understand. Somehow, her work with them helped her to see God more clearly:

> I'm learning what God's love is and really what unconditional love means.

She appreciated all the Christian volunteers and congregations that wanted to support her agency and its clients. They could be there for these families when her work has ended. She yearned for congregations to "wrap their arms around our clients and love them well." So it saddened—and angered—her when the support congregations offered was conditional; some only wanted to help those clients who would become a part of their worshipping community. Many of the refugees are Muslim or Hindu or have no religious faith. Some have left their countries fleeing religious persecution.

As a result, Karen reflects that her personal relationship with God is stronger, but "my relationship with people who claim to have the same relationship is just really not going well." Some days the church and the volunteers encouraged her; other times, the conditions they put on their care for families who are refugees deeply disappointed her. Karen said that her work has led her to believe that the way we put people in categories is not what God intends us to do. Karen finds herself increasingly affirming that Jesus' life showed us to care for one another, regardless of our differences:

> As I have done this work, I have found myself believing even more deeply that we are not called to love people because of their faith or because they share our beliefs. We are called to love others because that is what Jesus called us to do—it is our faith at work, to love those who are not like us.

Karen says that her calling to social work and to working with refugees is as strong as it ever was. She is confident that she is doing what God called her to do. At the same time, the work has challenged and changed her faith. She is constantly dealing with people who come from different cultural and religious backgrounds.

> Especially those three years I spent working directly with clients, I had to confront my own privilege that I had just taken for granted, as well as my biases. My calling has not changed, but it feels different because I have interacted with people that come from every corner of our world who have dealt with some really hard life experiences. It is impossible to not be changed by knowing them.

Her family, living in a rural southwestern area, has had trouble understanding her decision to work with people who are so unlike them and to move so far from home; her following her calling has felt like rebellion to them. Karen's response was to clench her jaw and say to herself:

> Because that is how you feel, I am going to rebel even more—I am going to love these people even more.

As a consequence, not only has Karen's worldview broadened, but so has that of her family. Back when she was working directly with clients, her mother began volunteering with the agency to befriend some of Karen's clients.

Just when she and her family had worked through to a new understanding of and even embracing Karen's calling and how it changed them, too, Karen presented them with a new challenge. Just months before our last interview, she married a man originally from Egypt and a Muslim. The cross-cultural relationship, particularly the fact that he is a practicing Muslim, was confusing and a source of conflict with her family; it has created a new source of stress for Karen as she tries to navigate her family's dismay. It helped that she had moved to the national office, far from home, located in an extremely culturally diverse city. The newlyweds are surrounded by other couples as culturally and religiously diverse as they are.

Karen says that her work and now her home life have been fertile ground for her to continue to grow in her understanding of God and faith:

> If I am not exploring my faith in the context of my experiences in this life, then my faith is dead. So I think about my faith against the backdrop of other cultures and religions. I begin to see how my culture has very much informed the religion of my family, and the religion that I have always called mine and is still mine.

Questions to Ponder

1. Karen went to Thailand to teach as an adventure. Instead, it exposed her to what she came to believe was a divine calling to serve people who are refugees. What kinds of experiences have shaped your life, like Thailand did for Karen?
2. What about Karen's work sounds most appealing to you? Are there parallels in work with other client groups with which you sense you would enjoy working?
3. What about Karen's work sounds most difficult for you? Is that challenge unique to work with this setting for practice, or might it be a thread in other settings for social work as well?
4. Karen believed that she needed to connect her client families to a supportive community that can be ongoing after her time-limited work

ends. How do you see the distinction between the role of the social worker and the role of neighbors and friends in this work? How might you imagine those roles, for example, in the preparation and initial arrival of a new family?

5. Given the non-Christian faith and experiences of persecution that characterize many of Karen's clients, what role, if any, should Karen consider for herself in working with congregations who only want to serve clients willing to join their faith communities? If you were Karen, how might you tackle this issue?

6. Karen found herself increasingly burdened by her work. Consider how she chose to handle the difficulty she had in setting boundaries around the responsibilities she carried for her clients. What other possible ways might she have addressed this struggle? How do you think she can use that struggle in her current work?

7. Karen has found her experiences with clients from other religions and cultures sending her to reexamine her own faith, saying, "If I am not exploring my faith in the context of my experiences in this life, then my faith is dead." What ramifications would this kind of openness to self-examination have for various areas of social work practice that you are considering?

Aurora Flores
Community Organizer, Immigrant Rights
Emily Bibb Mosher, Co-Author

Her mother remembers how Aurora Flores had a deep sense of compassion, even as a child. The family spent a couple of weeks each winter visiting relatives in Mexico. As they prepared for one such trip, little Aurora carefully covered all of her stuffed animals with blankets, worried that they might be cold in a house with the furnace turned down while the family was away. When the family was in the process of selling and replacing an old car, Aurora became sad, fearing that the car would think they did not like it anymore. Her mother reflected that Aurora's concern for inanimate objects was a sign of her calling to care for people who are suffering. She told Aurora that her compassion was not only a calling but also a gift.

Aurora followed her older brother and sister to a Christian university. She had no idea what to major in; she had never heard of social work as a profession. When she had completed her first year taking general studies courses, she knew she had to decide on a major. That summer, she had an experience she calls a "Godsend." An inner-city camp for at-risk teens invited her to serve as a counselor. One of the founders of the program had minored in social work at the university Aurora was attending. He and the other founder had played football in the NFL. When they retired, they designed a ten-day camp for at-risk inner city teenagers to experience what it is like to be a college student. Aurora loved every minute of those ten days. She said to one of the founders, "This is the kind of thing that I want to do for the rest of my life; what do I major in to do this kind of work?" The answer he gave was "social work."

That experience changed everything. Aurora declared social work as her major and earned her Bachelor of Social Work degree. She went on to another university to complete her Master of Social Work degree.

Immigrant Rights Collaboration (IRC)

After graduating, Aurora worked for three and half years at the Immigrant Rights Collaboration (IRC). Aurora served as the executive director with a full time staff of one—herself. The mission of the organization is to organize the immigrant community through human rights education with the goal of change in social policies and in practice, so that every human being's rights and dignity are recognized and protected.

Aurora believes that the history of the U.S. demonstrates that community organizing can bring about change, but "we have a long way to go." Aurora trained members of the immigrant community in her city to become "Human Rights Leaders." After an intensive training process, they each formed a Neighborhood Human Rights Committee of five to fifteen people. The Human Rights Leader organized the committee to learn about their rights and to plan their engagement in public and legislative campaign efforts. Instead of having one paid organizer—herself—trying to reach a whole community, Aurora was now consulting with ten volunteer leaders each reaching five to ten individual people, thus spreading the work—and the involvement.

Everyone in IRC was a volunteer except Aurora, although she was moving the organization toward having part-time Regional Coordinators who had already established their committees. They were coordinating the work of their geographical region and the committees within that region. IRC provided Regional Coordinators with small stipends because they dedicate so much of their time to the work.

Aurora learned this model of organizing from another grassroots organization. As an outcome of the model, IRC experienced significant victories with Aurora's leadership. They led a statewide campaign that successfully defeated more than eighty anti-immigrant bills in the state legislature.

When the legislative session ended, they thought their work was done, at least for that year. Then the governor of the state decided to call a special session of the legislature in an attempt to pass his own priority bill, the "Safe Harbors" bill. The bill would have given law enforcement greater permission to ask about a person's immigration status based on the officer's discretion—which could be based on the color of a person's skin and perceived ethnic group. Such a policy would have caused public safety issues by making immigrants less willing to come forward to police if they saw or experienced a crime, fearing questioning about their immigration status.

The decision rocked the hardworking IRC volunteers and Aurora. They thought they had experienced victory, but in a special session, bills can be approved with fewer votes, and it takes time to organize individuals across the state to contact their representatives, time that IRC now did not have. Aurora was determined, however, and she contacted and partnered with organizations across the state to bring pressure to defeat the bill. The bill died in committee. She said:

That victory was tremendous. The anti-immigration forces are so strong in the state and, indeed, in the nation; it felt like a miracle.

Aurora and her volunteer staff were very proud of their success. She believes that when people organize themselves, they can bring about real change.

Life at IRC

Aurora described a "typical" day at IRC to me—the day before our first visit. Knowing it would be a long day, Aurora chose to start the day with some personal time at home, and then arrived at work late in the morning. Her first task was talking with a researcher at the local university with whom IRC is collaborating to study the impact of a program called "Safe Neighborhoods." The program links local law enforcement to immigration officials. Their report will be published, and Aurora was in the last stages of preparing the document. Next, she completed a grant application to a local foundation that supports IRC. She then drove to the grocery store to buy snacks for the high school Human Rights Club that would meet later in the day—she was helping to organize the club.

Dashing back from the grocery store, Aurora joined a ninety-minute webinar provided by one of her funders on a campaign strategy. By then, it was time to head over to the high school for the Human Rights Club meeting.

At the meeting, Aurora taught the teenagers about the law enforcement violations of human rights that were the focus of the campaign. The students were shocked by the facts Aurora shared of recent abuses, and at the same time, they resonated with what they heard. All of them were either Hispanic or African American, and many had family experiences of their own that connected with the facts Aurora was sharing. Aurora facilitated the students' planning for meetings that they would be having during the rest of the school year.

After the meeting, Aurora caught up on some phone calls and reading before going to a *comité* (Spanish for committee) meeting a little early. The *comité* meets in a member's home. Aurora met with leaders, working with them in planning to divide the *comité* since it is becoming too large—thankfully—to operate optimally. Together they planned who would lead the new groups, meeting dates, and the agenda for the evening.

The meeting focused on their identity as an immigrant community, the rights they have based in the United States Constitution, as well as the Universal Declaration of Human Rights and the history of immigration in this country. Several were hearing about their rights for the first time, hearing that they should expect to be treated with greater justice and dignity than they had experienced. Believing that a larger group is a stronger group, the members came up with the idea: "Let's go to every house in our neighborhood that we know that has immigrants and let's tell them what we are doing and invite them to join us."

They divided into two-person teams, with one person to talk and the other to take notes. They then spent an hour spreading out, going door by door in the surrounding neighborhood. They spent about 10 minutes at each home, collecting names and phone numbers of interested community residents, as well as noting their concerns.

The group gathered back together, planned to call the new contacts to remind them of the following week's meeting, and then it was time to "hang out." They moved to the front porch; several parents had brought their children to the meeting, so as they talked, they rocked babies and watched the children play. In Mexico, Aurora said, people commonly visit on the front porch. Few people really have a back yard, and the front porch is more sociable, visible and engaged with the neighborhood. They talked long into the evening, eating fruit with lemon and chili powder, a common snack in Mexico. As the last *comité* members began to drift home, Aurora helped clean up and then headed home herself.

Inherent Dignity and Worth

Aurora receives great satisfaction from her work:
> I thrive on seeing the transformation in the minds of immigrants when they begin to realize that, despite what society tells them, despite what the news tells them, despite what legislators tell them, they have inherent dignity and worth because they are human beings.

That realization comes in these house meetings where people share their stories and begin to realize their collective power. Their focus becomes not just their struggles as individual immigrants but, more broadly, a shared human rights struggle. They see the connection of their struggles with other human injustices.

In the first *comité* meeting, since no one in the community knew her except the leaders, Aurora and the leaders decided that they would conduct a simulation. Aurora dressed to look like a law enforcement officer, wearing black clothing, boots, and pulling her hair back in a bun. The leaders started the meeting, and Aurora then came a few minutes later, pounding on the door. When someone opened the door, she said loudly and firmly to the group, "What are you doing here?" Everybody was quiet. Aurora continued, "You don't have the right to be meeting together." She began asking people individually where they were born and where they were from. People fixed their eyes on the floor; some answered her, and some were mute. She then stopped the simulation, and told the group who she was and she is not a law enforcement officer or immigration agent.

The group then talked about their feelings and what they had done in response. How should they have responded if she really had been an immigration official? The group realized that they did not have to invite her into the house.

They did not have to answer her questions about where they were born. She had no reason or right to ask them for that information, but as soon as they answered that they had been born outside the United States, she had permission to arrest them because there was a probable cause that they were undocumented. They discussed the meaning of documentation, of "that piece of paper" that gives people permission to be in the United States. Aurora put the question to the group, "When did we start believing the message that we should not be treated as human beings in this country just because we don't have that piece of paper?" One man said:

> I can't believe that I just answered so easily and that I was so afraid. That is the fear that we live in. That is a constant fear.

Others agreed. Someone said, "I knew that I wasn't supposed to answer but I still answered because I was so intimidated." Another recognized, "I could have been deported just because I answered a question honestly!" They acknowledged to one another what it was like to live in constant fear and intimidation.

People had come to the *comité* meeting simply because they had been invited by a neighbor or work colleague. They left galvanized for the work of securing human rights and dignity for immigrants, both documented and undocumented.

The Struggle

Aurora is quick to admit that as exciting as that meeting was and how much she enjoys community work, her days were also filled with mundane work because she had to do it as the only full-time staff member—bookkeeping, record keeping, maintaining the organization's databases. When she began the work, it was nothing like what she had expected. She says:

> Often times we think that if God has called you, that means everything is going to be all wonderful and easy because God did it for you, but that is not always the case; in fact, it usually is not.

A steering committee of representatives from organizations who had formed a coalition to address immigration issues had hired her. When she began, however, Aurora found herself faced with no staff, no secure income, no path forward. There was only enough money for three months of her salary. She knew that her first step was to survive, to provide herself with an income, and so fundraising became her priority. She faced the daunting task of securing IRC's financial future—and her own—by developing a business plan and securing grants from several foundations, as well as gifts from individuals.

Moreover, Aurora learned all too soon that interpersonal conflicts among steering committee members had deepened into mutual contempt for one another. Strong factions tried to pull her to their conflicting visions for the organization. Aurora knew it would take her a year to know the organization well enough to begin creating lasting changes. Although she had been clear in communicating that time line, several powerful steering committee members expected her to create change and a shared vision in the first month. In summary, Aurora found no organizational guidelines, no management systems, and a micromanaging board of people at war with one another.

She had been sure that God had brought her to IRC because its work fit her passion. She is an immigrant herself, and she had known since she started her social work courses that she wanted to work with her community. When IRC hired her, she was thrilled and excited, believing it to be an opportunity from God especially for her. But six months after she began, Aurora prepared her resignation. She was extremely stressed and anxious. Her parents also were going through a divorce at that time, so she felt like her life, "was pretty much at rock bottom."

Aurora was experiencing not only a crisis in her work and family but also a crisis in her faith. How could following God's will put her in such a difficult place? She meditated on the Psalms, where David said, in her words, "I will live to tell how God delivered me from this; I will live to tell of this." She would repeat that to herself, but she found it very difficult to hope. She sought counseling and shared her struggle with her church as well. She knew people were praying for her. She had a couple of mentors who were wise enough to tell her to hang on for two to three more months. Through it all, Aurora says that she knew that God was present. She believed that God had a purpose for her, and that purpose would be fulfilled even if IRC was not the place for her. She says:

> We are not called to be the savior of every organization that we go to. Nor are we called to be the leader of the next big movement. We are called just to seek God and to do the things that God asks us to do on a daily basis.

Methodically, she tackled the challenges; she wrote grants, she built trust, and she put organizational systems in place. She focused her efforts more on the grassroots organizing in the neighborhoods and less on trying to cajole the organizations to work collaboratively. When Aurora had difficult days and found herself being swept over with the weight of her responsibilities, she says she reminded herself:

> I am just here as a tool of God. I am not indispensable in this world. God is in charge of my life and God is good. I know I have a lot to do but what is more important than the doing is the stopping and acknowledging that I am not called to be the God of any of this work that I'm doing. I am simply an avenue through which God can work.

Back to School

After working about three and a half years at IRC, Aurora realized that she wanted to pursue justice and equality for immigrants from a different angle. She noticed that grassroots campaigns were effective at saying when a bill would be hurtful for immigrants or actually deny their rights. They were not good, however, at identifying and promoting social policy that furthered human rights. She sees a lack of connection "between research and what's happening in the real world or the people that are involved." Therefore, she resigned from her position at IRC and enrolled in a Ph.D. program in Public Policy. With her degree, she hopes to be able to bridge the gap between organizations and communities who are working for immigration reform and empirical studies on what kind of policies would be helpful. By using research to identify the policies that human rights organizations should be promoting, Aurora wants to be able to provide the extra support that these organizations need in order to accomplish their mission.

During her first year of her Ph.D. studies, Aurora was able to be a full-time student and not work, but now she works through the university as a Teacher's Assistant. Aurora did not want to go back to school if she was going to be in more debt, but the university offered her a fellowship that covered her tuition and gave her a living stipend. She saw that offer as a sign that God was opening this door for her. She admits that she is not completely sure what she will do once she graduates, but she is okay with that:

> I've never really been 100% sure about any of my career choices.
> I just know that I should be here.

Deepened Faith

Aurora wants the model for her work to be Christ, to be God's desire for mercy and justice. She says that she takes very seriously the passage of scripture in the Lord's Prayer that calls for God's kingdom to come and will to be done on earth as it is in heaven:

> We are called to impact the world that we are in, and not simply
> to long for or wait for a beautiful time in heaven.

She believes she has the spiritual gift of mercy, and that social work has operationalized that gift, has given her the ability to practice mercy. "I definitely chose the right profession for me." Through all that she experienced at IRC, she believed God was sustaining her. Because she stayed the course and relied on God, she believes she created a more productive organization that will have a much greater impact for justice. In the midst of the professional and personal difficulties she faced during her time at IRC, Aurora sees God's redemption at work in her life. She believes that God not only saves us from sin, "but also saves us from things that God doesn't want us to live with." During this period, Aurora was on several medications for anxiety and depression, and she views this medication as part of God's redemption. She says:

> Because I was on that medication, I was able to develop the coping mechanisms that I needed to deal with the anxiety that I have and that I've inherited. I think that all of this has really served to make me a stronger person, which I attribute to God.

Aurora's experiences remind her of Mother Theresa saying that in all of our lives, just as in the life of Jesus, the resurrection has to come, the joy of Easter has to dawn (Theresa & Kolodiejchuk, 2007). Jesus' resurrection is what gives Aurora hope and keeps her going through difficult times.

C.S. Lewis' writing about evil also has an impact on her thinking. She mused that, according to Lewis, people who are doing evil actually understand evil the least because they have not been able to resist it. "The only one who is fully able to understand the depth of evil is Christ Jesus, who never gave in to any temptation." Aurora thinks she has seen the depths of evil in her work. She remembers being appalled in a legislative session at what legislators said and how they manipulated one another for their own ends—yet they would not call what they were doing "evil." She believes that her work for human rights is a spiritual battle. She believes that only God's power can bring justice, "because we can never ever do it on our own."

Aurora does not know where her life path will lead. She feels called to promote human rights, particularly for immigrants. She believes a large, multi-sectored movement is brewing, and she wants to be a part of that. Whatever comes next, her work has brought her into a closer relationship with God. A friend sent her an email the other day, saying "Do you see God smiling down on you?" Aurora does. She is more confident that she is walking with God than she felt when she began this work, and she wants to continue walking the unfolding path.

Questions to Ponder

1. Her mother named Aurora's compassion demonstrated as a child as a "gift." Do you see compassion as a personality trait or a gift? Can it be learned?
2. What about Aurora's "typical day" at IRC appealed to you? What sounds challenging?
3. How effective do you think Aurora's pretending to be a law enforcement officer was in educating the group about their rights? What ethical issues are involved in a simulation like this one?

4. Put yourself in Aurora's place, hired by this steering committee to be Executive Director. What would you expect your work to be like as you began this work? What did she find to be her first challenges, and what kind of emotional reaction did she have? How do you imagine you would have reacted if you were Aurora?

5. Aurora couched the initial struggles she found herself in at IRC as spiritual in nature. In what ways did her faith contribute to her ability to understand and persevere?

6. Aurora draws on the Lord's Prayer in describing the motivation for her work. What teachings—biblical or otherwise—do you turn back to repeatedly as you contemplate your calling?

7. Aurora uses the term "evil," not a common term in social work books, to describe her experience with powerful societal leaders, such as state legislators. How does a theological concept such as evil contribute to social work assessment and intervention, if it does?

Criminal Justice

Laura Crawford
Clinical Forensic Specialist, The Refuge

Laura Crawford declared her major immediately when she started her undergraduate studies—psychology. She had been so sure of her path to become a counselor, but she soon found out that she did not enjoy the psychology classes. Although she had been a good student in high school, her first year college grades were C's and D's. During her sophomore year, she was walking through a campus building when she spotted a bulletin board flyer advertising the course Introduction to Social Work. The flyer asked, "Do you like to volunteer? Do you care about poverty? Do you want to work for social justice?" "I thought to myself," Laura said, "That's me." She went to an information session listed on the flyer to learn more and signed up. She loved the course; she felt at home among people who cared about the same ideas and issues she did. Even the history of social work was fascinating to her. She explained:

> Social work really spoke to me; I was doing something that made me proud. Social work is not a profession that everyone can do. You really have to come into social work wanting to help.

Based on her experience in the introductory course, Laura changed her major to social work. She reflects now that a mix of factors had guided her to social work—the environment in which she grew up, a compelling faith that drew her to service, and a simple desire to help others. Together, she says, those factors are what she means when she says that social work is a "calling":

> It was my choice, but it was not just me choosing—if that makes sense.

Laura completed her undergraduate degree and then chose a public university in a large city far from home, where she completed her Master of Social Work degree. She quickly found her first professional position at The Refuge, an agency providing assistance and shelter for victims of human trafficking, child abuse, domestic violence, crime, and for teenagers who have run away from home. Laura's responsibility was to investigate reports of child abuse for the

Child Advocacy Center of The Refuge, working closely with police, the district attorney, and the social services department of the City.

A Day at The Refuge

Laura's schedule at The Refuge varies day by day. She works 10:00 a.m.-6:00 p.m. two days a week, noon-8:00 p.m. two days, and 2:00 p.m.-10:00 p.m. one day a week. The Refuge building is open around the clock. The building also houses the police. A staff member from The Refuge is available until 10:00 p.m. each night, trading schedules so that usually no one has to do the evening shift more than once each week. Family violence does not typically take place during regular business hours, and the staff has to be ready to respond.

The services of The Refuge are free. The agency assigns a detective and a social services worker to each client. Clients decide if they want counseling; The Refuge's Child Advocacy Center offers confidential counseling services with a focus on brief intervention, using a "psycho-educational" approach and assessment for post-traumatic stress disorder (PTSD). In addition to counseling, there are support groups, parenting education groups, and treatment groups for children.

When someone calls 911 and reports that a child has been hurt, a police officer investigates immediately. If the officer finds evidence that abuse has occurred, the officer brings the child either directly to the Advocacy Center or, in severe cases, calls for an ambulance. Laura or someone else on her team is the first person the child sees at the Center. There are more than 3,000 cases of child abuse opened each year in The Refuge's area of the city.

The word "forensic" in her title means that Laura conducts interviews with children, especially those the police officers have difficulty interviewing because they are so young or so traumatized or frightened that a straightforward adult-like conversation is impossible. Laura is trained to interact with children in ways to encourage them to describe their experiences in their own words without leading them in one direction or another, so that the taped description can be used in court if charges are brought against an offender. If the interview reveals that a child was the victim of sexual abuse or another form of physical abuse, then the officer arrests the perpetrator based on the story Laura helps a child to tell.

If there is an arrest, the District Attorney then meets with the family, explaining the court process and describing what they can expect to happen in court. If the accused is the child's caregiver, then Child Protective Services relocates the child out of the home where abuse has occurred, often first to The Refuge's emergency child shelter and then to a family member's home, or if there is no one who can provide care, to a foster home.

Almost Thanksgiving

I asked Laura to tell me a story about a typical day for her. She told me that on the night before Thanksgiving, her day was supposed to end at 8:00 p.m. So at 7:30, as she began straightening her desk for the night and shutting down the computer, the phone rang. The police dispatcher was calling to say that three cases were coming in—a child whose mother had hit her and left marks; a young teenager who had been walking down the street when a stranger accosted her on the street and fondled her; and a child who said that her cousin had been "touching" her. Laura put her purse back in her bottom drawer, flipped the computer power switch to "on," and waited. She would handle the first case to arrive, and the social worker on the late shift would handle the other two.

The first family to arrive was the mother with her daughter who said that her cousin had been touching her sexually. As the mother and child waited in the outer waiting room, Laura talked to the detective to find out what the detective had learned about the child, the allegation, who the child had first told, and how she had described what had happened to her. After this brief conference, Laura observed via closed circuit television while the detective talked with the child alone, away from the listening ears of the mother. He then interviewed the mother as Laura observed.

After the police interview, Laura talked with the mother, who was understandably very upset. She had trusted her thirteen-year-old nephew, her sister's son, to watch out for her seven-year-old daughter in the afterschool hours, until she could arrive home from work. Now she had learned that he was making the little girl take her underwear off so he could touch her "private parts" whenever they were alone. The child had far more sexual knowledge than was appropriate for a seven year old. Laura shared with the mother how The Refuge could help her; she had decisions to make about how to keep her daughter safe. They could also provide her with counseling services and a support group with other parents facing such family crises. Meanwhile, the police officer left to arrest the cousin, who would face charges of sexual assault in juvenile court.

It was almost 11:00 when Laura finally turned off the computer after typing up her notes and headed home:

> It is hard work, and I was tired. But I am willing for it to be hard on me because I am helping provide a safe place to tell about these terrible experiences and I am helping secure the future safety of a child—isn't that worth a little lost sleep?

As hard as it can be sometimes, Laura loves working with people who have dedicated themselves to helping children. She knows that she is not alone; colleagues are there to listen when she is overwhelmed and to advocate with her for the needs of the children they serve. "I like that my agency really cares about the kids."

The agency is a warm and welcoming place for children. There are always snacks available, stuffed animals to hold and children's books to read. Bright and happy murals grace the walls. A big friendly therapy dog makes frequent visits. If a child has a toileting accident, they have a clothes closet where they can get new clothes. If a child is not able to go home because it is not safe, the staff packs a small overnight bag for them with pajamas, a stuffed animal, toothbrush and toothpaste, a change of clothes for the next day, and books to read from the supply closet. The agency never sends a child to a shelter or emergency foster home empty-handed.

The Challenges and the Signposts

The evening work is a challenge for Laura's ability to have a life outside of work. Most of her friends work "normal" hours; Laura has to deal with emergencies that come up, even if it interferes with her personal plans. A child in danger cannot wait until the next day—that child needs her assessment and decision immediately. Even when she is able to go home after a long day, she carries with her the terrible experiences that children have shared with her.

She realizes she is susceptible to "vicarious trauma" that she experiences through her exposure day in and day out to the trauma of others. So Laura is consistently committed to processing her experiences with her supervisor and co-workers. By putting words to her feelings, she can contain them rather than letting them define her. Her gym is just down the street from her office, and Laura can take breaks to go work off the stress, or to take a walk in the park and listen to music, to get perspective on her day. Sometimes she just takes a day off and lets a colleague cover for her. Of course, she does the same for her colleagues. She is thankful for meaningful work, and for colleagues who support one another in doing what they need to do so they can continue to be effective in helping traumatized children and families.

Laura's work with clients at The Refuge is almost always brief, beginning with that first investigation and then easing clients and their families to the longer-term services that they need. There are days when she is overwhelmed, when she wonders if she is doing any lasting good. Then a sign will come—what she does matter. Not often, but often enough, Laura receives a phone call from a parent or even a letter from a child, thanking her for being there to help when they were in the midst of overwhelming crisis.

Anna was one of those children that Laura remembers as a sign that she is doing what she was called to do. Anna was eight when the police brought her and her mother to The Refuge. Her stepbrother, age sixteen, had raped Anna. At their first meeting, Anna was understandably completely withdrawn, unwilling to talk—frozen in her trauma. Laura did not begin her work by trying to push Anna to talk, and certainly not by focusing on the traumatic experience. She brought out paper and crayons, and they simply colored together. Laura asked Anna about school and friends. In the third session, Laura drew a family tree while Anna coached her. Anna named the stepbrother who had hurt her—but said she did not want to talk about it. Laura said, "Okay, only when you want to," and they continued drawing. They played with paper dolls; Anna named a doll for each of her family members and colored them—and one of them was the stepbrother. Laura asked her to put Band-Aids on all the people who were hurt, smiles on those who had been brave, and red dots on those who had caused the hurt. And then they began to talk. Anna took the paper dolls home; she could remember in looking at them what Laura had taught her: that she had been brave to tell and that Band-Aids protect us while we heal, but they do come off and we are all better underneath.

Laura worked with Anna for four months. She helped Anna to trust her, and she helped her frame some of what she was experiencing as results of the trauma—her fear of being alone, fear of the dark, nighttime incontinence. Over the months they worked, Anna was able to leave her mother's bed and sleep alone again; her thoughts were not dominated by the trauma she had experienced—she declared herself "better." Laura referred Anna to a counselor in the community who would continue to work with her.

Half a year later, The Refuge held their annual Christmas party for the children they serve. Anna came with her mother. She was outgoing and funny, socializing with other children. Mom told Laura that Anna talked about Laura all the time. She was a typical eight year old girl again, not the frozen and traumatized victim whom Laura had met six months before.

A social worker who is the first responder to child abuse looks squarely in the face of evil. Laura finds herself praying her way through her days, silently breathing "God help me" as she does her work, when she does not know how to handle a situation, when she finds herself struggling with feeling compassion for people who have terribly hurt others. Laura believes that her faith in a God of goodness has helped her to confront evil with an assurance that God will win in the end. She is betting everything she can do on that assurance.

Questions to Ponder

1. Laura says that social work was her choice, but "not just me choosing." What do you think she means? In what ways can you identify with her explanation of calling?

2. Laura works evenings at least once each week. She also has flexibility in her job to care for herself—freedom to disappear to the gym for a little

while or to take a walk in the park. In what ways can you imagine that such a varied and flexible schedule is helpful—or not—in dealing with the stress of social work?

3. In addition to this flexibility, what other protective factors does Laura describe that help her cope with stress and the potential for vicarious trauma?

4. What are the Christian teachings and practices that relate to work in a situation like Laura's?

David Thomas
Family Therapist, Juvenile Court
David McClung, Co-Author

David Thomas is a family therapist in a large post-industrial city with a long history of segregation and racial unrest. David says that the city is adapting to a global market and attracting young professionals who are making good money and a good life. At the same time, the city's approach to growth is further marginalizing segregated, African-American neighborhoods of multi-generational poverty.

David's clients are teenagers living in those marginalized neighborhoods whose behavior has entangled them in juvenile court—truancy from school, illegal drug possession, and shoplifting. Some of his clients face more serious charges, such as assault and theft, including stealing motor vehicles. Although drug possession is the most common charge, it is usually because kids are selling drugs, mostly heroin and cocaine, and are not themselves users. In a city rapidly embracing technological business and industry in a global economy, his clients have no vision for college; many will not finish high school. Many have no role models in their community who have financially secure jobs. Their parents are the working poor who earn less than a living wage. The city's growth has come from attracting new young professionals, not from making a priority of the educational success and financial wellbeing of its long-term residents.

The influx of illegal drugs in the 1980s and 1990s and the community violence that co-occurs with high levels of drug trafficking devastated many of the families with whom David works. Grandparents are often raising David's clients because their parents are either dead or in such shambles from heroin or crack addiction that they are in no position to provide stable parenting. David says that the levels of trauma his young clients have experienced are higher than anywhere else he has ever been or known about—trauma from family violence, witnessing parental overdose, seeing a friend shot and killed, and sometimes multiple such experiences. Many children grow up without their fathers, who are serving long prison sentences for drug offenses.

David's day often begins at 10:00 in the morning in his favorite coffee shop at "his" table, where he drinks coffee and writes progress notes about his work with the client families with whom he met the day before. After lunch, he drops by the office to pick up any supplies he may need for the day's sessions. Those sessions will take place in the homes of teenagers, where he can work with the family.

He is sensitive to the schoolwork and activities the teens have been assigned by the juvenile court and their probation officers, as well as the work schedules of the family adults. Those adults may be single parents, foster parents, grandmothers, or older siblings who are providing care for their younger brothers and sisters. Some work evening and night shifts, so David has to take into account their sleep schedules as well as their outside responsibilities. David figures that just gathering the family for a conversation is often a significant accomplishment and symbolizes that they care about one another and the teenager. David's workday often does not end until early evening, but he loves the flexibility of being in the community and in homes. He thinks it is important that his clients know he cares about them, so much so that he builds his schedule around their needs and meets them where they are rather than expecting them to organize themselves and find transportation to travel across the city to his office. His coming to their home at a time that fits their lives is a symbol of his commitment to them. David has rescheduled appointments as often as three times in a single week because of the changing pressures on the family. As he notes, just hanging in there with the family is part of the work, part of joining them.

Many of the families with whom David works are living on the edge economically and socially. They are often poor and have experienced lots of disruptions, with children who have been in and out of the child welfare system and parents who have been in and out of relationships. Family adults may have dropped out of school and find it hard to find and keep well-paying jobs.

The challenges create tensions and sometimes a sense of hopelessness. David's work with a family often taps into hurts and disappointments that have accumulated over years. When tension arises, there may be times where family members yell and threaten violence. Some of the families with whom David works have been violent with one another in the past, so he takes seriously any signs that violence might erupt. There have been times he has stopped the conversation saying, "Do I need to call 911? Are you really threatening one another? Or is that just a figure of speech?"

Although the families live in impoverished communities that outsiders might consider unsafe, in all the years he has been driving and walking in the inner city, he has never experienced himself in danger, except when a kid threw a firecracker as a joke, and everyone, including David, laughed at how he jumped.

David works to help family members develop understanding and empathy for one another. It is a real breakthrough when family members shift from seeing one another as enemies to realizing that they share the same goals and dreams, and that, despite the challenges, they care for one another. David sees such moments as "beautiful," when a broken relationship is redeemed:

I love that I get to be with them in those moments.

David experiences awe when a family that seemed beyond repair when he first began working with them is now smiling and talking affectionately with one another, using the communication skills he has taught to tackle the challenges that face them. It often takes the full three months of weekly visits that David has to work with each family.

David uses functional family therapy as his theoretical approach to helping steer his clients away from future criminal behavior and toward life decisions that will lead to meaningful and productive adulthood. Functional family therapy presumes that all behavior has a purpose, and so to change behavior, we have to address the purpose behind the actions. A teenager can be carrying illegal drugs for many reasons, for example. If he is selling drugs to help his single mother buy groceries for the family, then David needs to work with the family's economic needs if he expects to help the teenager. If he is selling drugs as a way to gain entrance into a street gang, then the work with the teenager and family will take a different direction.

Daquan

I asked David to tell me about one of the families with whom he worked, and he told me about Daquan, an African American boy, age 14, who had been arrested several times for assault. His mother, Tamika, was unemployed and single; she has a lot of health issues and has great difficulty just getting out of bed. Daquan's father was physically violent with Tamika and Daquan until Daquan was big enough to fight back. When Daquan met violence with violence, his dad left. Since then, Daquan and his mother had lived on support from social services and contributions Daquan's older siblings make to the household.

Daquan's mother should qualify for disability, and David had connected her to Legal Aid to pursue that possible support for the family. After David began work with them, he learned that their overdue household utility bills now tallied to thousands of dollars, and he was working with public utilities to keep the family from having their electricity and gas discontinued. There simply were not enough financial resources to meet the family's basic needs.

In addition to the family violence Daquan had known his whole life, the family lived in one of the most violent neighborhoods in the community. In this context, Daquan's behavior was functional; it was protective to be known as explosive, for others to know that he would not put up with anything from anybody. That persona actually kept him safe—and also landed him in trouble at school, which was how he ended up in the juvenile justice system.

David began working with the school, where he learned that despite Daquan's learning disabilities, the Individual Education Plan the school is expected to have for each child with special needs, had not been updated. Tamika is a strong woman, and David says she took the lead in working with the school with David's encouragement. The meetings with the school were tense. Daquan had missed a lot of school, but Tamika said the school had not notified her until she received a warning from the truancy court threatening to fine her or even send her to jail if his truancy continued. Tamika had been doing everything she could to get Daquan to school, but once she sent him, either he just did not go, or he went and then slipped away later. Unless she rode the bus to school with him, and then stayed at school with him to make sure he stayed there, there was little else she could imagine doing. David successfully advocated for the truancy court to suspend the threats, vouching for Tamika that she was doing everything she could do and they were working together to address Daquan's school needs.

David summarized the systems with which he was working: truancy court, juvenile court, school, disability, and the public utilities company. In addition, Daquan had a reputation as a fighter and he was drawing a lot of negative police contact. Yet out of that contact, one officer seemed to care about Daquan, and David reached out to the officer to underscore this potential for being a protective factor Daquan's life. David coached Tamika to work with the officer to strategize keeping some eyes in the community on Daquan.

David pointed out that this family had strengths as well as problems associated with a long history of violence and multigenerational poverty. Tamika cared about her son, despite how frustrated she was with the poor choices Daquan had been making. One of the first challenges David addressed was how Tamika and Daquan talked with one another. He described one his first conversations with them:

> I told them, 'We've got to change the way the two of you talk to each other because every time the two of you begin to have a conversation, and there is a little fire between you, each of you are just throwing gas on it until it gets out of control.' In my very first meeting with them, Tamika said she wanted Daquan out of the house: 'He's out of control; I can't handle him.' And they got into a big argument.

> So I spent a lot of time sitting between them. I had to be very direct with them. I had to tell them sometimes that they were not allowed to talk, which felt very paternalistic, but it was because I was trying to prevent their conversation from blowing up. I would always explain that to them. I would apologize for being disrespectful and say, 'I'm sorry I'm cutting you off right now, but look, I need you to just not talk for a minute because this is about to just blow up again.' With persistence, we really developed a strong relationship. I actually matched their direct way of communicating; I told them, 'There's nothing wrong with

being direct, but you also want to make sure you say things in a way that the other person is going to hear it and know what you mean, and not just hear it and get upset and defensive."

Over the three months they worked together, David taught them conflict management so that he did not have to control their conversation. He helped them develop a safety plan for what to do when they felt violent impulses. He taught them to exit—use "time out"—before they said or did something that would make the situation worse instead of better. They worked hard to use what David was teaching them—and they learned:

It was a transformation; they were screaming at each other in that first meeting, and weeks later, they were laughing and smiling. They had learned to use words instead of physical threats and violence.

David said that first day, he thought, "Oh God, what am I going to do? This is too much." But he was relentless, and his treatment team supported and encouraged him:

The family and I just stayed at it. I always try to keep the "can do" hat on, and remind them that we were going to do this together. Somehow, some way we are going to find a way to get things better. Not perfect, but better.

The work is emotionally draining. After each visit, David takes a thirty-minute break as he drives to his next appointment, listening to music in the car and relaxing from the tensions of the last hour's work. He always reviews his notes from his last visit before leaving his car to knock on the next family's door, reminding himself of his plan for the coming session, and breathing a prayer for wisdom. He is very intentional about ending his workday early in the evening, heading for home to have some time with his family; caring for families includes caring for his own.

David also spends time each week collaborating with the juvenile probation officers responsible for his clients. Most of these discussions take place over the phone, but there are times that David arranges for meetings in person. There are also times that David attends court with the families in order to give updates, especially if they have made significant progress that the court needs to take into account. He sees himself as an advocate in the court for his clients. Because he knows them, he can help the court see his clients and the whole persons they are—teenagers who have been traumatized by life experiences and who are now acting out that trauma. He tries to leverage his role to help them get the services and resources they need rather than just the punishment that their actions may seem to warrant.

David says that he thinks he has actually seen change since his early time in the work in the court's attitude toward his clients. When he first started, if teenagers missed school for three days, they would be placed in detention for a week. The unintended outcome was to make school attendance even more a struggle, putting his clients even further behind and more likely to drop out as soon as they could do so legally. David can point to research that shows that the more a child is placed in detention, the more likely they are to continue to commit offenses. The practice of detaining teenagers has changed in the years of David's involvement—detention is now a last resort. I asked David what role he had in this change, and he said:

> There were some power players that were really pushing at the higher level to make that change occur. I was the person standing in front of the probation officers and judges arguing, "But if you keep detaining them, they're never home long enough to actually get the changes and support they need." I told them the research findings and said, "This is why I'm asking you not to do this; it's not that I'm just a bleeding heart social worker who thinks they all need a hug." So I would say I was very much part of the change at the court level.

David is also an advocate for teenagers in the community. He lives in a neighborhood that experiences a high rate of crime, and he speaks up for teenagers in community association meetings and other venues that have the potential for shaping public attitudes. In community meetings, when there is a push to crack down on juvenile crime by "not just putting these kids back out on the streets," David speaks with his authority about the research evidence that the more teenagers are detained for wrongdoing, the more like they are to reoffend. "What we need to do is actually find out what is driving them to crime and treat them in the community the best that we can," he argues. People know him as the guy on the community association's Facebook page that writes:

> It is unfortunate when someone's property gets vandalized. We rightfully want justice, but we need to rethink what justice looks like in this context for our teenagers.

There was currently a conversation about juvenile crime on the Facebook page, and David was writing to tie community-based services to his neighbor's self-interest, explaining the research about juvenile detention as a contributor to increasing recidivism:

> I may not win people's hearts over to recognizing all the trauma and violence that have led to the young person making poor choices and hurting others. I understand people are frustrated to see these kids just put back on the street. To help these teenagers become successful and contributing members of our city,

we have to take a different approach than a punitive approach that sends them away to 'scare them straight.' Fear tactics and punishment do not work. Youth boot camps do not work. We have plenty of research that shows that, and most of the time people are receptive to that. At least they bow out of the conversation when they see me as an expert.

David also meets with a team of colleagues each week, discussing their clients, problem solving together, and learning from one another. Sometimes David also works with other organizations and professionals who may be working with the same families. As his work with each family ends, he wants to make sure that they have the sources of support they need to sustain the changes he has helped them to make. Frequently, David helps teenagers develop connections to a community center where there are positive peers and recreational and educational activities.

From Direct Practice to Community Practice

Since the first interview more than three years before, David had taken a university teaching position, where he provides supervision full-time for students in their internships in agencies where there is no social worker on staff. But David has not left his work with teenagers; he continues to do that work contractually, which is easy to do since much his work is in the evenings. The university values his continued involvement in practice with families and his advocacy in the community, and so he continues to carry a caseload on a part-time basis. For David, this move is a next step in his passion for juvenile justice. He is using his experiences in direct practice through the juvenile court system to inform prevention and early intervention.

Part of the reason David took the university position is that it has given him the opportunity to be more engaged in community practice. The local community development corporation recently asked David to give a presentation on intergenerational relationship building. The neighborhood is currently struggling with gentrification; ten years ago it was all low income African American, but now that are lots of young professionals and Caucasians moving in, including David. But there are still three-generation families living there, and David thinks—and the research shows—that holding on to the cultural diversity will enrich the community for everyone. Therefore, in his presentation, David tackled building relationships not just across the human life course, but also across the ethnic and racial diversity of their neighborhood. His goal was to identify the assets they could gain as a neighborhood if they work together to bridge the generations and the ethnic and cultural differences. He pointed out the effects of institutional racism in how governments allocate public funding and other resources, such as the historic differences in the quality of schools in minority neighborhoods—but that is changing. He described tangible ways that neighborhood residents can contribute to the positive change. Not only does David have research to support what he is saying, but also he is given more authority as a university faculty member; people credit university faculty with expertise.

Thirty people from the neighborhood attended the session, which took place in the neighborhood public charter school that also hosts the neighborhood association meetings. David sees himself now as an advocate for teenagers not only in the juvenile court but also in the larger community.

David thinks that there needs to be an earlier response to trauma that kids and their families experience, and that the rich mental health services that his city already has need to be better connected to families through the two major institutions that have connections with families and trauma—schools and hospitals. The city has recently joined the Community Schools Movement, seeing their public school buildings as potential assets, turning them into community centers in the after-school hours, placing in them safe after-school activity programs for children and teenagers, parent education programs, mental health services, and employment services. The idea is not to have a pre-set list of programs, but rather, to determine with the neighborhood what services would be most helpful. Because row houses and apartment buildings densely populate the city's neighborhoods, services in neighborhood schools are close by and so accessible to virtually everyone.

David loves his work:

> I love being at that place in the juvenile system where I really have a shot at steering them away from becoming a statistic, becoming another adult who lives life in and out of the prison system.

His goal is to move to working in prevention and early intervention with teenagers and their families, doing so from a community asset building approach. Eventually, he wants to be in a place to develop programs that keep kids from ever getting into the juvenile justice system. He did not have much support for work at the community level in his clinical practice, but the university hired him to be part of their Center for Community Practice, a research and service unit of the School of Social Work. The goal is to connect the resources of the university to their city neighborhoods and, in turn, for the university to learn from engagement in the neighborhoods of the city in order to develop best community practices. The combination of clinical practice and community practice fits like a hand in a glove for David.

"No One is Beyond Redemption"

In the last interview with David before writing this chapter, I pointed out that the longer we talked, the more energized he became. I asked him where the energy comes from to persevere with complex systems and struggling families, families like Tamika and Daquan. He said that it comes from his firm belief that there is no person and no relationship beyond redemption, and he brings that belief with him to every home he visits. He believes that people want better lives, and their struggles are their attempts to achieve that for themselves.

> Even if they are hopeless, if I can give them a glimpse of hope somehow, then they will run with that. I am frustrated when, for whatever reasons, I cannot seem to connect people to that hope. With Tamika and Daquan, together we were able to get to hope, and it completely changed their family. That was two years ago. I ran into them about two months ago, and they were still smiling, and they remembered me, and they are still doing well.

David reminds his clients—and himself—of how far they have come and that relapses are to be expected. There will some tough days, but they can fall back on what got them this far.

David, too, faces tough days and discouragement—and remembers. When he graduated, he had the opportunity to make a speech to the graduating class. He encouraged his peers to remember that the people they work with are not numbers. It may be easy to forget that. If they are successful with eighty percent of their clients, that may be a great statistic, but it is not good enough for the other twenty percent. Every person, every family matters. Even if they cannot or do not change, they are still important:

> So many times, when I am working with a family, I find myself standing in a place of hopelessness. The only thing that keeps me going forward is knowing that even though it seems so bleak in this moment, that God can show up. Whether God gives me just the right skill or just the right statement at just the right time, it could mean all of the difference in the world to this family. So when I feel hopeless, I know that redemption can still happen.

David told me that staying involved in his urban Lutheran congregation fuels his own energy and hopefulness. Even there, he works with teenagers; many come from the same neighborhoods as David's clients. Even though his role may be different, the values are the same—he wants what is best for them. He wants them to know that they matter, every single one.

Questions to Ponder

1. How does David use research in his advocacy for his clients?
2. How has David used his role as a clinician in community practice?
3. David used the words "relentless" to describe his work with Daquan and Tamika. How do you see this word fitting other descriptions of his professional practice? Can being relentless be considered a Christian practice? If so, describe how.
4. Consider the story of Daquan. What description of David's work with Daquan's family do you find exciting? Daunting?
5. In what ways did David's clinical work with Daquan and his family lead to engagement with community systems?
6. How might David carry his experiences with Daquan into the community practice in which he is engaging, such as the development of community services in Daquan's school?
7. David says that two themes, hope and redemption, provide the energy and ability to persevere in his work. Describe the roots of these two themes in Christian beliefs and values.

Workforce Development

Joy Fitzgerald
Director,
Job Preparation Collaboration
of the Women's Missionary Alliance

Ally Matteson, Co-Author

Many of the activities of Joy Fitzgerald's childhood took place in her congregation. She particularly loved the missions organization for children, where they learned about, prayed for, and took up collections to support American missionaries serving across the globe. Those experiences, she says, "opened up a whole world for me." Her parents were very involved in missions, and her father was coordinating a partnership between their state denominational organization and Christian churches in Taiwan. Joy was twelve when she went with her parents to Asia for six weeks. It is a vivid memory:

> I remember being in the airport, the only White people in this throng of Asian people. I remember so clearly standing there, and people would look at us, and I remember thinking, "This is what it feels like to be a minority." That discomfort stuck with me. I remember thinking, "I have to be more careful when I'm at home; how I interact with people who are minorities because they may feel like this."

Her love of missions continued into her young adult years. As a college student, Joy decided to pursue a career in pastoral counseling, so that she could help missionaries with the challenges they encountered. She enrolled in a graduate seminary program. An ethics course she was required to take prior to beginning the pastoral counseling track radically altered her career path, however. A unit on a Christian response to poverty turned her world upside down.

That very week, she sought out the dean in the social work school and said to her:

> I think I'm on the wrong track; I want to do counseling, but I don't want to do it with middle class people.

The dean talked with her about systems theory and the importance of affecting the context in order to affect the person. Joy withdrew from the pastoral counseling track and started the application for social work school.

Joy completed her MSW and a certificate in graduate theological studies in 1996. The Women's Missionary Alliance (WMA), the national woman's organization of her denomination, was launching a new program, the Job Preparation Collaboration, nicknamed "Job Prep." One of Joy's social work professors had developed the vision for Job Prep; WMA leaders found the concept deeply exciting, a new way of engaging in mission activity in the local communities of congregations. They hired Joy, who had finished graduate school to launch the new program.

The goal of Job Prep is to equip women living in poverty with life and employment skills that are based in a Christian worldview. The program includes job training in classes where participants become friends and support and challenge one another over the one or two years they participate. Each client also receives the mentoring and friendship of a Christian volunteer. All participants also participate in Bible study, although participants do not have to be Christians or become Christians to participate in Job Prep programs. Job Prep assumes that Christian beliefs such as God's grace and loving involvement in our lives, and Christian values such as responsibility for the choices we make and treating others as we want to be treated, are strong foundations for success in life and work. Participants often are dealing with recovery from addiction, placement of their children in foster care because of family violence or neglect, and personal histories that include crime and imprisonment.

Joy began her work at Job Prep for women 14 years ago. In 2004, she launched a second "Job Prep" organization, this one targeting men and providing them with male mentors. She trained and supervised the leadership for each site across the country; today, there more than 200 certified Job Prep sites. The coordinators she trains then develop the program for their communities, recruit coordinating councils, and train and support mentors.

Obtaining job skills is something everyone needs in order to live well, support families, and participate in the community, but finding and keeping a job is not easy for many people who lack the educational preparation and do not have a strong network of persons who can encourage them and link them to possible employment. For those who dropped out of school, struggled to learn to read, do not know how to use a computer, lack the interpersonal skills to interview well and get along with colleagues, or have a prison record, the challenges may seem insurmountable. Addressing those challenges are the focus of Job Prep.

Workforce Development as Social Work Practice

From its beginnings, the profession of social work has been concerned with equipping persons with the means to lift themselves out poverty through employment. The ability to do work that is meaningful and provides needed financial support for self and family is profoundly important to persons' sense of worth and purpose. In the first decades of the profession, the volunteer "friendly visitors" served as mentors; the early settlement houses offered English classes for immigrants and sewing and other job skills classes. In addition, early social workers addressed the barriers to employment such as the need for preschool nurseries so that mothers could work, public transportation that enabled people to get to work, and a minimum wage (Keller, 2001; Midgley, 1995; Weissbourd, 1994).

By the 1920s, the armed services were developing vocational rehabilitation services in response to the needs of injured soldiers returning from the world wars. Social workers and other professionals worked with persons to overcome disabilities in preparation for employment. Social workers complemented job training with counseling based on their understanding of trauma to facilitate the development of resilience and renewed sense of life purpose. Soon, vocational training services began to be provided for civilians as well as military personnel—persons born with physical and developmental challenges as well as those that resulted as a consequence of accident or disease or life circumstances (Mizrahi & Davis, 2012).

In programs like Job Prep, social workers bring the knowledge and skills necessary for work with individuals and family whose lives have been challenged by addictions, imprisonment, multi-generational poverty, family violence and disruption, and immigration. Computer and other job skills are not enough; many program participants need help in learning how to interview for a job, the kinds of on-the-job behaviors that are necessary for success, and how to communicate and manage conflict in the workplace. Social workers also bring the community skills of networking to help program participants make connections with employers. The program components of both individual mentoring and a group of participants who are in classes together provide mutual assistance and encouragement that are so necessary in the daunting task of preparing for and then seeking employment. Together, participants are able to work through experiences such as rejection when one job interview after another ends in "no."

The Work of Directing Job Prep

Asked to describe a typical workday, Joy laughed. "There is no such day." Her work has included speaking and teaching at conferences, networking, recruiting and training new site coordinators, providing coordinators with counsel around the daily challenges of working with Job Prep participants and mentors, developing training materials for volunteers, writing for magazines, and writing devotional curricula to inspire other Christians to practice their faith. Joy said:

> I love helping people find the call to live out faith in tangible ways; my mission is to radically involve all believers in the mission of God.

As a leader in the larger WMA organization, she also has directed the multicultural curriculum team that develops educational programs and curricula for the adult mission organizations of congregations. WMA publishes the materials her team has developed and they are studied in congregational mission groups all over the country. For example, Joy has written materials targeting specific social issues such as human exploitation and trafficking. She takes pleasure in translating clinical and systemic topics into everyday lay language for Christians, to spur them on to think about what they can do as a body of believers in response.

Joy said that she has spent a great deal of her time responding to questions from other staff members and volunteers who call from sites across the country:

> Not long ago, I got a call from a Bible study leader. A young mother had shared in the Bible study that she tried to smother her baby the night before. She caught herself and stopped, and realized she needed help. She turned to her Bible study group, and the leader called in a panic, asking me what she should do. Our leaders know to call for help with challenges like this one, because they are not professional social workers.

Joy is one of the only staff members with a social work degree in the national office of WMA.

Day by day, Joy ponders how to equip team members as leaders, with a sense of ownership of the work they do together. She wants others to be as passionate about their work as she is, and she believes that feeling like the program is theirs to lead and shape fans the flames of the passion that brought them each to the work they do together. Joy makes it clear that she is always available to those she supervises:

> For example, a very intelligent and skillful member of my team needs to talk through decisions with others before she can make decisions. It is my responsibility to be available for that conversation, because once she figures it out, then she is committed to doing whatever is necessary to move forward.

Those conversations often come at inopportune times—when Joy is trying to prepare a workshop or conceptualize an article. But the conversation comes first and Joy's "to do" list is put aside.

While there are many uplifting moments, her conscious choice to communicate availability to her team means that somebody is always asking her for something. People are not afraid to ask—including text messages at nights and on weekends. Joy tries to protect her time with her family and for her own renewal:

> When you give a lot you cease to be creative because your mind and soul get tired.

Joy also misses the direct interaction with clients that she had when the Job Prep was small and she was involved in each site. As Job Prep grew, Joy had less time or role in the services with clients and mentors; she spent increasing amounts of time equipping staff and volunteers for their work with clients.

Living Her Faith

Joy says that her faith informs and fuels her work with people. In the same way, social work allows her to be in relationship with people she would never have encountered otherwise—and to help her staff and volunteers develop empathy and compassion for those they serve. She told me about a story of a site director who asked for her help with a woman who wanted to participate in their local Job Prep program. The director was not sure the woman was eligible, but she hedged when Joy asked her why she might not be eligible. Joy explained that the only reason for excluding a potential participant was if they were currently using drugs. The director said, "No, that's not an issue with this woman." After further questioning that led nowhere, Joy finally asked, "So help me out here, where is the dilemma?" The consultant says hesitantly, "Well five years ago she... used to be a he." Joy said she had to stifle a laugh, realizing why the director had been referring to the woman as "they" rather than "she"; evidently the client had been a male who had undergone gender-altering treatment to become female. Joy said she quickly recovered her composure:

> I explained that the first thing we need to do is recognize that who she is now is who God wants to be in relationship with now. It does not matter what decisions she made in the past. We need to love her now. I listened to her concerns and took them seriously.

The director admitted the woman to the program.

Joy loves that social work brings her into relationship with people who are often afraid of or feel unwelcome by the church.

> Social work has allowed me to embrace the grey and move away from black and white—I am less judgmental of others who have had different life experiences and challenges than I have had. When you really get to know people, they are just people not that different from me.

Joy is humbled not only by the genuineness and transparency she sees in the lives of the clients they serve, but also by the deep faith of volunteers:

They want to live their faith, to walk alongside a brother or sister who needs their friendship; God works in amazing ways through their sincerity and commitment to serve.

A Different Approach to Supporting Missionaries

When Joy struck off for seminary to prepare to live into what she thought was God calling her to a ministry of supporting missionaries, she thought those missionaries would be working in global settings in countries like India, Vietnam, and Kenya. Instead, the missionaries she has been supporting are U.S. Christians, program directors and volunteers working with neighbors seeking to escape addictions, poverty, and hopelessness. Joy has combined social work and her sense of calling to serve people who are oppressed, just as she believes Jesus taught. When I talked with Joy a couple of years after our first interview, she had read the first draft of this chapter, and she said it was really a moment of insight for her—she is really doing what she felt called to do when she sought training to support missionaries. She senses that God has used her, and it brings her great joy to see the people that she supervises grow in their understanding and skills.

I asked for an example, and Joy told me about Courtney, a new program director who was very focused on bringing about change in people's lives—and quickly. She was so focused on creating change that she did not assess whether program recipients *wanted* change. She ignored the dynamics of the group she led, trying to push them on in the direction she felt they should go. Over time, Joy helped her develop a deeper and longer vision, coming to appreciate that change comes slowly. Behavioral change that happens quickly, Joy says, is often a reaction to external forces—forces like Courtney herself—and not based in a real change in attitude. With Joy's guidance, Courtney learned patience and the concept of self-determination. And Joy silently celebrated the change over time in Courtney.

When Joy leads retreats for staff and helps new organizations form she emphasizes that a twelve week program is a beginning for program recipients, but it is only a beginning. Few people will be able to move out of poverty as a consequence of a time-limited program, no matter how dedicated the staff or determined the recipients are to change their lives. Poverty is not just about a lack of education; it is the consequence of a complexity of social systems that are slow to change. The volunteers and the staff of the agency have to be ready to stay in relationship with program recipients for the long term. That message has been Joy's message for more than a decade; again, she has modeled with the agency what she is seeking to teach them about their work with recipients.

The Next Chapter

That long commitment to the agency finally came to an end between the time of our first interview and the finishing of this chapter. Joy found herself presented with the opportunity to take a full-time faculty position in a newly developed social work program in a Christian college. She is sad to be leaving her work with her colleagues all over the country who have invested their lives in those they serve. The WMA has valued Joy's social work knowledge and skills, particularly her ability to think creatively about complex situations and create new approaches appropriate to the cultural context. Joy says:

> That is not something unique to me; that is just part of the skill set we learned in graduate school. Professionals can know a lot but if they cannot put that knowledge together in a meaningful way to fit an organizational culture, they can never be successful. They will be constantly frustrated. Regardless of the settings, that social work skill set is critical.

As much as she has loved her work at Job Prep, Joy found herself excited and challenged by this new opportunity, where she will be putting her previous experiences and knowledge and skills together to respond to her new context. She will be taking her work in supporting and preparing missionaries to a whole new level, preparing professional social workers to pursue the calling of God in their lives, just as Joy did when she left pastoral counseling to pursue social work with persons in poverty. One of the first courses she will teach will be Congregational Social Work.

Questions to Ponder

1. As the director of Job Prep, how has Joy developed her responsibilities at the micro, mezzo, and macro levels of practice?
2. Job Prep is a Christian program; in what ways did that make the integration of Joy's Christian faith with her practice easier than in non-Christian settings? What are the ways it might actually be harder?
3. How do you see Job Prep as an expression of Christian values? Of social work values?
4. The site coordinator called Joy to talk over how she should respond to a potential client who had a surgical procedure to change her gender. What are the Christian and social work ethical principles in how Joy addressed this issue and the coordinator's uncertainty?

5. What is appealing to you in the work Joy has done? What would be hard for you?
6. Much of her work at Job Prep was directly and indirectly as an educator. What is the relationship, if any, between her sense of calling to support missionaries and the career path that has unfolded for Joy over the past two decades?

Military

Ilene Borden
Military Social Worker, Air Force
Nicholas A. Wright, Co-Author

25

Ilene Borden received her undergraduate degree from a Bible college, where she majored in intercultural studies and Bible. During her last semester, she participated in Learning Venture, an overseas study program her college offered in Mexico. She loved it, and her college offered her a job in the study program, so she returned after graduation. She lived in Mexico for three years, teaching in the college, serving as a women's mentor, and arranging for U.S. students to live in the homes of families in the community. When school was not in session, she worked at Christian camps on a Mexican ranch. Ilene loved the work.

When Learning Venture needed help in the home office with administration, they pulled Ilene back to the United States to work. Ilene loved the program and her colleagues, but she did not particularly enjoy administration; it seemed to be a detour from her commitment to missions. She was restless, looking for where she needed to be. She was not sure, and she knew nothing about social work except the image she had that social workers were people who took babies out of abusive situations and placed them in adoptive homes—and that was not what she wanted to do.

Ilene's brother was in the Army, where he was a police officer. The U.S. was at war in the Middle East, and she learned from her brother about the high rates of family violence and Post-Traumatic Stress Disorder (PTSD) among soldiers returning from combat. She began to explore the possibilities of becoming a military chaplain or nurse, and then stumbled upon military social work—quite different from the child protective services stereotype she had held. She learned that the Air Force offered a residency, but they only accepted applications after the conclusion of the first year of social work school. She took a leap of faith, and enrolled in a graduate social work program in a Christian university. During the summer of the two-year program, she applied and was accepted into the Air Force residency program.

Later that year, Ilene fell in love with Mark, whom she met in an online dating service. They dated during her second year of graduate school. Ilene was commissioned the day she graduated. When she left for officer training more than a thousand miles away, she said goodbye to Mark, thinking that was the end of their relationship. The goodbye did not last; Mark contacted her and they began a long distance relationship that lasted throughout her residency.

Her first ten months in the residency she calls "Air Force social work indoctrination." There she learned that a century ago, during the horrors of World War I and later during World War II, the United States military relied on Red Cross social workers to help soldiers cope with the physical and emotional trauma of combat. During World War II, the Army began to respond to the physical and psychiatric trauma of combat by enlisting social workers in military units (Daley, 1999). By the end of the century, every military branch was commissioning social workers as officers as well as hiring them as civilians, where they carry a diversity of professional responsibilities: child and family services, family violence and the protection of vulnerable children, health and rehabilitation services, treatment for substance abuse and mental illness, suicide prevention, crisis intervention, critical event debriefing, hostage repatriation, and humanitarian relief (Gibelman, 1995; U.S. Department of the Army, 2007).

Part of her residency included observing the provision of clinical services. She still remembers one soldier, an Army Ranger, who had PTSD. He wanted desperately to cope better because of the impact his disorder was having on his family. Ilene remembers being struck by all he had suffered in service to the United States, and her deep desire to help him. That was confirmation; military social work was the right path for her.

Family Advocacy

After Ilene completed military officer training, the U.S. Air Force assigned her to direct the Family Advocacy Program at a stateside military base more than 1200 miles away from where Mark was living. They married and he moved to join her. He has been moving with her ever since.

The focus of the Family Advocacy Program that Ilene led was preventing and intervening in family violence and the other challenges that families face when they have one or more members in the military. Ilene's small team of three professionals and a secretary conducted an assessment with each family referred to them, then sent the assessment to the Central Registry Board, which determines whether or not the case meets criteria for maltreatment, whether of a child or an adult. The policies are similar to those of the state where they are located, except that the military has a lower bar for defining abuse. That is, Ilene's unit will intervene in a family at a lower level of abuse or neglect than would be required for state intervention, in an attempt to intervene early because of the high rates of family violence in the military.

Ilene laughed with recognition; she was doing work with families similar to her earlier stereotype about what social work is—protecting people from abuse. The difference is that Ilene's team had no authority to remove children; they provide counseling services, and if there was a truly dangerous situation, then they refer to the local police and to the military commander's office.

Deployed

After three years on the stateside military base, the Air Force reassigned Ilene, this time to a base in the Middle East. Her deployment was a great experience, she said, but also very hard—she had to leave behind everything familiar, including her husband. But she was working with people on the front lines of war. She knew she was really helping people, whether it was sending patients in crisis home or to a hospital in Europe.

Ilene saw military personnel struggling long distance with marriage problems or divorce. They were distressed, and distressed soldiers do not have their minds focused on the mission. Keeping minds on the mission was primary; otherwise, soldiers might put themselves or others in greater danger. So Ilene put together classes on how to maintain and strengthen family ties, even during deployment. She pieced together her own knowledge with the work of others. She said:

> Whenever you go to a base, you will find a file folder somewhere with power point and class outlines. I adapted.

Half of the base in the Middle East was Army personnel and the other half of it was Air Force—and Ilene was the only mental health provider for the entire base. Although she is in the Air Force, she also loves the Army, and she particularly enjoyed the day each week she spent with Army personnel, working with the medics in the clinic. She also spent time consulting with the Commanders and working with the liaisons that help evacuate people who need medical or mental health care beyond what the base could provide.

I asked Ilene to tell me about some of her patients that she remembers from her work in the Middle East. She described JoAnn, who had experienced a sexual trauma while in the military and was very anxious and distrustful of men. Ilene had learned Cognitive Processing Therapy and decided to try this new approach with JoAnn. They worked hard together, and JoAnn's stress improved dramatically, as well as how she saw herself and her ability to trust others. By the end of their work together, she was allowing herself to develop friendships with the men who were her colleagues. Together, they celebrated how much she had improved before JoAnn returned to the United States at the end of her deployment.

Not all stories have happy endings. Ilene was on call seven days a week around the clock while she was deployed. One night she received a middle-of-the-night call from an Army chaplain. He was bringing her a suicidal soldier. She met them at her office and learned that he had just completed two weeks of Rest and Recuperation (R&R) and was being sent back "down range" to where combat was taking place. Ahead of him was a year of deployment; he had already been in combat for several months, so he knew what he was facing. He was deeply depressed and anxious. Ilene described the situation:

> You could just look at him and see that he was very disturbed. He said his wife had called to say that she was leaving him, and he showed me pictures of his beautiful young children. He told me that he was planning once he got back down range to kill himself by getting in the way of sniper fire or the enemy so that they would shoot him. That way, he would die a hero in his kids' eyes instead of them knowing he had killed himself.

Instead of allowing him to be sent back on duty, Ilene sent him to a regional medical center in Europe, and, she guessed, from there he would be sent home. She was saddened: "Once soldiers left the combat zone, I lost contact; I never knew what happened to him."

PCS'd

"PCS" means permanent change of station. After two years in the Middle East without Mark, Ilene was PCS'd—reassigned, this time to a base in Europe. Mark could join her there. She returned to the States, where she and Mark packed everything, shipped the car, took a couple of weeks to visit their families, and then moved together to Europe.

Ilene now serves as a Mental Health Officer, supervising a staff of 15 professional mental health providers who are all licensed, as well as six technicians. She organizes programs such as the Disaster Mental Health Team to respond to crises. Ilene also carries a small caseload herself.

The clinic sees mostly active duty personnel, but they also work with spouses. Most often, they are dealing with depression, anxiety, adjustment disorders and, occasionally, PTSD. Although in general, the Air Force is not exposed to as much PTSD-causing trauma as there is in the Army or Marines, it does occur.

Ilene worked with one man who had run many convoys through hostile territory. He had observed unspeakable wounds to children. IEDs—improvised explosive devices—had injured him twice. He had lost friends in those explosions, and he felt guilty that they had died and he had survived. He was having nightmares, complicated by the after effects of an abusive childhood. He is a very large man who does a lot of bodybuilding, and he sees himself as a protector of others, particularly women. His desire to protect others meant that he would fight others if he perceived they were endangering someone or just not being respectful—and that landed him in trouble several times. Already an irritable, potentially physically violent man, his PTSD symptoms were exacerbating his problems. Ilene tried to connect him to the VA facility when he returned home; she hopes he followed through, but she has no way of knowing.

Even in a situation that makes her sad or frustrates her, Ilene has found her niche:

> I love wearing the uniform and am proud I can make a difference in people's lives.

The Challenges

Yet there are also challenges; the military is a large system that is hard to change. Ilene says that there are times when she has asked, "Why do we do it this way when it makes absolutely no sense?" The reply is always, "Because that is the way it is done."

Military social workers must practice not only under the guidelines of their professional code of ethics but also of the military code of ethics—and they do not always agree. Social work ethics focus on the well-being of humans and the meeting of their needs; military ethics emphasize duty to country and the military mission—and these duties take precedence even over the needs of clients. Military social workers have a sworn duty to support the military mission, even when it may mean physical or emotional harm to their clients (Daley, 1999). Military social workers also often find themselves isolated not only geographically but also with few or no other social work colleagues with whom to consult (Tallant & Ryberb, 1999).

Ilene's role as a commissioned officer as well as a military social worker creates some dilemmas. She lives by the military slogan, "Mission first; people always." According to the Air Force, Ilene is first an officer, then a social worker. But Ilene does not agree; she says that she is first a social worker and then an officer. Sometimes those two identities are congruent, but not always. Client confidentiality is one of those areas that sometimes create role conflict for her.

> When I first came into the military, I was committed to maintaining client confidentiality no matter what. But working with people who carry weapons on a daily basis, or who manage top-secret material, or who have sensitive duties, I soon realized that I have to share some information. The informed consent form we give our patients carefully describes the limits of confidentiality, and I also go over those limits verbally with

them, but still, sometimes they tell me information that I am
required to share with the commander.

If clients are suicidal or homicidal or otherwise a danger to the unit's mission, she has to inform their commander or their First Sergeant. Sometimes she has had clients who really want to be in the military, but because of mental illness or other chronic challenges, Ilene realizes that they are going to hamper the military mission. Then she has to initiate the process of moving that person out of the military. She reflects on her experiences:

> I thought I could change the world, but it is not going to change as fast as I would like it to. And maybe influencing smaller changes is a better place to have an impact.

Ilene described one opportunity to have just such an impact. There are instructions for virtually all of her activities, including suicide prevention. Suicide prevention has been a major focus in recent years because of high rates of suicide in the military. Ilene questioned some of the policies and procedures in the suicide prevention instructions and shared her critique with her commander. He thought about her critique and then learned that the instructions were to be rewritten, so he submitted Ilene's name to be one of the policy developers. Ilene went to Washington, D.C., and participated in revising the procedures.

Faith and Military Practice

Ilene believes God called her to military social work, and it has become her ministry—a way to share God's love—even as she is careful not to assume that those she serves share her Christian view of life and its meaning. She says:

> You don't have to be quoting Scripture to share God's love with someone. The military has strict rules that prohibit projecting your faith onto your patients.

Ilene says that the military is a very secular environment, and she believes she is where God wants her to be, but she is still trying to figure out how she lives her faith beyond simply being a nice person. Ilene believes that her professional care for those she serves is a respectful and powerful witness to her faith. She is in a very different place than when she went to engage in Christian mission work in Mexico.

She and Mark love living in Europe. Their daughter was born last year, and Mark is now a stay-at-home daddy. She also knows that her little family can experience a PCS at any point, and she has no idea where the military will send her next.

Questions to Ponder

1. Ilene began preparation and spent her first years of working in missions. What was her journey into military social work?
2. What drew Ilene to military social work and confirmed her path?
3. How has military social work responded to high rates of family violence and suicide in the military, according to Ilene? How do military and U.S. public child protection services relate to one another?
4. Ilene and her husband have made significant sacrifices for her work, including the long separation when she was in the Middle East and the moves in response to her assignments. How would such expectations influence your decisions for a career path?
5. In military social work, what is the primary goal of the work? How does that goal fit with or contrast with the purposes of the social work profession?
6. What are the challenges that a military setting creates for social work practice?
7. What about Ilene's work would seem to you to be most appealing? What would be hardest for you? Whether or not you ever serve in the military, what about those reactions to her work inform you about your own path?
8. How does Ilene describe her integration of faith and practice? What opportunities and challenges do you see for the military to be a place of Christian calling?

Step by Step

Social workers who are Christians serve in a rich diversity of organizations and agencies. I planned this book to be an exploration of the many professional settings in which social workers who are Christians fulfill their sense of calling. I teach an introductory course in social work, and I thought such a book would introduce students to the breadth of opportunities for Christian service throughout the social work profession.

Serving as dean and working with our school's external constituencies has taught me that seeing social work in action is the best way to teach people about our profession. For years, colleagues and I have taken new members of our school's advisory board as well as new students on field trips to visit our alumni in their places of service and learn about their work. We have also brought in panels of our alumni from around the world for this purpose, sometimes in person and sometimes virtually via computer link. Always, those who learn about the work of Christian social workers are excited to see that they are engaged in what church language would call ministry and missions. I believed a book of stories about how Christians are living their faith through social work might be another way to communicate how professional social work can be an expression of Christian ministry.

I thought I knew the book I wanted to write, but as I lived with this task over the years, the work unfolded as a path with its own twists and turns. As other demands slowed the writing process, I had the unexpected opportunity to follow these social workers over time. I no longer was simply exploring the settings for the social work profession that I thought they would represent. Now I was learning the stories of how their professional lives were journeys in themselves. Some moved from one organization to another or from one place within an organization to another. Several of these social workers moved beyond established job descriptions and charted new ways to respond to the challenges confronting the people they serve.

I had planned to describe the fields of professional practice and how social workers related their faith to their service in those settings. Instead, I found myself describing faith journeys, from one professional setting to another, placed in the context of lived life—career interruptions for the births of children or care of ill parents or sieges with cancer. Even when social workers stayed in the same organization, they often changed their focus and level of practice—from direct practice to supervision and management, for example.

As I listened to each story in all its uniqueness, I also heard common themes that resonated through these stories about how these Christians thought about social work not just as their occupation, but also as an opportunity to live out their Christian beliefs and commitments.

Themes that Resonate

Six themes of how Christian faith and the profession of social work can intertwine with one another resonated through these social workers' stories. (1) They regard social work as a calling and not just a career choice. (2) They believe that client need, not their organizational context, is the impetus for addressing issues of religion and faith in work with clients. (3) They are called to serve clients regardless of clients' life circumstances and choices. (4) They consider advocacy for change in systems to be integral to their work, even when the work is clinical practice with individuals. (5) They regard their role as being a conduit of hope, even in the most difficult situations. Finally, (6) they hold themselves responsible for providing the very best service possible, but not for producing ultimate outcomes.

(1) A Calling, Not Just a Career Choice

Not all of these social workers use the language of "calling" to describe their journey into social work, particularly if they associated "calling" with some extraordinary experience like hearing the audible voice of God directing them. At the same time, none of these social workers described social work as a simple vocational choice they made, weighing various career paths and ultimately choosing social work as their best option. The choice they did make was to follow *some impetus that came from beyond themselves*, even if experienced as a silent nudge, an intuition, a confirmation of their gifts, life circumstances that led them to social work, or the advice of trusted others.

For all of these social workers, the path unfolded over time, guided by life experiences—exposure to cultures and lifeways through travel, service projects, personal tragedies, mentors, parents' modeling, and/or engagement in congregational life. They usually did not recognize that guidance at the time. It is only as they reflect back on their work that they discern these experiences as God's calling.

For example, Patricia started out as a public school's secretary and nurse—and realized that many sick children were not physically ill but "sick at heart" with the challenges of their lives. She wanted to help, and over the next years, her path led to social work. Social work was the answer to God's call to ministry she had heard as a teenager, a path that took decades to unfold.

This lifetime of unfolding brought to my mind Bible stories to which I have returned repeatedly as I have wrestled with the concept of divine calling (e.g., Garland & Garland, 2007; Garland & Yancey, 2014). I have found much to guide me in understanding divine calling in the stories of Moses' life. Unlike most of us, Moses did hear God's audible voice calling him from a burning bush, instructing him to take God's message to Pharaoh and then to lead the Israelites out of Egypt (Exodus 3).

Much later, after the Israelites had indeed left Egypt on the dry ground of the Red Sea floor as God held back the seawater, Moses led the Israelites on a wandering wilderness journey. As he led, Moses asked God to "Show me your ways" (Exodus 33:13). Which way shall I lead? Where do I go next? God's answer was to place Moses in a crack in a rock wall and shield him from view as God passed in front of him. Only then did God allow Moses to see. What Moses saw was not the face of God, not God's presence beside him, but only the place where God *had been* (Exodus 33:18-23). I have heard this text explained as meaning that we cannot see where God will be in the future, nor even how God is at work in our lives right now. We can only look back and see God's path in our lives past, as we walked step by step.

In response to Moses, God gave Moses a pillar of cloud to follow by day (Exodus 13:21). God said, "Follow this cloud." At first, such a tangible directional sign sounds encouraging. But visually imagine what a "pillar of cloud" to follow would look like. A cloud on the ground is simply fog. Following a cloud meant picking their way along behind a fog. Fog does not point the way; instead, it conceals all but the most immediate surroundings. We can see just far enough to know where to put our feet next, but we have no idea where we are going. We only see the path by looking behind us, in where we have been and discern the Presence that guided us.

Following fog seems an apt picture of how many of these social workers have experienced God's calling and guiding them. They could have never imagined the journeys they have taken when they started.

(2) Client Need is the Impetus for Addressing Religion and Faith Issues, Not Organizational Context

Calling was no respecter of settings for practice. Those social workers in public agencies such as child protective services felt just as much called to their work as did those in congregations and religiously affiliated organizations. Faith as a motivation for serving is a different matter, of course, than religion and faith being an actual focus in the work with clients. Their faith not only motivated these social workers, but they ethically integrated religion and faith into their work with clients overtly when the work called for it, regardless of the organizational auspices.

For example, Martha's agency, a day treatment program for developmentally and physically disabled adults, is not religiously affiliated, yet she sees her development of its services and her advocacy for her clients and their families as her way of "sharing the good news." She prays with clients and with their families when that is what they want and need her to do; she has led funerals for clients who have died when that is what their families wanted. Allison assessed the faith of boys in a public residential treatment facility for juvenile offenders, helping them connect with the strength they could find in their faith tradition. Religion and faith are a significant dimension of life for many clients that can be part of a holistic approach to assessment and work, regardless of the organizational setting.

Perhaps the distinguishing difference between those in religiously affiliated settings and those in public settings was in the arena of programming. Social workers in public settings did not usually organize Bible studies or worship services the way those in congregations and religiously affiliated settings did, although they often did so in their own congregations. Even those like Diane in religious leadership roles in religiously affiliated agencies were careful, however, to be deeply respectful of the self-determination of clients. They ensured that clients understood that their participation was optional, even if they had sought services from a religious organization.

(3) A Commitment to Serve Regardless of Client's Life Circumstances and Choices

These Christians work with all kinds of clients living a variety of life choices and styles. Kate does couples counseling with non-marital couples, couples who are gay as well as heterosexual, and with marriages that are monogamous as well as "open" to sexual encounters outside the marriage. Christina works with teenagers in gangs. Adam and Christina both welcome persons who are transvestites.

Throughout this book, I have used "people first" language intentionally, because that is how these social workers see these clients. They look at clients and see people first, people God created to be cherished and loved, to be seen as "the image of God" (Genesis 1:26), regardless of their circumstances and life choices. They are not simply the disabled, gang members, homosexuals, delinquents, or terminal patients, identified primarily by their life circumstances and even their own choices. Instead, they are people who are . . . in gangs, living with disability, gay, convicted of criminal behavior, in the process of dying.

Less significant for these social workers than speaking about their faith *to* clients is their providing compassionate care *for* clients—all kinds of clients. Their care is a louder message than their words. As Kate said, "They experience something here with me and with each other that I believe is set apart and sacred because of how I frame our work and who I am."

At the same time, these social workers cannot and do not attempt to provide services to everyone. First, social workers may not be able to offer services to clients who insist that the social worker's values line up with their own, such as the potential client who quizzed Kate on her political orientation. The issue in that situation was that the potential client was judging Kate to be acceptable or not for what she needed—not the social worker judging the client.

Similarly, organizations may have guidelines to which clients must adhere in order to receive services. Diane described having to terminate services with clients who did not follow through in seeking treatment for chemical dependency, for example. In this case, again, the client decided not to use the services of the agency; the agency did not reject the client. The biblical narrative that comes to mind is Jesus' conversation with the rich young ruler who wanted to follow him (Mark 10:17-27). Jesus welcomed him, telling him what Jesus expected from him. It was the young man's choice, not Jesus' rejection, that caused him to walk away.

(4) Advocacy for Changes in Systems, Even when the Work is Clinical Practice

Decades into her career, Patricia is still engaged in direct practice with families. At the same time, she is organizing the community to make sure that children in poor families have adequate age appropriate school supplies, a community now unified instead of fractured around meeting the needs of its most vulnerable children. Allison's position was that of therapist in a public juvenile treatment program for children arrested for crimes, yet she brought about a major change in the organization. Locked wards were dismantled and the campus became "open," with a more effective method of providing client services. Joseph is not content to "go through the motions" as others seem to do in a large and unwieldy public school system. He is determined to make the system work for children. David is a "family therapist" who takes on changing community attitudes and juvenile court policies and processes.

In the more than 35 years I have been in social work education, I have always been in Christian institutions, teaching students who came to social work school because they felt called by God to help— to help abused children, or impoverished families, or beleaguered communities, or refugees from a war-torn country. At national conferences of social work professors and deans across all those years, I have listened to educators from other social work educational programs bemoan the lack of engagement of social work students in community development and social change—the macro side of the profession. Books have been written about our profession abandoning social causes to become more "clinical" in focus (e.g., Specht & Courtney, 1994).

I have been puzzled when I have considered our own students, therefore, who have not exhibited this trend toward clinical practice and away from a focus on social justice causes; our students seemed to care about big social issues as well as clinical practice. Our students all came with that desire to help people—

individual people and families—but they also seemed to make the critical connection between helping an abused child and doing something about the poverty and hopelessness of that child's family. Doing something about poverty and hopelessness ultimately means doing something to change the community and to change social policies that keep families poor and hopeless.

Of course, any generality like this one is undoubtedly only true in the abstract. Many non-Christian social workers educated in public universities have become powerful change agents in large systems. Similarly, I have had many Christian students who wanted to focus only on clinical practice with little interest in understanding, much less engaging, the larger systems that impinge on their clients. Nevertheless, I have seen a theme in the commitment of social workers who are Christians that resonated throughout my years of teaching as well as in these interviews. If social workers did not sense this calling to address systemic social issues as students, these interviews suggest that they find their path leading there over time.

Christian faith is a faith in Jesus, the Christ who lived his life as an example for his followers. Jesus cared deeply not only about healing sick people and feeding hungry people; Jesus also tackled the systems that oppressed people. In fact, Jesus launched his ministry with a call to system change. He did so by bringing to the minds of his hearers the teachings of Moses—and of God through Moses. In Leviticus 25:10-28, God's message to Moses was (loosely paraphrased): "Here's how I want you to take care of one another and take care of my land. Every seventh *day* is to be a Sabbath, a day of rest. Every seventh *year* is to be a Sabbath year. Then, not only are people to rest, but you are allow rest to the land." God promised that there would be a bumper crop in the sixth year so that there would be plenty to eat for two years. In that way, the land and the people could have a "sabbatical" during the seventh year. Not only that, but people were supposed to forgive one another's debts during the Sabbath year.

Then comes God's crowning economic policy: Every seventh Sabbath year—seven times the seven Sabbath years, or 49 years—the people were to proclaim the Year of Jubilee. In that year, not only were the land and the people to rest, but they were also to redistribute the money and the land. In a rural economy, every family needed land in order to thrive. Sometimes farmers had hard times and had to sell their land in order to pay their bills. Sometimes poor people even had to sell themselves as slaves because they could not pay their bills. In the Year of Jubilee, every 49 years, families who had to sell their land were to have it returned. In essence, every generation was to have a fresh start. The economic troubles of one generation were not to be allowed to condemn their children to poverty. Jubilee is God's economic institution, a way of protecting and caring for the smallest and weakest in society.

Building on the knowledge of this economic policy, Jesus launched his ministry with these words:

> The Spirit of the Lord is upon me,
> because he has anointed me
> to bring good news to the poor.
> He has sent me to proclaim release to the captives
> and recovery of sight to the blind,
> to let the oppressed go free,
> to proclaim the year of the Lord's favor (Luke 4).

The "year of the Lord's favor," Jesus' listeners knew, is the Jubilee Year. Jesus came to announce God's kingdom, to do away with the inequality and poverty that had spread across the land.

Jubilee describes how we are to order our society, making sure that every child, every generation, has opportunity to thrive. No society has actually fully practiced it, although there have been attempts such as the sharing that was done in the early church (Acts 2) and various other Christian communities throughout the centuries.

Taking Jesus' teaching to heart, it is difficult for social workers who are Christians to be exclusively micro or macro in focus. Perhaps as professionals, social workers frame their work at one level or another. As Christians, however, we cannot live comfortably in a micro world, drawing our salaries while others are unemployed and unemployable, sending our children to good private schools while children from families who are poor attend schools that are poorly resourced; or drinking coffee or eating fruit grown by farmers paid salaries so low they cannot provide adequately for their families. These social structures and our involvement in them haunt us. When social workers know the injustices because they know the clients—the people—those injustices oppress, they have the compelling stories to tell of the impact of social injustice. Like Nathan telling David the story of the rich man who took the poor farmer's ewe lamb (2 Samuel 12), social workers can speak truth to power.

Therefore, social workers use their professional skills as advocates, powered by the passion of their faith, to call for Jubilee wherever they find themselves. That passion is kindled by the One who proclaimed "This is the year"—not next year or the next year after that—this year.

(5) A Conduit for Hope

These social workers see themselves as channels of hope. Patricia believes that her Christian hope for the future can "carry clients until they can recover their own personal hope." Martha Ellington identified her role as an agent of hope—to the families who had despaired of help with their disabled members, and to social workers caught up in unresponsive social service systems that disempower people with charity rather than giving them opportunities to thrive.

In his work with teenagers caught up in the juvenile justice system and their families, David sees his role as connecting clients to hope. He believes in hope even when he does not feel it: "When I feel hopeless, I know that redemption can still happen."

In addition to hope for their clients, sometimes the hope these social workers claim is for themselves. Dianne talks about having "a serious commitment to hope." Laura confronts evil on a daily basis on the front line of care for children who have been abused. She fervently believes that God will win in the end, and she is betting her life's work on that hope.

Christian hope is not a feeling; it is a decision. The decision for hope rests on what we believe at the deepest levels—what our most basic convictions are about the world and about God and about the future. We choose hope, not as a naive wish, but as a choice, with our eyes wide open to the reality of the world and our responsibility to be at work in it.

As I write this final chapter, I have also been rummaging through the jumbled boxes of old family memorabilia that have finally overflowed the designated closet in our house. Therefore, I am finally going through and sifting that worthy of being kept from the less than enduring. In one of those boxes, I ran across a Christmas advent devotional that I had written for our congregation more than two decades ago and long forgotten.

Our family had just returned from a yearlong teaching assignment for my husband and me in Sydney, Australia. Our two children had attended Australian public schools for the year. Christmas comes in the middle of the hot Australian summer. In the devotional, I wrote about the oddity of that Australian Christmas season for our American family—pasta salads on the beach instead of a turkey and the trimmings; playing in the surf rather than in the snow; singing elementary school songs about Santa's sleigh being pulled by kangaroos and about three drovers instead of three kings. We sang what our Australian church called Christmas carols, but we did not know the tunes or the words. We were lost. It did not feel like Christmas to us. Then it had hit me, so I wrote in the devotional. Christmas does not depend on what we *feel*; the "Christmas spirit" is not ours to generate. God comes to us, ready or not. We do not have to get our feelings lined up or generate the appropriate mood. The shepherds were passing the night away like any other, and *God* brought the joy. In the same way, social workers do not have to generate feelings of hope. Sometimes we feel discouraged and even despairing. We may feel doubt, even of the principles of the faith we have chosen to believe most fervently. The hope comes from God. We just need to open ourselves to receiving it—and then pass it on, whether we *feel* it or not, to others.

(6) Responsible for Providing the Very Best Service Possible, but Not for Ultimate Outcomes.

For these social workers, their Christian calling means that their work is their worship, requiring their very best efforts. Providing the very best service possible is not just ethical professional practice, it is an expression of their love of God.

At the same time, the situations in which they are intervening are complex; their professional contribution is hardly the only factor at work influencing individual clients and the systems that are the target of their work. Most significantly, clients have the right to make their own life choices, even if they are not the choices their social workers would choose. Ultimately, as Joseph said: "There is no excuse for not staying abreast of research and new theory and techniques in practice, but I have to remember, too, that I am not in control of outcomes." Although some of these social workers felt their calling was justified when clients experience positive changes, their calling is not based on whether or not their work results in the changes for which they hope.

Adam described "success" as caring for people even when they continue to struggle and are not "successful" by external standards. Christian faith means that caring for the neighbor in need is how we can best show our love for the God who loves us whether or not we are successful. Or as Christina said: "There is no success; there is no failure; there is only accompaniment."

We are not "building God's Kingdom," as an earlier generation liked to put it. We simply lack the power to create change, sometimes even in our own agency much less the whole world. Jesus made it clear that God will bring God's reign in God's own time, and when we least expect it (Matthew 24:36, 44). The social gospel proponents at the turn into 20th century erroneously believed that they could Christianize the social order and so by their own efforts bring in God's kingdom (Evans, 2001; May, 2001). Their hopes dashed on the rocks of the horrors of the world wars. Evidence-informed practice only goes so far in working for justice. These Christian social workers believe in being the very best professionals they can be, in giving their clients the very best service possible—but they are not in control of outcomes.

These Christians are attempting to live their lives and serve professionally as pictures of what the kingdom of God is and will be. They have to have faith that God will use their efforts. If all our efforts resulted in success, then where is the faith in that? Christians merely prepare the ground and sow the seeds of mercy and kindness and justice. We did not create the seed—we just receive it, carry it, and plant it. The seed comes from God, and to God belongs the harvest (Mark 4:26-32). God wants us to *seek* justice, love kindness, and walk in humility with our God—ours is to work toward justice in everything we do, but recognize in humility that it is not ours to create (Micah 6:8). We seek justice; we do not create it.

Again, Moses' story has been one to which I have returned repeatedly to grasp what it means to live faithfully. When Moses' mother birthed him, two poor slave midwives—two women in a traditionally female occupation, much like social work—were delivering the Israelite babies in the community. Pharaoh had ordered those two midwives, Shiphrah and Puah, to kill every baby boy as he was born. They silently refused, defiantly risking their lives to save the babies. They colluded with mothers and sisters and a community that successfully hid infant boys—including Moses (Exodus 1:15-21). Because of these women and an Egyptian princess, Moses lived to become the leader of his people. Shiprah and Puah were likely dead by the time the Israelites escaped on dry ground through the Red Sea. Moses probably left his adoptive Egyptian mother, the princess, behind in Egypt if she was still alive. Moses lived the rest of his adult life leading a whining band of Israelite refugees as they wandered in the desert. He did not live to step foot in the promised homeland, himself dying in the wilderness (Deuteronomy 34:1-8). None of these faithful ones saw the end results of their actions. They gave their lives for a future they never saw.

Bertell (2004) tells a story from the holocaust of World War II. A truck was trundling from a German concentration camp toward the death ovens, loaded with a group of Jewish men. One of the doomed men suddenly grabbed another man's hand and read his palm with exuberance: "Oh, I see you have a very long lifeline; and you are going to have three children." Other men offered him their hands for reading. The spirit was contagious. With joy, he predicted more long lives, more children, and abundant joy. Laughter broke out, and an impossible hope became infectious—were they really about to die? The hope and laughter pouring forth from men they were supposed to kill unsettled the guards. Instead of marching the men to the ovens, the guards put them back on the truck and returned them to camp. The ovens continued to burn, and most of the men ultimately died—but no one died that day. Hope and faith cannot whisk us out of brutal reality; but at the same time, hopelessness can paralyze us into not acting at all.

Our comfort as Christians comes in knowing that we are not able to change hard realities—but God can. Our job is simply to sow the seeds of hope, to pick up the hand of another and read hope in it. Our human efforts cannot alone bring justice rolling down like a mighty river. It is *God's* river that will come pouring down (Amos 5:24). It is *God's* Kingdom that is coming. Aurora says, "I am not called to be the God of any of this work that I'm doing; I am simply an avenue through which God can work."

.... On Earth as it is in Heaven

The Lord's Prayer is the prayer of these social workers. These Christians are living and longing that God's will be done here, today, with the people and communities they serve. They recognize it is God's work to do, and they want to be a means. They are the tools, not the carpenter. They seek to be channels for

God's grace and working in the world. To change metaphors, they are like tube skylights, a pathway between the brightness of the sun and the darkness of the rooms their clients inhabit.

Moses led the Israelites to travel in a desert for 40 years, a journey that perhaps should have been walkable in months, not years. They seem to us to be wandering aimlessly. God's freeing of Israel from slavery was not just a single event but a process that took half a century—almost a lifetime. The babies and children who had walked or been carried across that dry seabed escaping Egypt with the sea piled up to give them passage were now the parent generation. Those years were not simply wandering, however. God was training a slave people to become a free people. If they had gone the most direct way to the Promised Land, they would have still acted and thought like slaves. They were born and raised to think of themselves as slaves. So God used years to train a new generation. They learned to trust God, not masters and not themselves, even for their next meal. They were not wandering aimlessly– they were learning to follow God.

Christians who are called to social work are similarly called to take the journey of a lifetime. Our calling is a path, not a destination. I have often prayed the following prayer as I send out newly minted social workers from our graduation convocation. I now pray it for you, readers I may never meet, and yet my brothers and sisters in this caravan seeking God's kingdom on earth, as it is in heaven:

> We are grateful, Lord God, that when you call us on this journey,
>
> You don't call us to walk it alone.
>
> We thank you for one another to share the journey,
>
> To comfort and encourage one another.
>
> Lord, hold our hands and steady us on the way.
>
> Don't let us trip over challenges seen and unseen.
>
> But if we do trip, pick us up and set us back on the path.
>
> Show us just the next three steps to take, or even just one—
>
> We don't need to see all the way, for we trust the destination to you.
>
> Give us courage to go, step by step, with one another and with you.

Appendices

Appendix A

Practice Settings—Organizational Auspices and Levels of Practice

This chart is designed to help you find social workers who work primarily at one or more levels of professional practice - I&F (with individuals and families), groups, and O&S (with organizations and social systems). The large bold X indicates their primary work; smaller Xs indicate work at other levels as well. The organizational auspices column refers to the nature of the organizational context. "RAO" stands for religiously affiliated organization (see Appendix B for a definition). "Public" refers to organizations that are agencies of the local, state, and national government. "PNS" refers to organizations that are "private" (governed by a nongovernmental entity) but "non-sectarian," i.e., not religiously affiliated. Some cells contain more than one of these designations; those using an ampersand (&) are in both settings simultaneously and those using a semi-colon (;) have moved from one kind of organization to another.

Chapter	Social Worker		Practice Level			Organizational Auspices	Description of Work Setting
			I&F	Groups	O&S		
1	Cummings	Patricia	x	x	**X**	RAO	Child and family services — family stabilization
2	Porter	Allison	**X**	x		Public	Juvenile residential treatment; county hospital
3	Armstrong	Joanie	**X**			Public	Child protective services— foster care and adoption
4	Martinez	Joseph	**X**	**X**		public	Primary and secondary schools
5	Martin	Kate	**X**	**X**		Self-employed & congregations	Self-employed—individual and couples therapy, relationship education
6	Hester	Myria	**X**			Public; RAO	Vulnerable adults—mental illness and physical disabilities
7	Bennett	Adam	x	x	**X**	Congregation & RAO	Community ministries— poverty, homelessness, gangs
8	McIntosh	Wes	x	x	**X**	RAO	Community organizing
9	Dobal	Christine	**X**	x	x	RAO	Gang intervention
10	Quintana	Heather	**X**	**X**	x	RAO & congregation	Global mission organization
11	Yindee	Chanphen	x	**X**		RAO	Global relief organization
12	Ellington	Martha	x		**X**	PNS	Day treatment agency— adults with physical and intellectual challenges
13	Barrett	Courtney	**X**	x		Public	Medical clinic; hospital
14	Terry	Kara	**X**	x		RAO	Nursing home

15	Black	Jon	x	x	X	PNS	Hospice care
16	Greer	Raelynn	X	X		Public	Community mental health center
17	Parker	Sunshine	X		X	RAO; public	Child welfare—foster care, residential treatment
18	Tarrington	Diane	x	x	X	RAO & congregation	Housing ministries and congregational social work
19	Arroyo	Kevin			X	PNS	Community organizing—food security
20	Richmond	Karen	X		X	RAO; PNS	Refugee resettlement
21	Flores	Aurora		x	X	PNS	Community organizing—immigrants' rights
22	Crawford	Laura	X			Public	Child advocacy center—child abuse intervention
23	Thomas	David	X	x	X	Public	Juvenile justice—family therapy; university
24	Fitzgerald	Joy	x	x	X	RAO	Job training
25	Borden	Elaine	X	x		Public	Military

Appendix B

Glossary[1]

Church social work: Professional social work practice in an organization, including congregations, whose mission is to put into action the teachings of Jesus.

Church: The society of all Christians, whatever tradition or time.

Cognitive behavioral therapy (CBT): A short-term, present-focused treatment approach that focuses on helping clients understand how their thoughts and feelings influence their behavior; CBT often used with phobias, addictions, depression, and anxiety.

Community: The interpersonal networks through which we attempt to find the meaning in our lives, meet one another's needs, accomplish our personal goals, and feel belonging.

Community ministry: Programs and services a congregation engages in alone or in partnership with other congregations and agencies to serve individuals and families locally (not in distant places). Those served are usually, but not always, persons who are not currently participants in the congregation, as a means of pursuing the congregation's mission.

Community practice: Social work practice whose goal is the strengthening of interpersonal connections of people and the development of communities and neighborhoods that support human thriving.

Congregation: The aggregate of people that gather regularly and voluntarily for worship at a particular place.

Congregant: A person, who, when asked, would say, "This is my congregation," regardless of membership status or frequency of attendance.

Congregational social work: Professional social work practice that takes place in or with a congregation.

Council on Social Work Education (CSWE): A nonprofit national association representing individual social work educators as well as programs of professional social work education. CSWE is the sole accrediting agency for social work education in the United States.

Denomination: Congregations and Christian agencies that share a name (e.g., Presbyterian), culture, and theology, that mutually support one another financially and with goods and services, and that collaborate in projects (e.g., missions, schools). Denominational agencies are a subset of religiously affiliated agencies.

Evidence-based practice (EBP): Using intervention approaches with client systems that are based on systematic scientific research.

Evangelism: Teaching others about Christianity and attempting to attract them to become Christians and/or participate in a congregation.

---

[1] This glossary was adapted from Garland and Yancey (2014) to provide consistency; it also includes additional terms relevant to this book.

Faith community:	A community created intentionally because people want to be in relationship with one another, often by going out of the way of home and work routines to share common faith commitments, mutual support in living their faith, and shared ideological perspectives.
Faith-based:	Organizations that have a religious mission, including both social service organizations and other business organizations and congregations. A term broader than "religiously affiliated" that does not distinguish between congregations and social service agencies, and a term used in some governmental policies.
Family Court:	A special court that deals with problems in family relations such as divorce, custody, and parental rights. A judge normally hears and decides cases without a jury. The purpose is to put the needs of children first and to help families resolve disagreements.
Hospice services:	A type of care for terminally ill persons, normally with a prognosis of six months or less to live, that focuses primarily on alleviating physical symptoms and pain, as well as addressing emotional and spiritual needs, rather than to seeking to cure the disease or to prolong life.
Ministry:	Service done in response to the Christian mission to love others as an expression of devotion to Jesus/God.
Missions:	All the ways that Christians and their congregations address human need wherever it exists as a way of responding to God's calling, whether the focus is individuals, families, neighborhoods, social systems or society. The focus of missions is on neighbors who are outside the congregation, although the boundary between neighborhood and congregation is a permeable one.
Neighborhood:	The geographical location in which people reside and/or work; the place where a person experiences belonging.
Non-sectarian organizations:	Organizations that do *not* identify with any religious group, including both private and public agencies.
Parachurch organizations:	Organizations with a Christian mission that operate autonomously from congregational or denominational oversight.
Preferential option for the poor:	The principle that serving those in poverty and seeking economic justice is a top priority because poverty is a primary concern of God.
Religiously affiliated organization:	Social service or business organization that identifies with one or more religious congregations or other religious organizations, often expressed in the organization's name and funding stream. Denominational agencies are a subset of religiously affiliated agencies.
Service:	Identifying and addressing a human need.
Stephen Ministry:	A training program for congregational mOembers to provide Christian care for persons in crisis. The name comes from the ministry of Stephen, one of the first deacons (Acts 6).

Appendix C

Interview Questions

I scheduled interviews with social workers after I had received their signed consent form that describes the purposes of the project and how I would protect their confidentiality. The interview began with the open-ended questions that follow. We used the "probes" as a means to encourage the interviewee to tell a story with detail. We made sure that the interviewee addressed all the questions by the end of the interview, but we encouraged them to tell the story as they chose, and not necessarily following the order of these questions. We began the interview by saying, "I have 13 questions I want to ask, and then at the end, I'll ask for some basic facts about you."

1. Tell me how you ended up in social work as a profession.
2. What kind of work do you do now? What is your title?
3. Pick a "typical" day during the past week and describe your day to me. Tell it as though you were scripting a movie. (Probe details—what did you think about on the way to work? What did you do first? With whom did you laugh? Cry? Paint the picture.)
4. What are some of the things you often do in your role that you did not happen to do that day?
5. What do you especially enjoy about your work? (Probe: Tell me a story about when that happened.)
6. What do you like least about your work? (Probe: Can you tell me a story about that?)
7. When the days are hard, what helps you keep on?
8. How do you relate social work to your Christian faith? (Probe: Can you tell me a story about that?)
9. How was your faith-life involved in your decision to become a social worker? (Probe: Tell me a story about when that happened)
10. Tell me about an experience that you knew that you were doing what you felt called to do.
11. How has your work affected your faith? (Probe: Tell me a story that illustrates that.)
12. What are your goals for your work; for yourself as a social worker?
13. As we write your story, may we call you back for additional information?

Demographic Data

At the end of the interview, I asked interviewees for any information needed to complete their record. This data was stored in a separate spreadsheet separate from the transcript; we changed all identifying information in the transcripts themselves.

1. Name
2. Interviewer's Name
3. Phone number
4. E-mail
5. Mailing address
6. Denominational affiliation
7. Name of employing organization
8. Type of employing organization (private nonreligious, public/government, religiously affiliated)
9. Title
10. State license as a social worker (yes or no)
11. If licensed, what is the license?
12. Highest SW degree (e.g., MSW)
13. Year obtained MSW
14. University attended
15. Any other graduate degree or certificate? (e.g., MDiv, MBA, etc.)
16. Gender
17. Ethnic identity (all that apply)
18. Age
19. Years in social work practice
20. Years in current employment
21. What you have read lately to help you with your work (book, journal, website)?
22. Date of interview(s)
23. Minutes of interview(s)

Appendix D

References

Action Network for Social Work Education and Research. (2009). *Social work reinvestment: A national agenda for the profession of social work.* from National Association of Social Workers http://www.socialworkers.org/advocacy

Bankson, M. Z. (1999). *The call to the soul: Six stages of spiritual development.* Philadelphia, PA: Innisfree Press, Inc.

Belcher, J. R., & Cascio, T. (2001). Social work and deliverance practice: The Pentecostal experience. *Families in Society, 82*(1), 61-68.

Bertell, R. (2004). In what do I place my trust? In P. R. Loeb (Ed.), *The impossible will take a little while* (pp. 191-195). New York, NY: Basic Books, Inc.

Bisno, H. (1952). *The philosophy of social work.* Washington, DC: Public Affairs Press.

Bridge, A. (2008). *Hopes's boy: A memoir.* New York, NY: Hyperion.

Buechner, F. (1993). *Wishful thinking : a seeker's ABC* (Rev. ed.). San Francisco, CA: HarperSanFrancisco.

Canda, E. R. (1989). Religious content in social work education: A comparative approach. *Journal of Social Work Education, 25*(1), 36-45.

Canda, E. R. (1995). Retrieving the soul of social work. *Society for Spirituality and Social Work Newsletter, 2*(2), 5-8.

Canda, E. R. (1999). Spiritual diversity in social work practice: The heart of helping. In E. R. Canda (Ed.), *Spiritual diversity in social work practice: The heart of helping* (pp. 97-105). New York, NY: The Free Press.

Canda, E. R., & Phaobtong, T. (1992). Buddhism as a support system for Southeast Asian refugees. *Social Work, 37 (1),* 61-67

Chamiec-Case, R. (2009). Ethical integration of Christian faith and social work practice: The motivation models. *Catalyst, 52*(3), 3, 5.

Chamiec-Case, R. (2012). Ethically integrating faith and practice: Exploring how faith makes a difference for Christians in social work. In T. L. Scales & M. Kelly (Eds.), *Christianity and social work: Readings in the integration of Christian faith and social work* (4th ed., pp. 337-359). Botsford CT: North American Association of Christians in Social Work.

Chamiec-Case, R. (2013). The contribution of virtue ethics to a richer understanding of social work competencies. *Social Work & Christianity, 40*(3), 251-270.

Chaves, M. (1999). Religious congregations and welfare reform: Who will take advantage of 'Charitable Choice'? *American Sociological Review, 64,* 836-846.

Cnaan, R. A., Boddie, S. C., & Danzig, R. A. (2005). Teaching about organized religion in social work: Lessons and challenges. In D. B. Lee & R. O'Gorman (Eds.), *Social work and divinity* (pp. 93-110). Binghamton, NY: The Haworth Pastoral Press.

Cornett, C. (1992). Toward a more comprehensive personology: Integrating a spiritual perspective into social work practice. *Social Work, 37 (2, March),* 101-102

Council on Social Work Education. (2012). Statistics on social work education in the United States. from http://www.cswe.org.

Daley, J. G. (1999). *Social work practice in the military*. New York, NY: Haworth.

Derezotes, D. S. (1995). Spirituality and religiosity: Neglected factors in social work practice. *Arete, 20*(1), 1-15.

Devine, E. T. (1939). *When social work was young*. New York, NY: Macmillan.

Dik, B. J., & Duffy, R. D. (2009). Calling and vocation at work: Definitions and prospects for research and practice. *The Counseling Psychologist, 37*(3), 424-450.

Evans, C. H. (Ed.). (2001). *The social gospel today*. Louisville, KY: WestminsterJohn Knox Press.

Farnsely, A. E. I. (2004). What congregations can and can't do: Faith based politics. *Christian Century, 121*(17), 27-33.

Farris, A., Nathan, R. P., & Wright, D. J. (2004). *The expanding administrative presidency: George W. Bush and the faith-based initiative*. Albany, NY: The Roundtable on Religion and Social Welfare Policy.

Frankl, V. E. (1969). *The will to meaning: Foundations and applications of logotherapy*. London: Souvenir Press.

Gallagher, S. V. (2007). Speaking of vocation in an age of spirituality. *Change, May/June*, 32-37.

Garland, D. E., & Garland, D. R. (2007). *Flawed families of the Bible: How God works through imperfect relationships*. Grand Rapids, MI: Brazos Press.

Garland, D. R. (2003a). Being Christian means being micro *and* macro. *Catalyst, 46*(1), 3-4.

Garland, D. R. (2003b). *Sacred stories of ordinary families: Living the faith everyday*. San Francisco, CA: Jossey-Bass.

Garland, D. R., & Yancey, G. I. (2014). *Congregational social work*. Botsford, CT: NACSW.

Gibelman, M. (1995). *What social workers do*. Washington, DC: NASW Press.

The Gottman Institute. (2015). from http://www.gottman.com/.

Hardy, L. (1990). *The fabric of this world: Inquiries into calling, career choice, and the design of human work*. Grand Rapids, MI: Eerdmans.

Hutchison, W. J. (1998). The role of religious auspiced agencies in the postmodern era. *Social Thought: Journal of Religion in the Social Services, 18*(3), 55-69.

Jeavons, T. H. (1998). Identifying characteristics of "religious" organizations: An exploratory proposal. In N. J. Demerath, P. D. Hall, T. Schmitt, & R. H. Willliams (Eds.), *Sacred companies: Organizational aspects of religion and religious aspects of organizations* (pp. 79-95). New York, NY: Oxford University Press.

John F. Kennedy Presidential Library. (2014). JFK and people with intellectual disabilities. Retrieved July 10, 2014, from jfklibrary.org.

Keith-Lucas, A. (1972). *Giving and taking help*. St. Davids, PA: North American Association of Christians in Social Work.

Keith-Lucas, A. (1985). *So you want to be a social worker: A primer for the Christian student*. St. Davids, PA: North American Association of Christians in Social Work.

Keith-Lucas, A., Kuhlmann, E., & Ressler, L. E. (1994). *Integrating faith and practice: A history of The North American Association of Christians in Social Work, 1950-1993*. St. Davids, PA: The North American Association of Christians in Social Work.

Keller, R. S. (2001). Women creating communities--and community--in the name of the social gospel. In C. H. Evans (Ed.), *The social gospel today* (pp. 67-85). Louisville: Westminster/John Knox Press.

Kline, C. (2013). *Orphan train: A novel*. New York, NY: Morrow.

Kolb, R. (2009). *Martin Luther: Confessor of the faith*. New York, NY: Oxford University Press.

Lovejoy, O. R. (1920). The faith of a social worker. *The Survey, May*, 208-211.

Marty, M. E. (1980). Social service: Godly and godless. *Social Service Review*, 463-483.

May, M. A. (2001). The kingdom of God, the church, and the world: The social gospel and making of theology in the twentieth-century ecumenical movement. In C. H. Evans (Ed.), *The social gospel today* (pp. 38-52). Louisville, KY: Westminster/John Knox Press.

Meinert, R. (1998). Consequences for professional social work under conditions of postmodernity. *Social Thought: Journal of Religion in the Social Services, 18*(3), 41-54.

Midgley, J. (1995). *Social development: The development perspective in social welfare*. Thousand Oaks, CA: Sage.

Mizrahi, T., & Davis, L. E. (2012). Human needs work and employment *Encyclopedia of Social Work* (20th ed.). London: Oxford University Press.

Moore, M. E. M. (2008). Stories of vocation: Education for vocational discernment. *Religious Education, 103*(2), 218-238.

NASW. (2013). *Guidelines for social worker safety in the workplace*. Washington, D.C.: NASW.

Netting, F. E. (2002). Reflections on the meaning of sectarian, religiously-affiliated, and faith-based language: Implications for human service consumers. *Social Work & Christianity, 29*(1), 13-30.

Palmer, P. J. (1991). *The active life: A spirituality of work, creativity, and caring*. San Francisco, CA: Jossey-Bass.

Pardeck, J. T., Murphy, J. W., & Min Choi, J. (1994). Some implications of postmodernism for social work practice. *Social Work, 39*(4), 343-346.

Pope John Paul II. (1981). *On human work: Encyclical laborem exercens*. Washington, D.C.: Office for Publishing and Promotion Services, United States Catholic Conference.

Reamer, F. G. (1987). Social work: Calling or career? *The Hastings Center Report, 17*(1), 14-15.

Scales, T. L. (2008). C. Anne Davis (1938-2006): Shaping an ethic of "Doing the Word". In L. McSwain (Ed.), *Twentieth-Century shapers of Baptist social ethics* (pp. 226-243). Macon, GA: Mercer University Press.

Scales, T. L., Harris, H. W., Myers, D., & Singletary, J. E. (2012). Journeys toward integrating faith and practice: Students, practitioners, and faculty share their stories. In T. L. Scales & M. Kelley (Eds.), *Christianity and social work: Reading on the integration of Christian faith and social work practice* (pp. 129-152). Botsford, CT: North American Association of Christians in Social Work.

Schuurman, D. J. (2004). *Vocation: Discerning our callings in life*. Grand Rapids, MI: William B. Eerdmans Publishing Company.

Sherman, A. L. (2011). *Kingdom calling: Vocational stewardship for the common good*. Downer's Grove, IL: InterVarsity Press.

Sherwood, D. A. (1999). Integrating Christian faith and social work: Reflections of a social work educator. *Social Work & Christianity, 26*(1), 1-8.

Sherwood, D. A. (2010). Acts of the loving imagination: Central themes of Alan Keith-Lucas. *Social Work & Christianity, 37*(3), 268-291.

Sherwood, D. A. (2012a). Doing the right thing: A Christian perspective on ethical decision-making for Christians in social work practice. In T. L. Scales & M. Kelly (Eds.), *Christianity and social work: Readings on the integration of Christian faith and social work practice* (4th ed., pp. 171-188). Botsford CT: NACSW.

Sherwood, D. A. (2012b). Ethical integration of faith and social work practice: Evangelism. In T. L. Scales & M. Kelly (Eds.), *Christianity and social work* (pp. 301-309). Botsford, CT: North American Association of Christians in Social Work.

Sherwood, D. A. (2012c). The relationship between beliefs and values in social work practice: Worldviews make a difference. In T. L. Scales & M. Kelley (Eds.), *Christianity and social work: Readings on the integration of Christian faith and social work practice* (4th ed., pp. 85-104). Botsford CT: NACSW.

Singletary, J. E., Harris, H. W., Myers, D., & Scales, T. L. (2006). Student narratives on social work as a calling. *Arete, 30*(1), 188-199.

Specht, H., & Courtney, M. E. (1994). *Unfaithful angels: How social work has abandoned its mission*. New York, NY: The Free Press.

Steger, M. F., Pickering, N. K., Shin, J. Y., & Dik, B. J. (2010). Calling in work: Secular or sacred. *Journal of Career Assessment, 18*(1), 82-96.

Tallant, S. H., & Ryberb, R. A. (1999). Common and unique ethical dilemmas encountered by military social workers. In J. G. Daley (Ed.), *Social work practice in the military* (pp. 179-204). Binghamton, NY: Haworth Press.

Theresa, M., & Kolodiejchuk, B. (2007). *Mother Theresa: Come be my light; The private writings of the Saint of Calcutta*. New York, NY: Doubleday.

U.S. Department of the Army. (2007). *Department of the Army pamphlet 600-4: Army medical department medical officer development and career management*. Washington, D.C.: Department of the Army.

United States Department of Justice, C. R. D. (2014). Olmstead: Community integration for everyone. Retrieved July 10, 2014, from http://www.ada.gov/olmstead/olmstead_about.htm

Veith, G. E. (2011). Vocation: The theology of the Christian life. *Journal of Markets & Morality, 14*(1), 119-131.

Volf, M. (1991). *Work in the spirit: Toward a theology of work*. New York, NY: Oxford University Press.

Walsh, J. (1995). The impact of schizophrenia on clients' religious beliefs: Implications for families. *Families in Society, 76*(9), 551-558.

Weick, A., & Saleebey, D. (1998). Postmodern perspectives for social work. *Social Thought: Journal of Religion in the Social Services, 18*(3), 21-40.

Weissbourd, B. (1994). The evolution of the family resource movement. In S. L. Kagan & B. Weissbourd (Eds.), *Putting families first: America's family support movement and the challenge of change* (pp. 28-47). San Francisco, CA: Jossey-Bass.